EVERYMAN, I will go with thee,

and be thy guide,

In thy most need to go by thy side

HENRIK IBSEN

Born at Skien, Norway, on 20th March
1828. Obtained work in connection with
theatres in Bergen and Christiania. Left
Norway in 1864 and lived abroad—mostly
in Germany—returning to Norway in 1891.
Died at Christiania on 23rd May 1906.

HENRIK IBSEN

Ghosts

The Warriors at Helgeland

An Enemy of the People

TRANSLATED BY
R. FARQUHARSON SHARP

DENT: LONDON
EVERYMAN'S LIBRARY
DUTTON: NEW YORK

NO. *552*

SBN: 460 00552 9

INTRODUCTION

(Revised for the 1941 edition)

The Warriors at Helgeland (*Hærmændene paa Helgeland*), the first of the three plays included in the present volume, was written in 1857, when Ibsen (who was then in his thirtieth year) was at Christiania. Both in conception and execution it is an enormous advance on the immature efforts which had preceded it; and, apart from its own very considerable merits, poetic and dramatic, it is noteworthy as foreshadowing two aspects of the later genius that could produce *Peer Gynt* and *The Wild Duck*. Judged as a poetic romance, it has great charm if approached in the necessary spirit of simplicity. As a piece of dramatic construction it is admirable, and already characteristic of the later Ibsen in its methods. A preface which Ibsen wrote in 1876 for a German translation of the play affords interesting evidence of his sane dramatic sense. After remarking that the Volsung Saga was the source of his inspiration for the play, he goes on to say that he was nevertheless convinced that " the idealised and, to a certain extent, impersonal figures in the Sagas " were unsuitable for representation on the stage of to-day, and that, apart from this, it had been his aim in this play to present " not mythical personages, but Scandinavian life in olden times." To realise the wisdom of this, one has only to compare the human interest possessed by the characters in *The Warriors at Helgeland* with the almost entire lack of it in the heroes and heroines of Wagner's *Ring der Nibelungen*.

Ibsen offered the play to the Royal Theatre at Copenhagen and to the Christiania Theatre, and both promptly rejected it as unsuitable to the tastes of the public. It was not until 1861, after a tentative performance at Bergen, that the play was produced at the Christiania Theatre. It was not seen in Copenhagen until some fourteen years later. The publication of the translation referred to above gave the play a footing in Germany where it was fairly often played after that date. Its only productions in London, so far, have been that at the Imperial Theatre in 1903, during Ellen Terry's management, when it was played under the title of *The Vikings*, and at the Old Vic in 1928 in connection with the celebration of the centenary of Ibsen's birth.

The remaining two plays here translated, *Ghosts* (*Gengangere*) and *An Enemy of the People* (*En Folkefiende*), are closely connected in their origin. *Ghosts* was written in 1881, when Ibsen was in Italy, and was published at the close of that year. Ibsen could not have expected—indeed did not expect—anything but a mixed reception for a play so aggressively daring in its defiance of all conventions. Thought has moved so quickly in the last sixty years, the boundary-posts (to use a favourite metaphor of Ibsen's) have been so often shifted in that time, that it requires a readjustment of one's point of view to realise fully how daring a thing it was to publish a play on such a theme as this and expect it to be performed. It is Ibsen's most remarkable polemical, and perhaps his most remarkable intellectual, effort; as a play it grips the mind and extorts a close interest despite any repugnance to its theme. Softening of the brain as the result of disease inherited from a licentious father is a subject æsthetically repulsive, and must perhaps become especially so upon the boards of a theatre. No doubt the play teaches lessons that social teachers cannot emphasise too strongly; and in none of his works has Ibsen diagnosed a social malady (a proceeding which he was fond of claiming as his aim in writing these plays) with more terrible skill. But it is still open to question whether the acted drama—which, after all, is a form of art distinguished by peculiar conditions—is a legitimate medium for the exposition of such truths. There is much virtue in the old artistic canon as to what may fitly be displayed *coram populo*.

Another criticism that may fairly be made upon *Ghosts*, judged as a play, is that it is rather too obviously a work with a didactic purpose. The dramatist seems more interested in his thesis than in his characters. Except for the dominance of Mrs. Alving's personality, the characterisation is a shade conventional, for a writer of Ibsen's rare ability in that respect: his personages perhaps appearing to expound the dramatist's views rather than voice thoughts that are their own. And yet Ibsen wrote to a friend of his, at this time, that "in none of his plays did the author stand so entirely apart from the action as in *Ghosts*"!

However prepared he may have thought he was for the reception of the play, Ibsen was nevertheless considerably taken aback by the bitter storm of abuse it aroused in Norway. Björnson was the only public man who would say a word in his defence; and the "Liberal" press, on whose professions of broadmindedness Ibsen had more or less relied, threw him over altogether. The result was the writing, at white heat, of *An Enemy of the People*, in which Ibsen sought to chastise his opponents with satire. Dr. Stockmann, the protagonist of the play, is not intended as a portrait of the author; but the picture of his relations to his fellow-townsmen, to the Liberal press, and to the "damned compact majority"—his account of himself as "fighting at the outposts of thought," and standing at a point which in ten years' time the majority would have reached, while he himself would be far ahead again—obviously depict Ibsen's own position towards his countrymen in the matter of *Ghosts*. Writing to his friend Brandes at this time about the controversy, Ibsen complains of the Liberal press prating of freedom of action and thought, and then letting themselves become merely the slaves of their subscribers' opinions and following the crowd instead of leading it; and, again, writes of himself as being always ten years ahead of the great mass of the people— expressions identical with those used by Dr. Stockmann.

Despite its satirical intention, *An Enemy of the People* is in many ways more genial than most of Ibsen's "social dramas," thanks to the leavening of humour which he has permitted himself to mix with his scorn. The result of this, and of the fact that the play contains some theatrically effective scenes, was that it became immediately popular on the Scandinavian stage—the audience, wherever it was played, no doubt considering the satire peculiarly applicable to any other community than their own.

Ghosts was at first refused a hearing either in Norway, Denmark or Sweden; but in 1883 the Swedish actor August Lindberg was attracted by the play's possibilities, and toured with it—with the result that soon afterwards it was played at the Royal Theatre at Stockholm. It was a good many years, however, before it was seen in Norway or in Denmark. It was first performed (privately) in Germany in 1886; in Paris, by the Théâtre Libre, in 1890; and in London, by the Independent Theatre, in 1891. Since then it has been played in most European countries. For many years the censor refused to remove his veto on its public performance in this country, possibly on account of the fact that the plot of the play involves even uglier questions than hereditary disease.

An Enemy of the People was published in the winter of 1882, and performed early the following year in Norway, Sweden and Denmark, and since then has been widely played on the continent. It was produced in England, in 1893, at the Haymarket Theatre, by Sir (then Mr.) Herbert Beerbohm Tree, who more than once revived it.

For the verse translation of Örnulf's funeral chant over his dead sons in Act IV. of *The Warriors at Helgeland,* I am indebted to the kindness of Mr. Ernest Rhys.

R. Farquharson Sharp.

SELECT BIBLIOGRAPHY

SEPARATE PLAYS (titles in English; dates of first Norwegian editions). *Catalina*, 1850; *The Warrior's Barrow*, 1850; *Norma*, 1851; *Olaf Liljekrans*, 1856; *The Feast at Solhoug*, 1856; *Lady Inger of Østeraad*, 1857; *The Vikings at Helgeland*, 1858; *Love's Comedy*, 1862; *The Pretenders*, 1864; *Brand*, 1866; *Peer Gynt*, 1867; *The League of Youth*, 1869; *Emperor and Galilean*, 1873; *The Pillars of Society*, 1877; *A Doll's House*, 1879; *Ghosts*, 1881; *An Enemy of the People*, 1882; *The Wild Duck*, 1884; *Rosmersholm*, 1886; *The Lady From the Sea*, 1888; *Hedda Gabler*, 1890; *The Master Builder*, 1892; *Little Eyolf*, 1894; *John Gabriel Borkman*, 1896; *When We Dead Awaken*, 1899.

COLLECTED EDITIONS. *The Collected Works of Henrik Ibsen*, edited and translated by W. Archer, 12 vols., 1906–12; *The Correspondence of Henrik Ibsen*, translated by Mary Morison, 1905. *Lyrics and Poems from Ibsen*, translated by F. E. Garrett, 1912.

BIOGRAPHY AND CRITICISM. G. B. Shaw, *The Quintessence of Ibsenism*, 1891; expanded 1913; P. H. Wicksteed, *Four Lectures on Henrik Ibsen*, 1892; G. M. C. Brandes, *Henrik Ibsen, Critical Studies*, translated by J. Muir, 1899; E. W. Gosse, *Henrik Ibsen* (Literary Lives Series), 1907; H. Macfall, *Ibsen: the Man, his Art and his Significance*, 1907; A. E. Zucker, *Ibsen the Master Builder*, 1930; H. Koht, *Henrik Ibsen*, 1931; B. W. Downs, *Ibsen: The Intellectual Background*, 1946; J. Lavrin, *Ibsen: an Approach*, 1950; B. W. Downs, *A Study of Six Plays by Ibsen*, 1950; B. Ibsen, *The Three Ibsens*, translated by G. Schjelderup, 1951; J. R. Northam, *Ibsen's Dramatic Method*, 1953; G. W. Knight, *Henrik Ibsen*, 1962; F. L. Lucas, *The Drama of Ibsen and Strindberg*, 1962; M. C. Bradbrook, *Ibsen the Norwegian: A Revalation*, 2nd (revised) edition, 1966; M. Meyer, *Henrik Ibsen: The Making of a Dramatist, 1828–64*, 1967; D. Grene, *Reality and the Heroic Pattern: Last Plays of Ibsen, Shakespeare and Sophocles*, 1968.

CONTENTS

xi

THE WARRIORS AT HELGELAND

A Play in Four Acts

DRAMATIS PERSONÆ

Örnulf of the Fjords, a chieftain in Iceland.
Thorolf, his youngest son.
Sigurd the Strong, a Viking.
Dagny, his wife (daughter of Örnulf).
Gunnar, a rich yeoman of Helgeland.
Hjördis, his wife (foster-sister to Dagny).
Egil, his son, four years old.
Kaare, a Helgeland yeoman.
Örnulf's six elder sons.
Örnulf's and Sigurd's Men, Guests, Servants, Wait-
ing-Women, Outlaws, etc.

*The action takes place in the time of Eric Bloody-Axe; at, and
in the neighbourhood of, Gunnar's house at Helgeland, in northern Norway.*

ACT I

(SCENE.—*The top of a high cliff, which in the background drops sheer down into the sea. On the left is a boat-shed, on the right hills covered with pine woods. The masts of two ships of war can be seen down in the creek below; far out on the right, rocks and islands. The sea is very rough. It is winter, with storms of wind and snow.*

SIGURD *comes up from the ships. He is dressed in a white tunic with silver belt, a blue cloak, loose hose, fur boots and a steel casque, with a short sword hanging at his side. A moment later,* ÖRNULF *comes into sight on the hillside, dressed in a dark lambskin tunic, with breastplate, greaves worn over woollen hose, and fur boots; over his shoulders he wears a cloak of brown frieze, with the hood drawn over his casque in such a way as partly to conceal his face. He is tall and powerfully built, but has a long white beard, and is a little bent with age. He is armed with a round shield, a sword and a spear.* SIGURD *advances first, looks around and sees the boat-shed, goes quickly up to it and tries to burst open the door.* ÖRNULF *comes down from the higher ground, starts when he sees* SIGURD, *appears to recognise him, strides forward and calls out to him.*)

Örnulf. Stand back, warrior!

Sigurd (turns, and lays his hand on his sword). If I did that, it would be the first time!

Örnulf. You must and shall! I need this boat-shed for a night's shelter for my men, who are half frozen.

Sigurd. And I need it for a weary woman.

Örnulf. My men are of more worth than your woman!

Sigurd. Outlaws must be of great value in Helgeland, then!

Örnulf (raising his spear). You shall pay dearly for those words!

3

Sigurd (*drawing his sword*). It shall go ill with you, old man!

> ÖRNULF *falls upon him;* SIGURD *defends himself.* DAGNY *and some of* SIGURD'S *men come up from the shore;* ÖRNULF'S *six sons appear on the higher ground on the right.* DAGNY, *who is dressed in a red kirtle, blue cape and fur cap, is a little in advance of the others.*)

Dagny (*calls down towards the ships*). Up, all Sigurd's men! My husband is at blows with a stranger!

Örnulf's Sons. To our father's help! (*They come down.*)

Sigurd (*to his men*). Stay where you are. Surely I can deal with him alone!

Örnulf (*to his sons*). Let me fight in peace! (*Closing in upon* SIGURD.) I will draw your blood!

Sigurd. You shall see your own first!

> (*Wounds him in the arm, so that his spear falls from his hand.*)

Örnulf. A good stroke, warrior!—

> Swift the sword thou swingest,
> Keen thy weapon's aim;
> Sigurd's self, the Strong One,
> It would put to shame!

Sigurd (*with a smile*). Then would he have shame and honour at the same time!

Örnulf's Sons (*in tones of surprise*). It is Sigurd himself! Sigurd the Strong!

Örnulf. But it was a keener stroke you dealt me the night you stole away Dagny, my daughter! (*Throws back the hood from his face.*)

Sigurd and his Men. Örnulf of the Fjords!

Dagny (*happily, but with some signs of uneasiness*). My father and my brothers!

Sigurd. Get behind me.

Örnulf. There is no need. (*Approaches* SIGURD.) I knew you as soon as I saw you, and that was why I provoked a quarrel; I wanted to try whether they speak truly who say of you that you are the best swordsman in Norway. Now let there be peace and reconciliation between us!

Sigurd. I ask nothing better, if it may be arranged.

Örnulf. There is my hand. You are a doughty hero; such swashing blows has no one before exchanged with old Örnulf.

Sigurd (grasping his outstretched hand). Then may it be the last time we exchange blows! And therewith I beg you to give judgment on the matter that lies between us. Are you willing to name conditions on which we may be at one?

Örnulf. That I am, and the dispute shall forthwith be settled. *(To the others.)* Now shall you all know what is the matter in question. Five winters ago Sigurd and Gunnar, on a Vikings' quest, came to Iceland and received from me free hospitality for the winter. So it was that Gunnar, with craft and force, carried off my foster-daughter, Hjördis; but you, Sigurd, took Dagny, my own child, and sailed away with her. To atone for that you shall be sentenced to pay three hundred pieces of silver, and so shall you expiate your deed of violence.

Sigurd. The conditions you choose seem to me easy indeed. The three hundred pieces shall be paid, and to them I will add a broidered cloak of silk that was a gift to me from King Athelstan of England—such a cloak as no man in Iceland has ever worn.

Dagny. Well said, my brave husband; and my thanks, my father, to you; this is the first day I have known real happiness! *(She grasps her father's and brothers' hands and talks to them aside.)*

Örnulf. Now peace is fully established between us, and from to-day Dagny shall be in every way as honourably esteemed as if you and she had been wedded lawfully and with her kinsmen's consent.

Sigurd. And now can you depend upon me as upon one of your own blood.

Örnulf. Of that I am assured, and instantly mean to make trial of your goodwill.

Sigurd. You shall find me ready. Say on—what do you require of me?

Örnulf. Your help in word and deed. I have steered hither to Helgeland in search of Gunnar, to demand of him reparation for the carrying-away of Hjördis.

Sigurd (in surprise). Gunnar!

Dagny. And Hjördis! Where are they to be found?

Örnulf. At home in Gunnar's house, I imagine.

Sigurd. And that is—?

Örnulf. Not many bow-shots away. Did you not know that?

Sigurd (repressing a movement). Not I! It is seldom that I have sought news of Gunnar since last we sailed from Iceland together. A Viking's life has led me afar and I have served many kings in foreign lands, while Gunnar has sat at home. Before the stress of the storm I came under the lee of this land at daybreak to-day; and though it is true I knew that Gunnar dwelt here in the north in the home of his fathers, still——

Dagny (to ÖRNULF*).* So that was the errand on which you set forth from home?

Örnulf. It was. *(To* SIGURD.*)* Our meeting has been the work of the Mighty Ones above; they have willed it so. Had I been minded to seek you, I should have had but little knowledge where I should find you.

Sigurd (thoughtfully). Very true, very true!—But now about Gunnar—tell me, Örnulf, are you resolved to press him to the uttermost, with all your power, by fair means or foul?

Örnulf. That I must do. Listen, Sigurd, to what I have to say. Last summer I rode to the meeting of the Thing, where many men of high honour sat with me in council. When that was over, I sat in the hall and drank with the men of my own Hundred, and it happened that our talk turned upon the carrying-off of women; and then was I reproached with scorn for having let my disgrace go so long unavenged. Thereupon my anger rose; and I swore to go to Norway and seek out Gunnar, and demand amends from him, or vengeance,

for his deed, and never to journey home again to Iceland
till I had accomplished my purpose.

Sigurd. Ah, well—if that is how it stands, it is clear
that the matter must be hotly pursued in whatever way
is needful.

Örnulf. It must; but I shall not be unreasonable, and
Gunnar is reputed an honourable man. I am glad, too,
to have set out upon this journey; time has hung very
heavily upon my hands in Iceland of late. It was on the
blue waters that I had grown old and grey, and I yearned
to be out upon them once more before I——. Ah,
well!—Bergthora, my good wife, is long since dead; my
eldest sons have left me every summer to go on Vikings'
quests; and now, as Thorolf was growing up—

Dagny (happily). Is Thorolf with you? Where is he?

Örnulf. On board my ship, out there. (*Points to the
background on the right.*) A fine lad—you shall see. He
has grown big and strong and comely since you were at
home. He will make a splendid man, Sigurd; he will
be like you some day.

Dagny (with a smile). It is just as it always was, I see.
Thorolf was ever the nearest to your heart.

Örnulf. He is the youngest, and like his mother; that
is why it is.

Sigurd. But tell me, now—your errand with Gunnar—
do you mean this very day——?

Örnulf. Rather to-day than to-morrow. I shall be
well content with a reasonable sum paid as penalty; but if
Gunnar refuse such an offer of reconciliation, then must
he take the consequences that will follow.

> (KAARE *enters hurriedly from the hillside. He is
> dressed in a coat of grey frieze and a felt hat, and
> carries a broken staff in his hand.*)

Kaare. Well met, warriors!

Örnulf. Warriors are seldom good to meet.

Kaare. If you are honourable men, let me find safety
among you. Gunnar's men are after me and would kill me!

Örnulf. Gunnar's men!

Sigurd. Then you must have done him some harm!

Kaare. I did no more than I had a right. We had set our cattle to graze together on an island just off the shore. Gunnar's people drove off my best oxen, and one of his men abused me, calling me a thrall. For that I took my sword to him and slew him.

Örnulf. That you had the right to do.

Kaare. But now this morning his men came to make an attack on me. By good luck I was warned in time and got away; but I can look but for a short respite, for my enemies are seeking me.

Sigurd. I can put but little faith in your story, fellow! In days gone by I knew Gunnar as well as I know myself; and this I know, that never would he attack a peaceable man.

Kaare. Gunnar has no hand in the matter; he is away southwards. No, it is Hjördis, his wife—

Dagny. Hjördis!

Örnulf (muttering). Yes, it would be just like her!

Kaare. I offered to pay Gunnar a penalty for the killing of his thrall, and he was willing to accept it; but then came Hjördis and goaded her husband with scornful words, and prevented our peace-making; so Gunnar went away to the south, and this morning—

Sigurd (looking out to the left). Are those not men coming on the road northward?

Kaare. It is Gunnar himself!

Örnulf. Take comfort; I fancy I shall be able to make your peace with him.

(GUNNAR, *with some of his men, enters from the left. He is in home dress; brown tunic, woollen hose, a blue cloak and wide-brimmed hat; the only weapon he carries is a small axe.*)

Gunnar (stopping in wonder and uncertainty at the sight of the gathering). Örnulf of the Fjords! Yes, in truth—!

Örnulf. Yes, it is he.

Gunnar (approaching). Then welcome to my land!— if you are come in peace.

Örnulf. If you be of the same mind as I, there shall be peace between us.

Sigurd (coming forward). Well met, Gunnar!

Gunnar. Sigurd—foster-brother! (*Grasps his hand.*) Nay, if you are with him, I know for certain that Örnulf is come in peace. (*To* ÖRNULF.) Give me your hand, old man! It is not difficult to guess what errand has brought you here in the north. It concerns Hjördis, your foster-daughter.

Örnulf. It is as you say. It was a great wrong you did me when you sailed away with her from Iceland without asking my consent.

Gunnar. You have right and custom on your side. A man must pay for his youth's wild deeds. I have expected you this many a day, Örnulf, for that deed of mine; and if paying a penalty can make peace between us, it shall soon be done.

Sigurd. That is what I think. Örnulf will be reasonable.

Gunnar (with warmth). That must you be, old man; for if you were to esteem her at her true worth, all that I have could not pay the price.

Örnulf. I shall go by law and custom, be assured of that. But now there is another matter. (*Points to* KAARE.) Do you see this man?

Gunnar. Kaare! (*To* ÖRNULF.) Do you not know there is enmity between us?

Örnulf. Your men have raided his cattle, and amends should be made for a raid.

Gunnar. And for killing also. He has killed my thrall.

Kaare. Because he insulted me.

Gunnar. I told you I was ready to arrange an agreement with you.

Kaare. But Hjördis was in no mind for that; and this morning, while you were away, she fell upon me, and seeks me now to take my life.

Gunnar (in an irritated tone). Are you speaking the truth? Did she—?

Kaare. Every word is true.

Örnulf. And for that it was that this fellow craved my help, and he shall surely have it.

Gunnar (after a moment's thought). You have dealt honourably with me, Örnulf; it is only right, therefore, that I should conform to your will. Listen to me, Kaare. I am willing to let my thrall's death, and all the injury that you have suffered, acquit one another.

Kaare (holding out his hand to GUNNAR*).* That is fairly spoken; I agree to that.

Örnulf. And he shall be at peace with you and yours?

Gunnar. At peace in my house or wherever else he may choose to go.

Sigurd (pointing to the hillside). Look there!

Gunnar (displeased). It is Hjördis!

Örnulf. With armed men!

Kaare. She is seeking me!

(*Enter* HJÖRDIS *with a train of followers. She is dressed in black kirtle, cloak and hat. Her followers are armed with swords and axes; she carries a light spear in her hand.*)

Hjördis (stopping abruptly). We are mustering strong here, it seems!

Dagny (advancing towards her). Greeting to you, Hjördis!

Hjördis (coldly). Thank you. I heard that you were not far off. (*She advances, casting a keen glance on the men who are standing together.*) Gunnar—and Kaare, my enemy—Örnulf and his sons, and—(*as her glance falls on* SIGURD *she gives an almost imperceptible start, is silent for an instant, then recovers herself*). I see many faces that I know; but this I do not know—which of you is best disposed towards me.

Örnulf. Indeed we are all well disposed towards you.

Hjördis. If that is so, you will not refuse to hand Kaare over to my husband to deal with.

Örnulf. There is no need.

Gunnar. There is peace between us, and a reconciliation.

Hjördis (with stifled derision). A reconciliation? I see. I know you are a prudent man, Gunnar; Kaare has fallen in with a goodly number of friends, and I can easily understand that you thought it safest—

Gunnar. Taunts are of no avail! (*Decisively.*) Kaare is at peace with us.

Hjördis (*restraining herself*). So be it; if you have promised him peace, you must keep your promise.

Gunnar (*firmly, but without heat*). I must and shall do that.

Örnulf (*to* HJÖRDIS). And another reconciliation was half accomplished, before you came.

Hjördis (*sharply*). Between you and Gunnar?

Örnulf (*nodding his head*). It has to do with you.

Hjördis. I know full well what it has to do with; but this I tell you, foster-father, never shall it be said that Gunnar allowed himself to be frightened because you came with armed men to his shores. Had you come alone, as a traveller seeking shelter in our house, the breach between us might have been easier healed.

Gunnar. Örnulf and his sons are come in peace.

Hjördis. Maybe; but the people will have a different tale to tell. And you yourself, Gunnar, had no such great trust in this peace yesterday, when you sent our son Egil to the south as soon as it was noised abroad that Örnulf's war-ship lay in the fjord.

Sigurd (*to* GUNNAR). Have you sent your son to the south?

Hjördis. Yes, so that he should be safe if Örnulf fell upon us!

Örnulf. It is no matter for jesting, Hjördis. What Gunnar has done may prove to have been the deed of a prudent man, if you prevent our reconciliation.

Hjördis. Fate rules our lives. What must be, will be; but for my part I would rather die than save my life by a cowardly reconciliation.

Dagny. Sigurd is making due amends, and none will deem him a man of less account for that.

Hjördis. Sigurd should know best what his honour can stand.

Sigurd. As to that I shall never need another's telling.

Hjördis. Sigurd is a renowned slayer of men; but Gunnar did a bolder deed when he slew the white bear at my door.

Gunnar (with an embarrassed glance at SIGURD). Yes, yes, but no more of that !

Örnulf. In very truth that was the boldest deed that ever man did in Iceland, and therefore—

Sigurd. So may Gunnar all the easier make a pact without being called a craven.

Hjördis. If he pay a penalty, he shall demand one too. Remember, Gunnar, the promise that once you gave !

Gunnar. It was an ill thought of mine to make the promise. Do you mean to hold me to it ?

Hjördis. Indeed you shall hold to it, if we two are to live under the same roof after to-day. Listen to me, Örnulf; if amends are to be made for the carrying-off of your foster-daughter, you too shall make amends for having murdered my father Jökul and laid hands on all he possessed.

Örnulf. Jökul fell in fair fight, in a duel between us. Your kinsmen did me a worse wrong by sending you to Iceland without telling me who you were, and causing me to adopt you.

Hjördis. It was an honour, and no wrong done to you, to be foster-father to Jökul's daughter.

Örnulf. It brought me nothing but trouble; *that* I know.

Hjördis. Worse trouble may befall you now, if—

Örnulf. I am not come here to wrangle with women ! —Gunnar, for the last time, are you willing to make amends for her carrying-off ?

Hjördis. Remember what you promised !

Gunnar (to ÖRNULF). You have heard that I have given a promise and I must—

Örnulf (in an exasperated tone). Enough, enough ! Never shall it be said of me that I made amends for killing in fair fight !

Hjördis (proudly). Then we defy you and yours !

Örnulf (with growing anger). And who is there here that has the right to demand amends for Jökul's death ? Where are his kinsmen to be found ? Not one of them is alive ! Where is his lawful champion ?

Hjördis. That Gunnar is—on my behalf!

Örnulf. Gunnar! Undoubtedly, if you had been wedded to him with your foster-father's consent, or if he had made amends for your carrying-off, he might have been your lawful champion; but—

Dagny (pleading anxiously). Father! Father!

Sigurd (quickly). Do not say it!

Örnulf (raising his voice). Yes, I shall cry it aloud! A captured woman has no lawful husband!

Gunnar (vehemently). Örnulf!

Hjördis (in a wild outburst). Insulted! Shamed! (*In a trembling voice.*) You—you shall come to repent this!

Örnulf (continuing). A captured woman may only lawfully be esteemed a man's mistress! If you wish a more honourable name, you must—

Hjördis (restraining herself). No, Örnulf, I know better what is seemly. If I am only to be esteemed Gunnar's mistress, well and good; then must he regain my honour for me by his deeds—by deeds so mighty that my position shall mean no shame to me! Have a care now, Örnulf! Here our ways part, but our swords shall be drawn against you and yours without respite; life and limb, you shall always be in danger, and so shall all who — (*turns angrily upon* KAARE) Ah, Kaare! Örnulf has taken your part, and there is peace between us, but I would counsel you not to go home yet awhile. The man you slew has many to avenge him, and it might easily happen that—well, I have warned you of the danger, now take the consequences. Come, Gunnar— to arms! You did a splendid deed in Iceland, but you must do greater deeds now, unless your—your mistress is to be ashamed of you and of herself!

Gunnar. Curb yourself, Hjördis; these are unseemly words you speak!

Dagny (pleading with her). Foster-sister, stay—stay; I will bring my father to reason!

Hjördis (without listening to her). Let us home, let us home! Never was it foretold to me that I should spend my life as a wretched wanton; but if that is the life and that the shame that I have to endure, even for a single day more, then must my husband do some deed that shall make him more renowned than all other men! (*Goes out to the right.*)

Gunnar (*sadly*). Sigurd, one thing you must promise me; we must speak together before you leave these shores. (*Goes out, with his followers, to the right. Meanwhile the storm has ceased. The midday sun is seen like a red disc far out on the horizon.*)

Örnulf (*threateningly*). Dear shall this day cost you, foster-daughter!

Dagny. Father! Father! Surely you cannot mean them harm!

Örnulf. Let me be!—Now, Sigurd, there will be matter more serious than the mere paying of a penalty, betwixt Gunnar and me!

Sigurd. What do you mean to do?

Örnulf. I do not know; but it will be enough to set men talking, far and wide, of the visit of Örnulf of the Fjords to Gunnar.

Sigurd (*quietly and firmly*). Perhaps. But this I tell you, Örnulf, you shall never take up arms against him as long as I am alive.

Örnulf. Not! But suppose I say I will?

Sigurd. It shall not be—no matter how much you may will it.

Örnulf (*impetuously*). Very well. Even if you side with my foes, I shall not fear to face you all!

Sigurd. Listen to me, Örnulf. Never shall you see the day when you and I meet as enemies. There is an honourable peace between us; Dagny is dearer to me than victories or gold, and never shall I forget that you are her nearest kinsman.

Örnulf. That is no more than I expected of your noble heart, Sigurd.

Sigurd. But Gunnar is my foster-brother. We have sworn peace and friendship. Both in battle and in times of peace we have taken life's chances together, and he is dearer to me than any other man. Brave as he is, he has no lust for fighting. And as for me, you all know me, and know that warfare has no terrors for me; but here I stand forth, Örnulf, and entreat you to be reconciled to Gunnar. Let me have my way in this!

Örnulf. I cannot. I shall be the laughing-stock of all my peers if I go empty handed back to Iceland!

Sigurd. Empty handed you shall not go. Here in the creek lie my two ships of war, with all the spoils I have won on my Viking quests. There are many costly gifts from kings, coffers full of goodly weapons and other precious things. Take one of the ships; choose whichever you prefer, it shall be yours with all that it contains; let that pay the penalty for Hjördis' carrying-off, and so let Gunnar go in peace.

Örnulf. Worthy Sigurd, would you do that for Gunnar!

Sigurd. No man can do too much for a trusty friend.

Örnulf. You would give half of all you have!

Sigurd (urgently). Take all I have, both my ships and all that is in them, and let me go with you to Iceland as the poorest man in your following. What I give, I can win again; but if you take up arms against Gunnar, I shall never again be happy. Now, Örnulf, what is your answer?

Örnulf (thoughtfully). Two good ships of war, weapons and precious things—a man cannot have too much of such things, but—(*vehemently*)—no, no! Hjördis has threatened me! I will not! It would be a dishonourable thing if I took your gifts!

Sigurd. But listen to me—

Örnulf. No, I say! I must enforce my rights alone, and take my chance of the issue.

Kaare (approaching). It is kindly advice that Sigurd gives; but if you are minded to enforce your rights to the best advantage, I can advise you better. Count upon no satisfaction while Hjördis has any word in the matter; but revenge may be yours, if you will follow my counsel.

Örnulf. Revenge? What counsel is this of yours?

Sigurd. An evil counsel, I dare swear!

Dagny (to ÖRNULF). Do not listen to him!

Kaare. Hjördis has made an outlaw of me, and with guile she will seek my life. Do you but promise to protect me afterwards, and this night I will go to Gunnar's house and burn it down over their heads. Is that to your mind?

Sigurd. Miscreant!

Örnulf (quietly). To my mind? Shall I tell you, Kaare, what is far more to my mind? (*In tones of thunder.*) To cleave the nose and ears off you, you miserable thrall! Little do you know of old Örnulf if you deem that he will have part in such a deed of infamy!

Kaare (recoiling). If you do not set upon Gunnar, he will set upon you!

Örnulf. I have fists and weapons to hinder that.

Sigurd (to KAARE). And now, be off! It is a disgrace to an honourable man to hold converse with you.

Kaare (going). So be it. Then I must defend myself as best I can. But this I tell you—you will repent it, if you persist in gentle dealing. I know Hjördis—and I shall find a way to strike at her! (*Goes down to the shore.*)

Dagny. He is plotting some revenge. Sigurd, it must be prevented!

Örnulf. (angrily). Oh, let him do what he likes. She deserves nothing better!

Dagny. You do not mean that. Remember, you have been her foster-father.

Örnulf. It was a baleful hour for me when I took her under my roof. Things begin to fall out as Jökul prophesied.

Sigurd. Jökul?

Örnulf. Jökul, her father. When I gave him his death-stroke, he fell back upon the sward, looked at me, and chanted:

> "Jökul's seed their father's slaying
> Shall avenge in fullest measure;
> Nor shall he find any gladness
> Who hath taken Jökul's treasure!"

Then, when he had chanted this, he was silent for a while; then he laughed, and with that he died.

Sigurd. You should take little account of that.

Örnulf. Who knows? Who knows? Men tell it for a true tale that Jökul gave each of his children a wolf's heart to eat, to make them fierce. Hjördis certainly had her share; one can see it in her. (*Stops as he looks out to the right.*) Gunnar!—Are we two to meet again?

Gunnar (*entering*). Yes, Örnulf; think what you will of me, but I cannot part from you as an enemy.

Örnulf. What do you want?

Gunnar. To grasp your hand in friendship, before you go. Listen to me, all of you. Follow me to my house, and be my guests there as long as you have a mind to. Sleep and good food shall not be lacking; and none shall speak of the dispute between us, either to-day or to-morrow.

Sigurd. But Hjördis?

Gunnar. She is obedient to my will. She is of a different mind since we went home, and thinks with me that we may yet be reconciled if you will be our guests.

Dagny. Yes, yes—if only that could be!

Sigurd (*irresolutely*). But indeed I do not know whether—

Dagny. Gunnar is your foster-brother; surely you will not refuse—if I know anything of your nature.

Gunnar (*to* SIGURD). You have been my friend in all our wanderings; you will not set yourself against me now!

Dagny. And to sail away and leave hatred in Hjördis' heart—no, no, we could never do that!

Gunnar. I have done Örnulf a great wrong; till that is righted my mind will know no peace.

Sigurd (*vehemently*). I will do anything else for you, Gunnar, but I cannot remain here. (*Recovers himself.*) I am King Athelstan's vassal, and must be with him in England before the end of winter.

Dagny. But you can be that nevertheless!

Gunnar. No man knows what the future has in store

for him; it may be, Sigurd, that this is the last time we shall meet; and, if that be so, you will regret that you did not grant my last request.

Dagny. And it will be long ere you see me happy again, if you sail away to-day.

Sigurd (decisively). So be it, then! It shall be as you wish, although—. However, I have decided. There is my hand. I will stay here and be your guest and Hjördis'.

Gunnar (grasping his hand). Thanks, Sigurd; I knew well you would.—And you, Örnulf, do you say the same as he?

Örnulf (sullenly). I will think on it. Hjördis has offended me bitterly—I will give you no answer to-day.

Gunnar. Ah well, old warrior, Sigurd and Dagny will know how to smooth the wrath from your brow. Now I go to prepare the feast; peace be with you, till we are well met in my halls! *(Goes out to the right.)*

Sigurd (to himself). Hjördis has changed her mind, he said! He knows her but little, then; I should be more ready to believe that she is plotting—. *(Breaks off and turns to his men.)* Come, follow me all to the ships; I will choose goodly gifts to take to Gunnar and his folk.

Dagny. Gifts of the best we have. And you, my father—I shall let you have no peace until you relent. *(She goes with* SIGURD *and his men down to the seashore at the back.)*

Örnulf. Relent? Truly, if Gunnar had no women-folk in his house, I might—. Ah! if only I knew how I could strike at her!—Thorolf, you here?

Thorolf (who has entered hurriedly). As you see! Is it true what they say, that you have met with Gunnar?

Örnulf. Yes!

Thorolf. And are now at strife with him?

Örnulf. Well—at all events with Hjördis.

Thorolf. Be of good cheer, then; you shall have your revenge.

Örnulf. Revenge? Who will avenge me?

Thorolf. Listen. I was standing on shipboard, when

there came a man, with a staff in his hand, running and crying out: "Listen, you who are on Örnulf's war-ship; greet him from Kaare and tell him that I am going to take vengeance for us both." Thereupon he got into a boat, and, as he rowed away, he said: "Twenty outlawed men lie out upon the fjord; with them I am going southwards, and before nightfall Hjördis shall have no son to glory in."

Örnulf. Did he say that! Aha, now I understand! Gunnar has sent his son away, Kaare is at enmity with him—

Thorolf. And now he is rowing after the boy to kill him!

Örnulf (with sudden decision). Let us away! That is a prey we will fight for!

Thorolf. What do you mean to do?

Örnulf. Leave that to me. It shall be I, and not Kaare, that will take revenge!

Thorolf. I will go with you!

Örnulf. No, you will follow Sigurd and your sister to Gunnar's house.

Thorolf. Sigurd? Is he in these parts?

Örnulf. You can see his war-ships there. We are reconciled; you will follow him.

Thorolf. To your enemies' house?

Örnulf. Go only to the feast. Now Hjördis shall learn to know old Örnulf! But listen, Thorolf; say no word to anyone of what I have in my mind—do you hear, to no one!

Thorolf. I promise that.

Örnulf (taking him by the hand and looking affectionately at him). Farewell, then, my noble boy. Bear yourself modestly in the banqueting-hall, that you may do me honour. Avoid unnecessary talk, but let what you say be keen as a sword's edge. Be friendly to all that treat you well; but, if you be attacked, do not sit silent under it. Drink no more than you can carry; but do not put the drinking-horn away from you if it be offered in moderation, lest you be deemed womanish.

Thorolf. No, set your mind at ease!

Örnulf. Well, now, away to the feast in Gunnar's house. I am coming to the feast too, and that in a way that is least looked for. (*Cheerfully, to the others.*) Up, my wolf cubs! Sharpen your fangs!—you shall have blood to drink now! (*Goes out with his other sons by the background on the right.* SIGURD *and* DAGNY, *dressed in handsome festal garments, come up from the shore, followed by two men carrying a coffer; the men go back again at once.*)

Thorolf (*looking after his father*). Now are they all away to fight, and I must not go with them. It is hard to be the youngest.—Dagny! Greeting and hail to you, sister!

Dagny. Thorolf! By heaven—how you are grown!

Thorolf. Well, in five years I suppose—

Dagny. Of course, of course.

Sigurd (*offering him his hand*). Örnulf will have a doughty helpmate in you, or I am much mistaken.

Thorolf. If only he would try me—

Dagny (*with a smile*). But he takes more care of you than is to your liking. I know he is almost too fond of you.

Sigurd. Where is he gone?

Thorolf. Down to the ship. Let us go now; he is coming later.

Sigurd. I am waiting for my men; they are bringing up some things and making fast the ships.

Thorolf. I will go and help them. (*Goes down to the shore.*)

Sigurd (*after a moment's thought*). Dagny, my wife— now we are in private, I have something to tell you which may no longer be concealed.

Dagny (*in astonishment*). What do you mean?

Sigurd. This visit to Gunnar's house may prove perilous!

Dagny. Perilous? Do you think Gunnar—?

Sigurd. Gunnar is an honourable man. No, no—but it would have been better had I sailed away from here without being his guest.

Dagny. You frighten me! Sigurd, what is it?

Sigurd. Answer me one thing first. The gold bracelet that once I gave you—where is it?

Dagny (showing it to him). Here on my arm; you bade me wear it.

Sigurd. Throw it into the depths of the sea, so deep that it can never be found!—because it may mean the doom of many men.

Dagny. The bracelet!

Sigurd (in a low voice). The night when you were carried off from your father's house—you remember?—

Dagny. Do I remember!

Sigurd. It is of that I wish to speak.

Dagny (anxiously). What is it? Tell me!

Sigurd. You know, there had been a feast; you went early to your chamber, but Hjördis still sat at table with the men, who were drinking. The cup went freely round, and all sorts of brave oaths were sworn. I swore to carry off a fair maid with me from Iceland; Gunnar swore the same, and offered Hjördis the drinking-cup. Taking it, she stood up and swore that no warrior should have her to wife save he who should go to her chamber, slay the white bear that stood chained at her door, and carry her off in his arms.

Dagny. Yes, yes, I know that.

Sigurd. But all thought it was an impossible task; for the bear was the fiercest of wild beasts. None save Hjördis could come near it, and it had the strength of twenty men.

Dagny. But Gunnar slew it, and became famous far and wide for the deed.

Sigurd (in low tones). He became famous—but—I did the deed!

Dagny (with a cry). You!

Sigurd. When the men left the banquet-hall, Gunnar bade me withdraw to his bedchamber with him to talk with him in private. Then said he: " Hjördis is dearer to me than all other women; I cannot live without her." I answered him: " Go to her chamber, then; you know

B 352

the terms she has set." But he said: "A man who is
in love prizes his life dearly. The issue would be doubtful, if I attacked the bear, and I am fearful of losing my
life now—for I should lose Hjördis with it." For long
we talked together; and the end of it was that Gunnar
got ready his ship, but I drew my sword, put on Gunnar's armour and went to Hjördis' chamber.

Dagny (*with proud happiness*). Then it was you—you
who slew the bear!

Sigurd. It was I. In her chamber it was dark and
black as a raven's wing. Hjördis thought it was Gunnar
that was at her side—her head was heavy with wine.
She drew a bracelet off her arm, and gave it to me—it is
that you wear now.

Dagny (*hesitatingly*). And you were all the night
through in Hjördis' chamber?

Sigurd. My sword lay drawn between us. (*Short silence.*)
Before the day dawned, I bore Hjördis to Gunnar's ship;
she never perceived our trick, and he sailed away with her.
Then I went to your chamber and found you there among
your women. What followed afterwards, you know. I
sailed away from Iceland with a fair maid, as I had
sworn, and faithfully since then have you followed me
wherever I have steered my course.

Dagny (*excitedly*). My brave husband! You did the
mighty deed—oh, I might have known it! None but
you were strong enough! You might have won Hjördis,
that proud and splendid woman, and yet you chose me!
Ten times dearer would you be now, were you not already
the dearest thing in the world to me!

Sigurd. Dagny, my dear wife, now you know—all
that there is need you should know. I had to warn you,
because of the bracelet—. Never let Hjördis set eyes
upon it. If you will do as I desire, you will cast it away
—into the depths of the sea!

Dagny. No, Sigurd, it is too dear to me for that; it
is a gift from you! But be at ease, I shall hide it from
every eye, and never shall I betray what you have told
me.

(THOROLF *comes up from the ships with* SIGURD'S *men.*)
Thorolf. All is ready; let us go to the feast!

Dagny. Come, Sigurd—my brave and noble warrior!

Sigurd. Softly, Dagny—softly! It depends on you now, whether our journey shall end in peace or slaughter! (*Quickly, to the others.*) Now away, all, to the feast in Gunnar's halls! (*Goes out with* DAGNY *to the right; the others follow him.*)

ACT II

(SCENE.—*The Banqueting-hall in* GUNNAR'S *house. The main entrance is at the back; there are smaller doors in the side walls. In the foreground on the left, the chief seat of honour; opposite to it, on the right, the lesser seat of honour. A fire of logs is burning on a stone hearth in the middle of the floor. In the background, on both sides of the door, are platforms for the serving-women. From the seats of honour two long tables, with benches, stretch along the walls to the background. It is dark without; the log fire lights up the hall.* HJÖRDIS *and* DAGNY *enter from the right.*)

Dagny. No, Hjördis, I do not understand you. You have shown me your home; I can see nothing lacking there, and everything that you have is fine and handsome. How can you complain as you do?

Hjördis. Ah!—set an eagle in a cage and it will bite at the bars, whether they be iron or gold.

Dagny. At any rate in one thing you are richer than I; you have Egil, your little son.

Hjördis. Better far to have no child than one born in dishonour.

Dagny. In dishonour?

Hjördis. Have you forgotten your father's words? Egil is a bastard—that is what he said.

Dagny. A word spoken in anger—why do you pay heed to that?

Hjördis. Oh, Örnulf was right. Egil is a poor creature; he has not the look of a free-born lad.

Dagny. Hjördis, how can you—!

Hjördis (without paying attention to her). Doubtless infamy of that sort may be absorbed into the blood, like the venom from a snake-bite. The free-born sons of heroes are of different stuff. I have heard of a queen who took her little son and sewed his tunic fast to his flesh, and he never so much as stirred an eyelid. (*With a malignant expression.*) Dagny, I should like to try that with Egil!

Dagny (in disgust). Hjördis! Hjördis!

Hjördis (with a laugh). Ha, ha, ha! Did you think I was in earnest? (*Changing her tone.*) But, believe me or not as you will, there sometimes comes over me an overwhelming desire to do things like that. I daresay it is born in me; for I am descended from a race of giants, they say.—Come, sit down, Dagny. You have journeyed far and wide in these five long years. Tell me, have you often been a guest in kings' houses?

Dagny. Yes—especially at the court of Athelstan in England.

Hjördis. And were received with the highest honour everywhere—and everywhere sat in the highest seats at table?

Dagny. Of course. As Sigurd's wife—

Hjördis. Yes, quite so. Sigurd is a man of great renown, though Gunnar outranks him.

Dagny. Gunnar?

Hjördis. Gunnar did a deed which Sigurd dared not attempt—but let that pass. Tell me, when Sigurd has been on a Viking's quest and you have been with him—when you heard the blades whistling in keen sword-play, when the decks of the ship reeked red with blood—were you never filled with a wild desire to join with the men in the fight?—did you never put on armour and take a sword in your hand?

Dagny. Never! What are you thinking of? I, a woman?

Hjördis. A woman, a woman—I tell you, no one knows of what a woman is capable!—At all events there is one thing you can tell me, Dagny, because in truth you must know it well. When a man embraces a woman, loves her—is it true that then her blood is on fire, her breast throbs—that she swoons with a strange joy?

Dagny (blushing). Hjördis, how can you—!

Hjördis. Well, but tell me!

Dagny. I think there can be little doubt you have known it yourself.

Hjördis. Yes, once—once only. It was that night Gunnar sat beside me in my chamber; he crushed me in his embrace till his coat of mail burst apart, and then, then—!

Dagny (with a cry). What! Sigurd—?

Hjördis. Sigurd? Who spoke of Sigurd? I said Gunnar—the night he carried me off—

Dagny (recovering herself). Yes, yes, I remember—of course I know—

Hjördis. That was the only time. Never again—never! I thought I had been bewitched, because for Gunnar to embrace a woman in such a fashion—(*stops, and looks at* DAGNY). Are you ill? Your colour comes and goes.

Dagny. It is nothing, it is nothing!

Hjördis (without heeding her). No, I ought to have gone out to taste the joy of battle! It would have been better for me—better, maybe, for us all. It would have been a full and glorious life! Are you not amazed, Dagny, to find me still alive here? Would you not be afraid to be alone with me here in my chamber, when all is dark? Would you not imagine that I had died long since, and that it was the ghost of me that was here with you?

Dagny (uneasily). Come—let us go—and join the others!

Hjördis (taking her by the arm). No, stay! Can you understand, Dagny, how anyone can be alive after sitting here for five nights?

Dagny. Five nights?

Hjördis. Here in the north it is night all the winter long. (*Quickly, and in an altered tone.*) But you must not think it is not splendid enough here sometimes. You shall see sights here such as you have never seen in the halls of England's king. We shall be as sisters together while you are my guest. We will go down to the sea when the storms begin to rage; you shall see the billows breaking on the shore like wild white-maned horses— and the whales far out at sea! They rush on one another like foemen clad in steel! What joy to sit like a witch on a whale's back and ride before the ships, rousing the storm and luring men into the depths with spells of witch-craft!

Dagny. For shame, Hjördis, how can you speak so!

Hjördis. Do *you* know any witches' spells, Dagny?

Dagny (*with horror*). I!

Hjördis. I had thought you did; how did you entice Sigurd?

Dagny. What you say is shameful—let me go!

Hjördis (*holding her back*). I was but jesting! Nay, but listen! Think of it, Dagny—to sit at night here by the door, and listen to the kelpies wailing by the boats; to sit and wait, listening for the dead men to pass on their last journey homewards, for their path must lie past these northern shores—heroes who have fallen in battle, noble women who have not spent their life tamely as you and I have. In the storm and tempest they hurtle through the air on black horses, to the sound of bells! (*Throws her arms round her and clasps her wildly to her.*) Ah, think of it, Dagny! To ride one's last ride on so goodly a steed!

Dagny (*shaking herself free of her*). Hjördis, Hjördis! Let me go! I will not listen to you!

Hjördis (*laughing*). You are a poor thing, and easy to scare!

(GUNNAR *enters from the back, with* SIGURD *and* THOROLF.)

Gunnar. Yes, in truth, I could wish for nothing better than this. I have found you again, Sigurd, my brave and noble brother, faithful and true as ever; I have a son of Örnulf's under my roof, and Örnulf himself will be here ere long—is it not so?

Thorolf. He promised to come.

Gunnar. The only thing I lack is to have my little Egil at home.

Thorolf. You must love the boy dearly; you speak of him so often.

Gunnar. That I do. He is the only one, and has the makings of a well-favoured and warm-hearted man.

Hjördis. But not of a hero.

Gunnar. Come, come—you have no right to say that.

Sigurd. And yet you sent him away—

Gunnar. I would I had not done so! (*In a lower voice.*) But you, Sigurd, know that a man is apt to play the woman sometimes when there is one thing dearer to him than all else in the world. (*Raising his voice again.*) I had but few men about the house; and there was not one of us but felt that his life was in danger, when we heard that Örnulf lay off the shore with his ships of war.

Hjördis. I know one thing that a man should think of first, before his life.

Thorolf. And that is?

Hjördis. His honour and repute.

Gunnar. Hjördis!

Sigurd. No one will ever say of Gunnar that he has forfeited his honour by what he has done.

Gunnar (severely). It is a bootless task to try and embroil me with Örnulf's friends!

Hjördis (with a smile). Hm!—tell me, Sigurd, can your ship sail before any wind?

Sigurd. Yes, if it be shrewdly steered.

Hjördis. Good!—I shall steer my ship shrewdly, too, and shall know how to reach the port I am making for. (*Goes further into the room.*)

Dagny (in a low, uneasy voice). Sigurd, let us go away from here—this very night!

Sigurd. It is too late now; it was yourself that—

Dagny. I felt fond of Hjördis then; but now—I have heard her say what I am afraid to think of. (SIGURD's *followers and other guests, men and women, serving-men and maids, come in at the back of the hall. Salutations are exchanged among the guests.*)

Gunnar. Now, to table! My most honoured guest, Örnulf of the Fjords, comes later; that Thorolf promises me.

Hjördis (to the serving-folk). Pass round ale and mead, that tongues may be loosened and hearts made merry.

(GUNNAR *leads* SIGURD *to the seat of honour on the right.* DAGNY *sits on* SIGURD's *right,* HJÖRDIS *opposite to him at the same table.* THOROLF *is given a similar place at the other table, and sits facing* GUNNAR, *who takes his seat in the chief seat of honour. The others take their places further back. There is a short pause, while the guests drink and talk together.*)

Hjördis. It is not often that so many brave men sit together as are gathered in this hall to-night; it would seem a suitable occasion to practise an old pastime. Let each man tell of his exploits, and all here shall judge who is the best man among us.

Gunnar. That is an ill custom when the drinking-horn is passing round; often it breeds quarrels.

Hjördis. I did not think that Gunnar was afraid.

Sigurd. That no one can think; but so many are we here that it would be late ere we had finished, were we to tell our exploits. Rather do you tell us, Gunnar, of your journey to Bjarmeland; it was a goodly exploit to journey so far northwards, and we would gladly hear of it from you.

Hjördis. The journey to Bjarmeland was nought but a journey, and scarcely worth mention among heroes. No, do you begin, Sigurd!—unless you would have me think that you can ill bear to hear my husband praised. So begin! Tell us which you esteem the finest of the deeds you have done.

Sigurd. Well, since you force me, so be it. It may be worth the telling, that once on a Viking quest, as I lay

off the Orkneys, enemies attacked us, but we cleared
their ships and I fought alone against eight men.

Hjördis. It was a goodly exploit; but were you fully
armed?

Sigurd. Fully armed, with axe, spear and shield.

Hjördis. It was a goodly exploit, nevertheless. Now,
husband, must you say what you deem the bravest deed
you have ever done.

Gunnar (reluctantly). I slew two berserkers that had
seized a merchant vessel, and thereupon sent the captured seamen home and gave them their ship freely and
without ransom. The king of England thought well of
the exploit and said I had done what was worthy of
honour, and gave me thanks and goodly gifts.

Hjördis. Truly, Gunnar, you could tell us of a nobler
exploit than that.

Gunnar (vehemently). I will boast of no other exploit!
Since last I journeyed from Iceland, I have lived at peace
and been nought but a traveller. So there is no more to tell!

Hjördis. If you conceal what is your glory, then must
your wife speak.

Gunnar. Hjördis, be silent— I command you!

Hjördis. Sigurd fought with eight men when he was
fully armed; but Gunnar came to my chamber in the dead
of night and slew the bear that had the strength of twenty
men, and he had nought but a short sword in his hand.

Gunnar (deeply agitated). Woman, not another word!

Dagny (in a low voice). Sigurd, will you endure this—?

Sigurd (to her). Be still!

Hjördis (to the guests). And now, good friends—which
is the braver man, Sigurd or Gunnar?

Gunnar. Silence!

Hjördis (raising her voice). Speak on, I have the right
to ask!

An Old Man (among the guests). If truth be told, Gunnar's deed stands above all other deeds men have done;
Gunnar is the bravest hero, and Sigurd the next to him.

Gunnar (glancing across the table). Oh, Sigurd, Sigurd,
if only you knew— !

*B 552

Dagny (in a low voice). It is too much—even for a friend!

Sigurd. Silence, wife! (*Aloud, to the others.*) Yes, indeed is Gunnar the most worthy of honour among all men; and that would I deem him till my last breath, even had he never done that brave deed—for that I esteem less highly than you.

Hjördis. There speaks envy in you, Sigurd!

Sigurd (smiling). There you are much mistaken! (*In a friendly tone, to* GUNNAR, *while he pledges him across the table.*) Your health, noble Gunnar; our friendship shall stand fast, whoever may attempt to sever it.

Hjördis. That no one is attempting, so far as I know.

Sigurd. Do not say that. I am almost tempted to believe that you invited us to this feast in order to stir up strife.

Hjördis. That is like you, Sigurd; you are wroth now, because you cannot be looked upon as the best man here!

Sigurd. I have always thought more of Gunnar than of myself.

Hjördis. Well, well—to be second to Gunnar is an honour, too; and— (*with a sidelong glance at* THOROLF) —if Örnulf had been here he might have had the third place.

Thorolf. Then if Jökul, your father, were here, he would have to take a lowly seat—for he had to bow low before Örnulf, as we know.

(*The subsequent dialogue is carried on with a growing, if restrained, excitement.*)

Hjördis. You have no right to say that! We know that Örnulf is a bard; and there are those who whisper that he has taken credit for greater deeds than he has done.

Thorolf. Then let those that whisper such things have a care that it does not reach my ears!

Hjördis (with a provoking smile). Would you avenge it?

Thorolf. Yes, and in such a way that men should know it far and wide!

Hjördis. Then I drink to you, with the wish that you may first grow a beard on your smooth chin.

Thorolf. Even a beardless boy is too good to bandy words with women.

Hjördis. But too weak to fight with men! That was why your father let you sit still by the fireside at home, while your brothers went forth to fight.

Thorolf. It was ill done of him that he did not keep as watchful an eye on you; for then you would not have left his shores as a captured woman!

Gunnar and Sigurd. Thorolf!

Dagny (at the same time). Brother!

Hjördis (in a low voice, trembling with rage). Ah—wait! Only wait!

Thorolf (holding out his hand to GUNNAR). Do not be angry with me, Gunnar; they were evil words that my tongue let slip—but your wife provoked me to it!

Dagny (in a low, entreating voice). Foster-sister, if ever you had any love for me, do not stir up strife!

Hjördis (with a laugh). One must jest at a feast, if there is to be any merriment.

Gunnar (who has been talking aside to THOROLF). You are a brave lad. *(Takes down a sword that is hanging above his seat, and gives it to him.)* There, Thorolf— there is a good gift for you. Use it well, and let us be friends.

Thorolf (examining the sword). Thanks for the gift, Gunnar; it shall never be used in a dishonourable fight.

Hjördis. If you mean to keep that promise, never lend the sword to your brothers—

Gunnar. Hjördis!

Hjördis (continuing). Nor hang it on your father's walls either, for there it would hang beside the weapons of a dishonoured man.

Thorolf. True enough, Hjördis—your father's axe and shield have hung there these many years.

Hjördis (restraining herself). You are for ever boasting of Örnulf's having defeated my father; but, if rumour speaks truly, that exploit was not so honourable as you think.

Thorolf. What rumour?

Hjördis (with a smile). I dare not tell you; it would make you angry.

Thorolf. Then be silent; that is what I should prefer. (*Turns away from her.*)

Hjördis. Oh, I may as well tell you. Is it true, Thorolf, that your father, before he dared go out to meet Jökul in the duel, put on a woman's clothes and sat for three nights brewing spells with the witch of Smalser-horn?

(*All rise; consternation spreads among the guests.*)

Gunnar, Sigurd and Dagny. Hjördis!

Thorolf (provoked beyond endurance). So foul a lie have you never heard spoken of Örnulf of the Fjords! You have invented it yourself; only a mind so poisoned as yours could invent such infamy! You have accused my father of the basest thing a man could do! (*Throws the sword away from him.*) There, Gunnar, take back your gift! I take no gifts from a house where my father is insulted!

Gunnar. Thorolf, only listen to me!

Thorolf. Let me go! But have a care, both you and Hjördis; for my father has in his power at this moment one that is dearest of all to you both!

Hjördis (with a start). Your father has—!

Gunnar (with a cry). What are you saying!

Sigurd (quickly). Where is Örnulf?

Thorolf (with a scornful laugh). Gone to the south—with my brothers!

Gunnar. Gone to the south!

Hjördis (impetuously). Gunnar! Örnulf has slain Egil, our son!

Gunnar. Slain!—Egil slain! Then woe betide Örnulf and all his house! Thorolf, tell me—is this true?

Sigurd. Gunnar, Gunnar, listen to me!

Gunnar. Tell me, if you value your life!

Thorolf. You cannot frighten me! Wait till my

father comes. He will brand Gunnar's house with shame. But you, Hjördis—do you, meantime, make the most of the words I heard to-day: "Before nightfall, Gunnar and his wife shall have no child to glory in!" (*Goes out at the back.*)

Gunnar (*in deepest grief*). Slain—slain! My little Egil slain!

Hjördis (*wildly*). And you—you have let him go! Are you going to let Egil, your own son, be unavenged! You will be the mock of every man if you—

Gunnar (*as if beside himself*). A sword—an axe! He has spoken his last word! (*Snatches an axe from one of the bystanders and rushes out.*)

Sigurd (*trying to follow him*). Gunnar, hold your hand!

Hjördis (*holding him back*). Let him be! Let him be! They will separate them. I know Gunnar!

(*A cry is heard from among the crowd which has gathered round the door.*)

Sigurd and Dagny. What is that?

A Voice from the Crowd. Thorolf is killed!

Sigurd. Thorolf! Ah, let me go!

Dagny. My brother! Oh, my brother!

(*As* SIGURD *turns to rush out, the crowd parts and* GUNNAR *comes in, throwing his axe away from him at the door.*)

Gunnar. It is done. Egil is avenged!

Sigurd. Aye, if only your hand has not struck too soon.

Gunnar. Maybe, maybe; but Egil, Egil, my beautiful boy!

Hjördis. We must arm ourselves now, and claim our friends' help, for there will be many that will seek to avenge Thorolf.

Gunnar (*darkly*). He himself will be his grimmest avenger; he will be in my thoughts night and day.

Hjördis. Thorolf got what he deserved. One of a family must suffer for the misdeeds of another.

Gunnar. True; but this I know, that I was happier in my mind before I slew him.

Hjördis. The first night after a killing is always the

worst; when that is past, all goes well again. Örnulf
has accomplished his revenge with shameful cunning;
he would not come against us in open fight, but made as
though his mind were set on reconciliation, that he
might fall thus upon our defenceless child! I saw
more clearly than you all; I knew Örnulf to be evil-
minded and crafty, and good cause had I to stir you to
enmity with him and his false brood!

Gunnar (excitedly). That had you! My vengeance
is but a little thing compared with Örnulf's crime. He
has lost Thorolf, but he has still six sons left to him, and
I not one—not one!

A Serving-Man (rushing up from the back of the hall).
Örnulf of the Fjords is here!

Gunnar. Örnulf!

Hjördis and some of the Men. To arms! To arms!

Dagny. My father!

Sigurd (as if seized with misgiving). Örnulf—! Ah,
Gunnar, Gunnar!

Gunnar (drawing his sword). Up, all of you! Vengeance for Egil's death!

       (ÖRNULF *strides in with* EGIL *in his arms*.)

Gunnar (with a shriek). Egil!

Örnulf.   Here is your little Egil come back to you!

All (in amazement). Egil! Egil alive!

Gunnar (letting his sword fall out of his hand). Woe is
me—what have I done?

Dagny. Oh, Thorolf, my brother!

Sigurd. I was sure of it!

Örnulf (setting EGIL *down)*. There, Gunnar, there is
your splendid boy for you!

Egil. Father! Old Örnulf was not going to do me
any harm, as you said he would when I went away!

Örnulf (to HJÖRDIS*)*. Now I have atoned for your
father's death; now I think we may be reconciled.

Hjördis (restraining herself). That may be!

Gunnar (as if waking from a dream). Is it a horrible
dream that is bewildering me! You—you have brought
Egil home!

Örnulf. As you see; but this let me tell you, that he has been very near death.

Gunnar. I know it.

Örnulf. And yet you show no more happiness than this over his return?

Gunnar. Had he but come sooner, I would have shown more happiness. But tell me everything—all that has happened!

Örnulf. It is soon told. Kaare, the peasant, had an evil design against you; together with some other wretches he went southwards after Egil.

Gunnar. Kaare! (*In a low voice.*) Ah, now I understand what Thorolf said!

Örnulf. His plot came to my ears, and such a crime was not to be permitted. I would have refused all atonement for Jökul's death, and willingly, Gunnar, would I have slain you in a duel if fate had so decreed —but I could not but defend your child. So with my sons I went after Kaare.

Sigurd (*to himself*). A terrible deed has been done here!

Örnulf. When I came up with them, Egil's attendants had been captured, your son was at the mercy of his enemies, and they would not long have spared him. Fierce became the fighting then! Keener blows has my sword seldom dealt! Kaare and two of his men escaped inland; the rest are sleeping soundly and will be hard to wake.

Gunnar (*in the greatest anxiety*). But you—you, Örnulf?

Örnulf (*grimly*). Six sons of mine followed me into the strife.

Gunnar (*breathlessly*). And there came back—?

Örnulf. Not one.

Gunnar (*in terror*). Not one! (*Softly.*) And Thorolf, Thorolf!

(*Profound sensation among the crowd.* HJÖRDIS *appears to be fighting a hard fight with herself.* DAGNY *is weeping quietly.* SIGURD, *deeply moved, stands beside her.*)

Örnulf (*after a short pause*). It is hard to stand like

a green and vigorous tree, and then to be stripped of all one's branches by a single storm. Nevertheless, one man must die and another live. Give me a cup; I will drink to the memory of my sons. (*One of* SIGURD's *men brings him a drinking-horn*). Hail to you on your last ride, my noble sons! The copper gates shall not be shut upon your heels, because ye are come to the halls of Walhalla with a goodly following! (*Drinks, and gives back the horn.*) And now, home to Iceland; Örnulf's fighting days are over. The old tree has but one green branch left, and that he must protect. Where is Thorolf?

Egil (*to his father*). Yes, show me Thorolf! Örnulf told me he would carve me a wooden ship with lots and lots of warriors.

Örnulf. I should thank the good gods that Thorolf was not with me; because if he too—no, strong as I am, that would have been too hard for me to bear. But why does he not come? He has always been the first to greet his father, for it seemed to both of us as if we could not live a day without the other.

Gunnar. Örnulf, Örnulf!

Örnulf (*with growing uneasiness*). You all stand silent, as I now see—. What has happened? Where is Thorolf?

Dagny. Sigurd, Sigurd—this will be the cruellest blow to him!

Gunnar (*fighting with himself*). Old man!—no—no—and yet it cannot be concealed—

Örnulf (*vehemently*). My son! Where is he?

Gunnar. Thorolf is slain!

Örnulf. Slain! Thorolf? Thorolf? You are lying!

Gunnar. I would give the last drop of my blood to see him alive again!

Hjördis (*to* ÖRNULF). Thorolf had but himself to blame for what came to pass. He told us a dark saying, that you had fallen upon Egil and killed him. It was half in enmity that you and we parted last, and you have already dealt death among my race—and, besides, Thorolf behaved like a pert boy, at the feast; he took every jest amiss, and spoke many an ill word. It was only then that Gunnar was moved to anger—only then that he raised his hand against your son. I should say indeed that he had good cause for what he did.

Örnulf (*calmly*). It is easily seen you are a woman; you use many words. What is the use? If Thorolf is slain, then the book of his life is closed.

Egil. If Thorolf is slain, I shall not get my warriors.

Örnulf. No, Egil—we have both lost our warriors, you and I. (*To* HJÖRDIS.) Your father sang:

> " Jökul's seed their father's slaying
>   Shall avenge in fullest measure."

You have taken good care that his words should come true. (*After a moment's silence, he turns to the men.*) Where did he receive his death-blow?

A Man. Over the brow.

Örnulf (*happily*). Ah!—that is an honourable place; he did not turn his back on his foe. But did he fall to the side, or in towards Gunnar's feet?

A Man. Half to the side and half towards Gunnar.

Örnulf. That bodes only half a vengeance. Ah, well— we shall see!

Gunnar (*drawing near*). Örnulf, well do I know that all my possessions could not make up for your loss; but demand what you will of me—

Örnulf (*coldly, interrupting him*). Give me Thorolf's body, and let me go! Where is he lying? (GUNNAR *points silently to the back.* ÖRNULF *takes a few steps, then turns and says in tones of thunder to* SIGURD, DAGNY *and others who are following him compassionately:*) Back! Do you think Örnulf needs to be followed by a train of mourners, like a whining woman! Back, I say!—I can tend Thorolf alone. (*With quiet dignity.*) Childless I go; but none shall say he saw me bowed in grief! (*Goes out slowly.*)

Hjördis (*with a bitter laugh*). Let him go as he likes. There will be no need for us to be many here, if he should come again as a foe! Well, Dagny—I should think this were the last time your father would sail from Iceland on such an errand!

Sigurd (*indignantly*). For shame!

Dagny (*in the same tone*). Have you the heart to mock at him!—to mock at him, after what has passed!

Hjördis. When a deed is done, it is wise to make the best of it. I swore hatred and vengeance on Örnulf this morning. Jökul's death I might have forgotten, and all else—but not his insults to myself. Gunnar's mistress, he called me; if that be so, I count it no shame, because Gunnar is a mightier man than your father now. He is nobler and more renowned than Sigurd, your husband!

Dagny (*deeply stirred*). There you are wrong, Hjördis—and this moment all shall know that you live under a coward's roof!

Sigurd (*hastily*). Dagny, what are you going to do!

Gunnar. A coward!

Hjördis (*with a mocking laugh*). You talk like one out of her wits!

Dagny. It shall be concealed no longer. I was silent until you mocked at my father and my dead brothers; I was silent while Örnulf was here, so that he should not hear that Thorolf had fallen by the hand of a dastard. But now—never again praise Gunnar for his brave deed in Iceland, for Gunnar is a coward! The sword that lay drawn between you and the man that captured you, hangs at my husband's side—and the bracelet that you drew off your arm, you gave to Sigurd—(*draws it off her arm and holds it high in the air*) and here it is!

Hjördis (*wildly*). Sigurd!

The Crowd. Sigurd! It was Sigurd that did it!

Hjördis (*trembling with emotion*). He—he! Gunnar, is it true?

Gunnar (*with quiet dignity*). It is all true —except that I am a coward. I am neither coward nor dastard.

Sigurd (*moved*). That you are not, Gunnar! That you have never been! (*To the others.*) Away, my men! Let us away from here!

Dagny (from the doorway, to HJÖRDIS). Who is the best man among us now, my husband or yours!

(*She goes out with* SIGURD *and his followers.*)

Hjördis (alone). Now I have but one thing left to do—but one thing to think of. Either Sigurd or I must die!

ACT III

(SCENE.—*The hall in* GUNNAR'S *house. It is day.* HJÖRDIS *is sitting on a seat in front of the lesser seat of honour, busy twisting a bowstring. A bow and some arrows are lying on the table.*)

Hjördis (stretching the string). It is tough and strong. (*Glances at the arrows.*) The arrows are sharp and well-weighted. (*Lets her hands fall into her lap.*) But where is the hand that will—! (*Impetuously.*) To be made a mock of—by him—by Sigurd! It is he that deserves my hate more than anyone—that is certain—and the day is not far off when I shall—. (*Brooding.*) Yes, but where—where is the hand that will do the deed?

(GUNNAR *enters from the back, silent and deep in thought.*)

Hjördis (after a short pause). How goes it with you, husband?

Gunnar. Ill, Hjördis; I cannot rid myself of the burden of yesterday's deed. It lies heavy on me.

Hjördis. Do as I do; get yourself some work to do.

Gunnar. Yes, I must. (*A pause.* GUNNAR *walks up and down, then looks attentively at what she is doing and draws near.*) What are you doing there?

Hjördis (without looking up). Making a bowstring, as you can see.

Gunnar. A bowstring—of your own hair!

Hjördis (with a smile). Great things happen every hour nowadays; you killed my foster-brother, and I have been twisting this since daybreak.

Gunnar. Hjördis, Hjördis!

Hjördis (looking up). What is it?

Gunnar. Where were you last night?

Hjördis. Last night?

Gunnar. You were not in your chamber.

Hjördis. Do you know that?

Gunnar. I could not sleep; I dreamed restlessly of—of what happened to Thorolf. I thought I saw him before me—. Well, at last I woke, and heard the sound of strange and beautiful singing through the house. I got up, peeped in through this door, and here you sat by the fire, which was burning blue and red, sharpening your arrows and crooning witches' spells over them.

Hjördis. There was good need; for it is a stubborn heart that must be pierced to-day.

Gunnar. I understand you well enough. You would have Sigurd dead.

Hjördis. Hm! Perhaps.

Gunnar. You shall never have your will, then. I am Sigurd's friend, however bitterly you may incite me against him.

Hjördis (smiling). Do you mean that?

Gunnar. Certainly.

Hjördis (holding out the bowstring to him). Tell me, Gunnar—can you undo that knot?

Gunnar (trying). No, it is tied too well and cleverly.

Hjördis (getting up). The mesh that the Norns weave is knotted even tighter than that; it will not be in your power to undo it.

Gunnar. The ways of the Mighty Ones are strange; neither you nor I know aught of them.

Hjördis. One thing I know well. Sigurd will bring misfortune to us both.

(*A pause.* GUNNAR *stands buried in thought.* HJÖRDIS *watches him silently.*)

Hjördis. What are you thinking of?

Gunnar. Of a dream I had lately. I dreamt I had done the deed you are set upon; Sigurd lay dead upon the ground, and you were standing by him, as pale as

death. Then I said: " Are you glad now, when what
you wished is done ? " But you laughed and answered:
" I should be gladder if you, Gunnar, lay there in Sigurd's
stead."

Hjördis (with a constrained laugh). Little do you
know me, if so senseless a dream can stay your hand !

Gunnar. Ah !—Tell me, Hjördis, are you happy
here ?

Hjördis. If I must tell you truth, Gunnar, there are
times when I feel cramped in these halls.

Gunnar. Just as I thought. We are one too many
here.

Hjördis. Perhaps two.

Gunnar (not hearing her last remark). But that shall be
remedied.

Hjördis (looking at him questioningly). Remedied ? Do
you mean—?

Gunnar. I mean to arm my ships of war and sail
away from here. I mean to win back the honour that
I lost because you were dearer than all else to me.

Hjördis (pensively). You are going away ? Yes—
maybe that will be best for us both.

Gunnar. Ever since the day we sailed away from
Iceland, I have known that we should not be happy
together. You are proud and resolute; there are times
when I am almost afraid of you—and yet, strangely
enough, it is most of all on that account that I love you
so dearly. You seem to cast a terrible spell upon me;
I feel as if you could tempt me to any crime, and that
I should think anything good that you bade me do.
(Shaking his head slowly.) Inscrutable are the ways of
the Norns !—Sigurd should have been your husband.

Hjördis (with a cry). Sigurd !

Gunnar. Yes, Sigurd. If you were not blinded by
hate and vengeance, you would see his worth better. If
I had been like Sigurd, I might have made your life happy
for you.

Hjördis (with deep, but restrained emotion). And do
you mean that—that Sigurd could have done that ?

Gunnar. He is a man of resolute mind, and wellnigh as proud as you.

Hjördis (impetuously). If that is so—. (*Restrains herself.*) No matter, no matter! (*With a wild outburst.*) Gunnar—kill Sigurd!

Gunnar. Never!

Hjördis. By cunning and deceit you got me for your wife—that shall be all forgotten! Five joyless years have I spent here—that shall be all forgotten, on the day when Sigurd shall cease to live!

Gunnar. No harm shall come to him at my hands. (*Starting back involuntarily.*) Hjördis, Hjördis, you shall not tempt me!

Hjördis. Then must I find another avenger; Sigurd shall no longer be able to heap insults on me and on you! (*Clenching her fists convulsively in her passion.*) Perhaps he is sitting alone with her now—with that fool of a woman—dallying with her and laughing at us, telling over again the tale of the disgrace he wrought me when he carried me off in your stead; telling her how craftily he laughed when he stood in my chamber in the dark and I did not know it was he!

Gunnar. That he would never do—never!

Hjördis (violently). Sigurd and Dagny must die! I can never breathe freely till they two are dead! (*Comes closer to him, with glittering eyes, and speaks in a passionate whisper.*) If you could help me to that, Gunnar —then I would live lovingly with you; I would clasp you in my arms with such passionate caresses as you have never dreamt of!

Gunnar (vacillating). Hjördis! Would you—!

Hjördis. Set your hand to the work, Gunnar—and there shall be no more unhappy days for you; no longer will I go out of the room when you come in—never speak an unkind word, or quench your smile when you are happy; I will deck myself in furs and costly silken dresses; if you go fighting, I will follow you—if you ride out on peaceful journeys, I will ride beside you; at the feast I will sit at your side, and fill your drinking-horn and drink to you, and sing goodly songs to you to make your heart glad!

Gunnar (almost won over). Is it true? Would you—!

Hjördis. I would do more than that—ten times more —I swear it! Only avenge me! Avenge me upon Sigurd and Dagny, and then I will— *(breaks off, as she sees the door opened).* Dagny—you!

Dagny (from the back of the hall). Haste, Gunnar—call your men to arms!

Gunnar To arms? What for?

Dagny. Kaare is coming with a rabble of outlaws. He means you harm. Sigurd has checked him for the moment, but who can tell—

Gunnar (moved). Sigurd has done that for me!

Dagny. Sigurd is indeed a faithful friend to you.

Gunnar. And we, Hjördis—we that were thinking—! What I said was true; there is witchcraft in every word you speak; any kind of deed seems fair to me when you urge it.

Dagny (in amazement). What do you mean?

Gunnar. Nothing, nothing! Thanks for your warning, Dagny; I will away and collect my men. *(Turns towards the door, but stops and comes forward again).* Tell me—how goes it with Örnulf?

Dagny (drooping her head). Do not ask. Last night he bore Thorolf's body to his ship; now he is on the shore digging a grave—for his sons to lie in. (GUNNAR *is silent, and goes out.*) There is no danger before the evening. *(Approaches* HJÖRDIS.) Hjördis, I have one task still to perform in this house. It was you I was seeking.

Hjördis. Me? After what passed yesterday?

Dagny. Just on that account. Hjördis, my foster-sister, do not nourish hate against me. Forget the words that grief and a wicked impulse brought to my lips. Forgive me the wrong I have done you—for, believe me, I am now ten times more wretched than you.

Hjördis. Wretched? You—Sigurd's wife?

Dagny. I am to blame for all that has happened—for

the strife that arose, for Thorolf's death, and for all the shame that Gunnar and you have suffered. It was all my fault! Alas, alas—I was so happy; but never shall I know happiness again after this.

Hjördis (as if seized by a sudden thought). But before this—all these five long years—were you happy all that time?

Dagny. Can you doubt it?

Hjördis. Hm!—yesterday I did not doubt it, but—

Dagny. What do you mean?

Hjördis. Oh, nothing much. Let us talk of something else.

Dagny. No, indeed. Hjördis, tell me—!

Hjördis. It will do you no good; still, if you wish it—. *(With a malicious expression.)* You remember how once, in Iceland yonder, we had been to the meeting of the Thing with Örnulf, and were sitting with our companions in the council hall, as usual; then there came two strangers into the hall.

Dagny. Sigurd and Gunnar.

Hjördis. They greeted us courteously, sat down beside us, and there was much jesting talk between us. And there were some who asked why these two warriors had come to Iceland, and if it were not to find themselves wives there. Then Sigurd said: "It will be difficult for me to find the woman my heart will cleave to." Örnulf laughed, and said that in Iceland there was no lack of high-born maidens, or of rich ones either. But Sigurd answered: "A hero needs a high-souled wife. She that I shall choose must not be one to be content with an ordinary woman's lot. She must think no honour too great for her to aspire to. When I go on Viking's quest she must be willing to follow me; she must go armed in steel, and spur me on to the fight, and her eyes must be able to bear the flash of sword-blades; for if she should be a craven, she would bring me but small renown." Is it not true that Sigurd spoke so?

Dagny (uneasily). He did—but—

Hjördis. Such a woman should she be, who should

make his life happy; and then—(*with a contemptuous smile*) he chose you!

Dagny (with a painful start). Ah, you mean that—?

Hjördis. And, no doubt, on that account you have borne yourself proudly and imperiously, and have demanded honour from every one, so that Sigurd should be honoured through you—is it not so?

Dagny. No, Hjördis, but—

Hjördis. No doubt you have incited him to heroic deeds, have followed him in arms, and have taken joy in being where the fight was thickest—have you not?

Dagny (deeply moved). No, no!

Hjördis. Then have you been a craven, such as would bring shame to Sigurd?

Dagny (overcome). Hjördis, Hjördis!

Hjördis (with a scornful smile). And yet you have been happy all this time; do you suppose that Sigurd can say the same!

Dagny. Let me be. Alas, you have made me see myself only too clearly.

Hjördis. One jesting word, and you are in tears immediately! Think no more of it. See, what I have been doing to-day. (*Takes some arrows from the table.*) See how keen the points are! Do not I know well how to sharpen arrows!

Dagny. And how to use them, too! You know how to strike home, Hjördis! All that you have just said to me—I never thought of before. (*More courageously.*) But to say that Sigurd—! To say that all this time I have made his life unhappy and unhonoured—no, no, that cannot be true!

Hjördis. No, no, be comforted, Dagny—indeed it cannot be true. Certainly, if Sigurd were of the same disposition now as he was then, it might be true. Then, all his aim and desire was to be the foremost man in the land—now he is content with a lesser happiness.

Dagny. No, Hjördis, Sigurd's mind is set on as great things as ever. I see quite well that I am not a fitting

wife for him.   He has hidden it from me, but it shall be
different now.

Hjördis. What do you mean to do?

Dagny. I mean to be a burden and a hindrance to him
no longer.

Hjördis. Are you thinking of—?

Dagny. Silence, someone is coming.

(*A servant comes from the back of the hall.*)

Servant. Sigurd the Viking approaches.

Hjördis. Sigurd!   Then let Gunnar be summoned.

Servant. Gunnar has ridden out to assemble his neighbours, because Kaare the yeoman is—

Hjördis. Yes, yes, I know.   You may go.   (*The
servant goes out.*   HJÖRDIS *turns to* DAGNY, *who is per-
paring to go also.*)   Where are you going?

Dagny. Out of here, so as not to meet Sigurd.   The
only end there can be to this is our separation, I see
that well enough; but to meet him now—no, no, I cannot!   (*Goes out to the left.*)

Hjördis (*looks after her for a moment in silence*). And it
was she that I was going to—(*continues her train of
thought, with a glance at the bowstring*). That would
have been a paltry vengeance—no, now I have struck a
keener blow than that!   It is hard to die, but sometimes
to go on living is even worse.   (SIGURD *comes in from the
back.*)   It is Gunnar you are seeking, I suppose.   Sit
down, he will be here directly.   (*Turns to go.*)

Sigurd. No, stay.   It is you I am seeking rather than
him.

Hjördis. Me?

Sigurd. And it is well that I have found you alone.

Hjordis. If you have come to insult me, a hall full
of men and women would be no protection to me.

Sigurd. Ah, I know very well what you think of
me.

Hjördis (*bitterly*). Perhaps I am doing you an injustice!   No, no, Sigurd, you have poisoned my whole life.
Remember, it was you that played me that shameful
trick; it was you that sat with me in my chamber and

fooled me with talk of love, while all the time you were laughing craftily at me; you flung me to Gunnar, because I was good enough for him—and then you sailed away from Iceland with the woman you loved!

Sigurd. There is much that the will of man can accomplish; but great events are directed by fate—and thus it has been with us two.

Hjördis. Very true—the cruel Norns rule the world; still, their power is but slight, if they do not find our own hearts respond to them. Happiness waits for whoever is strong enough to defy the Norns—and that I mean to do.

Sigurd. What do you mean?

Hjördis. I mean to risk a trial of my strength with them, though they be greater than I. But let us talk no more of it; I have much to do to-day. (*Sits down at the table.*)

Sigurd (*after a short pause*). You are making good weapons for Gunnar.

Hjördis. Not for Gunnar, but against you.

Sigurd. It may prove to be the same thing.

Hjördis. That may be so; for, if I become as the Norns, then shall you and Gunnar sooner or later—. (*She stops, leans backwards against the table, looks at him with a smile, and continues in an altered tone.*) Do you know what I think of sometimes? I often take pleasure in devising imaginary scenes. At such times I sit and shut my eyes and think: Now Sigurd the Brave is come to our shores—he threatens to burn down our house and us in it. All Gunnar's men are slain; only he and I are left. They are setting light to the house. "One bowshot," says Gunnar, "a single shot will save us"—and his bowstring breaks. "Hjördis, cut off a tress of your hair, and make a bowstring of it—it will mean saving our lives!" But I laugh, and say: "Let it burn, let it burn—life is not worth a handful of hair to me!"

Sigurd. There is a strange power in all you say.
(*Draws nearer to her.*)

Hjördis (*looking coldly at him*). You—you sit beside me !

Sigurd. You think I bear wrath in my heart. Hjördis, this is the last time we shall talk together; there is something that lies like a canker on my soul, and I cannot go away thus; you must know me better before I go.

Hjördis. What do you want?

Sigurd. To tell you a tale.

Hjördis. A sad one?

Sigurd. Sad as life itself.

Hjördis (*bitterly*). What do you know of the sadness of life?

Sigurd. Judge of that, when my tale is told.

Hjördis. Tell it then; I will work meanwhile.

(*He sits down on a stool by her side.*)

Sigurd. Once there were two young warriors, who sailed away from Norway to win riches and fame. They had sworn friendship together, and stood honourably by one another wherever their wanderings led them.

Hjördis. And the two young warriors' names were Sigurd and Gunnar?

Sigurd. Well, we may give them those names. After some time they came to Iceland, where dwelt an old chieftain who had gone thither from Norway in King Harald's time. He had two fair maidens in his house; but one of them, his foster-daughter, far surpassed the other, for she was stout of heart; and the two warriors used to talk of her, and agree that neither of them had seen a goodlier woman.

Hjördis (*anxiously*). Both of them? Are you mocking me?

Sigurd. Gunnar thought of her night and day, and so did Sigurd; but neither spoke of their love. On her part, she gave no sign that Gunnar pleased her; on the other hand it was easier to see that Sigurd found no favour in her eyes.

Hjördis (*breathlessly*). Go on, I entreat you—!

Sigurd. Well, this only made Sigurd think the more of

her, but he showed it to no one. Then it happened that one evening, at a feast, this proud maiden swore that no man should possess her save the one who should perform a great task that she named. Sigurd's heart beat high with joy, for he felt in him the strength to do the deed; but Gunnar took him apart, and told him of his love—Sigurd said naught of his own, and so it came about that—

Hjördis (interrupting him). Sigurd, Sigurd! (*Controls herself.*) And this tale—is it true?

Sigurd. It is. One of us had to give way. Gunnar was my friend; I could not have done otherwise than I did. Thus it was that you became Gunnar's wife, and I married another woman.

Hjördis. And came to love her?

Sigurd. I learnt to esteem her; but there is only one woman Sigurd has ever loved, and that is the woman who set her face against him from the first day they met. (*Rises.*) And so ends my tale, and now let us part.— Farewell, wife of Gunnar; we shall never meet again.

Hjördis. No, stay! Alas for us both—Sigurd, what have you done?

Sigurd (astonished). What have I done? What ails you?

Hjördis. And you tell me all this now! No, no—it cannot be the truth!

Sigurd. This is the last time we shall talk together; every word of it is the truth. I wish d you to judge more kindly of me, and that is why I had to tell you now.

Hjördis (clasping her hands involuntarily, and looking at him in calm amazement). Loved me—you loved me— you! (*Impetuously, going close up to him.*) I do not believe you! (*Fixes her eyes on him and says in an outburst of wild agony.*) Yes, it is true—unhappily for us both! (*Covers her face with her hands and draws back.*)

Sigurd (in dismay). Hjördis!

Hjördis (quietly, struggling between tears and laughter).

Take no notice of me. All I meant was—. (*Lays her hand on his arm.*) Sigurd, you have not told all the tale! That proud maiden you spoke of—she loved you too!

Sigurd (recoiling). You!

Hjördis (with composure). Yes, Sigurd, I loved you—I know it now. You said I was silent and ungentle with you—what else could a woman do? If I had let my love be seen, you would have thought but little of me. You always seemed to me the goodliest of all men—and to see you the husband of another gave me a bitter pain that I scarcely understood!

Sigurd (shaken). It is a web of woe that the Norns have weaved around us two.

Hjördis. You have yourself to blame for it! A man should act firmly and bravely!   When I set that hard condition on which I was to be won, in very truth I was thinking of you—and then you could—!

Sigurd. I knew Gunnar was heart sick; I alone could cure him—how else could I have chosen? Besides, had I known what I now know, I could not have answered for myself; the power of love is too strong.

Hjördis (quickly). Well, then, Sigurd—a wretched trick has separated us for these long years; now the knot is untied; the days that are to come shall requite us.

Sigurd (shaking his head). That can never be. We must part again.

Hjördis. We must not. I love you, and dare say so now without a blush, for mine is not the light love of a weak woman. If I were a man—by all the Gods, my love could not be stronger than it is! Up, Sigurd! Happiness is worth some great deed to win it. We are both free, if we ourselves will it, and so we may win the game!

Sigurd. Free? What do you mean?

Hjördis. What is Dagny to you? What can she ever be to you? No more than Gunnar is to me in my inmost heart. What compulsion is there to spoil two wretched lives!

Sigurd. Hjördis, Hjördis!

Hjördis. Let Gunnar stay here; let Dagny go back to Iceland with her father; I will put on my armour and follow you wherever you choose to go. (SIGURD *moves uneasily.*) It is not as your wife that I will follow you—for I have belonged to another, and the woman still lives who has been your bedfellow. No, Sigurd, not as your wife, but like a splendid Valkyrie will I follow you—urge you on to the fight and to a hero's deeds, so that your name may be famed abroad; when swords are flashing I will stand by your side, and will go with your warriors across the stormy seas wherever fate may lead you; and when your funeral song is sung, it shall honour Sigurd and Hjördis together!

Sigurd. That was what I used to dream of once, but now it is too late. Gunnar and Dagny stand between us —as they have both the right to do. I wasted the love of my youth for Gunnar's sake—if I must suffer for that, at least it must not have been done in vain. And Dagny —who left her home and her own people, suspecting nothing and full of trust—never must she think that I yearned for Hjördis as often as she took me in her arms.

Hjördis. And for such reasons as this would you burden your whole life? What is the good of your power and strength and all your splendid gifts of mind? Do you think that now I could endure to live in Gunnar's house any longer? No, Sigurd, believe me, there is much here that a man like you could achieve. Erik is King of Norway; pit yourself against him. There are many doughty fighters will range themselves with your own men. We will go forward with invincible might, to fight and strive and never rest until you are seated in the King's throne!

Sigurd. Hjördis, Hjördis, it was what I used to dream of in my wild youth; let it be forgotten—do not tempt me!

Hjördis (in exaltation). The Norns have decreed that our lives should be bound up together; it cannot be otherwise. Now I see clearly my task in life—to make you famous. You have been in my thoughts every day, every hour I have lived here. I tried to tear you out of my mind, but had not the power. Now there is no need—now that I know you love me.

Sigurd (forcing himself to speak coldly). If that is so— then, listen; I did love you, but that is all over now—I have forgotten those days.

Hjördis. It is a lie, Sigurd! This much worth I know I have—that if you once loved me you can never forget it.

Sigurd (vehemently). I must—I will!

Hjördis. Maybe—but you cannot! Thwart me if you will, it will do you no good—for before nightfall Gunnar and Dagny shall know all.

Sigurd. You would not do that!

Hjördis. I would!

Sigurd. Then I have known you but ill; I have always imagined you noble-hearted.

Hjördis. Evil days beget evil thoughts. You have put too great a trust in me. I will and must follow you, out into the battle of life! The roof of Gunnar's house is too low for me.

Sigurd (with emphasis). But you have always held men's honour in such high esteem. There is reasonable ground of quarrel between Gunnar and me. Suppose he were to fall by my hand—would you even then disclose everything and follow me?

Hjördis (with a start). Why do you ask that?

Sigurd. Answer me first. What would you do if I slew your husband?

Hjördis (looking fixedly at him). I should keep silence, and never rest until I had brought about your death.

Sigurd (with a smile). That is well, Hjördis—I knew it would be so.

Hjördis (quickly). But that can never happen!

Sigurd. It may; you yourself have cast the die that may decide Gunnar's death or mine.

(GUNNAR *and some of his men enter from the back.*)

Gunnar (gloomily, to HJÖRDIS). Well—the seed you have sown is sprouting!

Sigurd (approaching). What has gone amiss with you?

Gunnar. Sigurd, is it you! What has gone amiss with me? Nothing but what I might have expected. As soon as Dagny had brought me the news of Kaare, I mounted my horse and rode to seek help among my neighbours.

Hjördis (anxiously). Well?

Gunnar. A surly answer met me everywhere. My quarrel with Kaare was an unworthy affair, they said—other things they said, too, that I cannot repeat. I am a dishonoured man; I am accused of having played a coward's part, and it is thought a disgrace to have anything to do with me.

Sigurd. It shall not be thought a disgrace long. Before nightfall you shall have plenty of men to go with you against Kaare.

Gunnar. Sigurd!

Hjördis (in a low voice, triumphantly). I knew it!

Sigurd (with forced sternness). But it means also that peace is broken between us. Listen to me, Gunnar—you have slain Thorolf, my wife's kinsman, and for that I challenge you to a duel to the death to-morrow at sunrise!

(HJÖRDIS, *torn by her emotions, takes a step towards* SIGURD, *but controls herself and remains motionless during the rest of the scene.*)

Gunnar (in profound amazement). A duel!—With me! You are jesting, Sigurd!

Sigurd. I formally challenge you to a duel. It will be a question of life and death—one of us must fall!

Gunnar (bitterly). Ah, I understand. You were talking alone with Hjördis when I came in; she has insulted you afresh.

Sigurd. Perhaps. (*Turning slightly towards* HJÖRDIS.) A noble-spirited woman must defend her husband's honour. (*To the men standing at the back.*) And you, fellows, do you go now to Gunnar's neighbours and tell them that to-morrow he is to fight me; none will call that

man a coward who will stand up in fight against Sigurd
the Viking.

(*The men go out.*)

Gunnar (*goes quickly up to* SIGURD *and grasps his hand
in obvious emotion*). Sigurd, my noble brother, I understand now. You are risking your life for my honour,
just as once you risked it for my happiness.

Sigurd. Thank your wife. She has had most to do
with what I have done. To-morrow, at sunrise—

Gunnar. I will meet you. (*Affectionately.*) Foster-
brother, will you accept a good sword at my hands? It
is a gift of some value.

Sigurd. I thank you—but let it hang where it is.
Who can tell whether to-morrow night I shall have need
of a sword?

Gunnar (*grasping his hand*). Farewell, Sigurd!

Sigurd. Farewell—and may good fortune go with you!

(*They part.* GUNNAR *goes out to the left;* SIGURD
casts a glance at HJÖRDIS *and goes out at the back.*)

Hjördis (*after a pause, in a low and thoughtful voice*).
A duel to the death in the morning! Which of them
will fall? (*Is silent for a short time; then cries out, as if
possessed by a sudden resolve:*) No matter which of them
falls—Sigurd and I shall never be separated!

ACT IV

(SCENE.—*The seashore. It is evening. Glimpses of
the moon are seen in a dark, storm-swept sky. At the back
is a lofty, newly-made grave-mound.* ÖRNULF *is sitting
on a rock to the right of the foreground, bareheaded, his
elbows resting on his knees and his face hidden in his hands.
His men are at work on the grave-mound, to the light of
torches. After a short pause* SIGURD *and* DAGNY *come out
of the boat-shed, in which a fire is burning.*)

Dagny (*in a low voice*). There he sits, still. (*Holds*
SIGURD *back.*) No, do not speak to him!

Sigurd. You are right, it is too soon; let us leave him alone.

Dagny (*crosses over and looks at her father with quiet sorrow*). He was so brave yesterday, when he bore Thorolf's body upon his back, and so brave while the grave was being dug; but when they had all been laid in it, and the earth and stones heaped over them, then his grief was too great for him—it seemed to crush him. (*Wipes away her tears.*) Tell me, Sigurd, when do you mean to sail home to Iceland?

Sigurd. As soon as this storm is over and I have finished with Gunnar.

Dagny. And then you will buy land and build yourself a house, and never go to war again?

Sigurd. Yes, yes—I have promised you so.

Dagny. And I may really believe that Hjördis was deceiving me when she said I was no fit wife for you?

Sigurd. Yes, yes, Dagny—you may believe me.

Dagny. Then I am happy again, and will try to forget all the horrors I have seen here. In the long winter evenings we will often talk of Gunnar and Hjördis, and—

Sigurd. No, Dagny, as you value our happiness, never let me hear Hjördis' name again when we are home in Iceland!

Dagny (*gently reproachful*). Your hatred of her is unreasonable. Sigurd, that is not like you!

One of the Men (*approaching*). The grave-mound is finished.

Örnulf (*as if waking from a dream*). The grave-mound? Is it—then we must—

Sigurd. Speak to him now, Dagny.

Dagny (*going to her father's side*). Father, it is cold out here, and a storm is brewing.

Örnulf. What matter if it is? The grave-mound is solidly built; they will lie warm.

Dagny. Yes, but you—

Örnulf. I? I am not cold.

Dagny. You have eaten nothing to-day. Come into the shelter—there is food ready there.

Örnulf. Let it bide—I am not hungry.

Dagny. But do not sit here like this—believe me, it can do you no good; it is not what you are wont to do.

Örnulf. You are right; there is something gripping me at the chest; I cannot draw my breath. (*He buries his face again in his hands. After a pause,* DAGNY *sits down beside him.*)

Dagny. To-morrow, will you hoist sail and away to Iceland?

Örnulf (without looking up). What should I do there? No, I shall stay with my sons.

Dagny (with a cry of pain). Father!

Örnulf (lifting his head). Go in, and let me be. Wher one or two nights of storm have beaten upon me, there will be an end.

Sigurd. How can you have such thoughts!

Örnulf. Do you wonder that I long for rest? My day's work is done; I have buried my sons. (*Impatiently.*) Leave me alone!—Go, go!

Sigurd (in a low voice, to DAGNY, *who has got up).* Let him sit awhile longer.

Dagny. No, I must try one more appeal—I know him. (*To* ÖRNULF.) Your day's work is done, you say—but it is not done yet. You have buried your sons; but are you not a bard? Then you must chant a funeral song in their honour.

Örnulf. A funeral song? No, no. Yesterday I might have done that; to-day I am too old.

Dagny. You must do it. Your sons were all men worthy of honour; they must have their funeral song, and none of their kin can make it but you.

Örnulf (looking questioningly at SIGURD). A funeral song? What do you say, Sigurd?

Sigurd. I think Dagny is right; you should do as she says.

Dagny. It will seem to your neighbours in Iceland ill done if, when they drink to the memory of Örnulf's

sons at the funeral feast, there is no funeral song to
chant.   There is no need to think of following your
sons yet.

Örnulf. Well, I will try; and do you, Dagny, listen to
it, so that afterwards you may carve it in runes!

(*His men group themselves round him with their torches.
He is silent for a little, in thought; and then begins:*)

> The heart with woe wounded
> Cannot laugh with the Song-God;
> Heart-broken, the bard then
> Makes a song of his hardship.

> To me, too, the Song-God
> Gave the gift of the glee-men;
> Let me make with my heartstrings
> My loss loud and mournful.

> The Norns, stern and wrathful,
> Have laid waste my life-way;
> Have scattered my gladness;
> Have wasted my housegear.

> Seven sons were to Örnulf,
> By the gods freely given:
> Now he fares forthright lonely:
> Not a son left hath Örnulf.

> Seven sons, seven swordsmen,
> Like a bulwark about me;
> Like a built wall to harbour
> The white-haired old Viking.

> Now the wall it is wasted,
> Laid low; and my sons lie
> Dead, all; while an old man,
> In a lone house sits Örnulf.

> Thorolf, youngest, and bravest
> Of brave ones; oh Thorolf!
> I could yet be contented,
> Had my youngest been left me.

Fair like spring thou wert, Thorolf,
Fair and kind to thy father;
With a light in thy forehead,
The promise of heroes.

But a mortal wound, baleful
And heavy, has crush'd me,
As if my old bosom
Were crush'd between shields.

A jealous Norn leaves me
No rich gift, god-given;
She has sprinkled my pathway
With pain and with trouble.

Weak, worn, my old weapon:
Had I only the gods' arm,
One thing would be left me—
On the Norn to take vengeance!

One thing left to Örnulf:
To fight for her downfall
Who hath seized all he held dear,
And hath taken, last, Thorolf.

Hath she seized all?   Nay, one thing
The Norn hath not taken:
For Örnulf at birth had
The gods' gift, the song-mead.

My sons she took from me:
But power hath my tongue still
To sing with the Song-God—
Ay, my grief turn to singing.

On my lips did the Norn lay
The fair gift, the song-gift:
Loud my song shall resound, then,
Even here, by my sons' grave.

> Hail ye! my bright riders!
> Hail ye! while ye ride there,
> My sons! Let the gods' gift
> Heal the woe, the world-anguish!

(*He draws a deep breath, pushes the hair back from his fore-head, and says calmly:*)

Ah!—now Örnulf is himself again. (*To his men.*) Come to supper, my lads; we have had a heavy day's work. (*Goes with them into the boat-shed.*)

Dagny. Thanks to the gods above, that put such good counsel into my mind! (*To* SIGURD.) Are you not going in.

Sigurd. No, I have no fancy to. Tell me, is everything ready for to-morrow?

Dagny. Everything. A shroud, sewn with silk, lies upon the bench within; but I have shed no tears over it, for I know well that you will be a match for Gunnar.

Sigurd. May the gods grant that you may never shed tears on my account. (*Stops and looks into the distance.*)

Dagny. What are you listening to?

Sigurd. Do you not hear—over there? (*Points to the left.*)

Dagny. Yes, it sounds like a storm over the sea!

Sigurd (*going towards the background*). There will be hard hailstones from this storm. (*Calls.*) Who comes there?

Kaare (*from without*). Folk that you know, Sigurd! (KAARE, *with a rabble of armed men, comes in from the left.*)

Sigurd. Where are you going?

Kaare. To Gunnar's house!

Sigurd. As foes?

Kaare. Yes, trust us for that! You hindered me before; but now I expect this will be to your liking.

Sigurd. Maybe.

Kaare. I have heard of your business with Gunnar; but, if I have my way, it will be with weak weapons that he goes to the duel.

Sigurd. It is dangerous work you are thinking of; have a care, Kaare!

Kaare (with a defiant laugh). Leave that to me! If you want to rig your ship to-night, I will furnish you with a light to see by!—Come, all of you, here is the path! (*They go out.*)

Dagny. Sigurd, Sigurd, you must prevent this disaster!

Sigurd (goes to the door of the shed, and calls in). Up Örnulf—avenge yourself on Kaare!

Örnulf (coming out with his men). Kaare!—where is he?

Sigurd. He is making for Gunnar's house, to burn it down over his head!

Örnulf. Aha—let him, then! That will avenge me on Gunnar and Hjördis at one stroke. I will look for Kaare later.

Sigurd. No, that is profitless talk! You must look for Kaare to-night, if you wish to strike at him. As soon as he has done this foul deed, he will take to the hills. I have challenged Gunnar to a duel; he will not escape you, even supposing I do not—. Well, it is no matter; to-night he must be protected from his foes, for it would be a disgrace if an outlawed wretch like Kaare were to steal my vengeance from me!

Örnulf. That is true. I will protect Gunnar to-night; but to-morrow he must die.

Sigurd. Either he or I—of that you may be certain.

Örnulf. Vengeance, then, for Örnulf's kinsmen!
          (*Rushes out with his men.*)

Sigurd. Dagny, go with him! I must stay here, for the news of our duel has spread far and wide, and I must not meet Gunnar before the time has come. But you must guide and advise your father. He must act honourably. In Gunnar's house there are many women; no harm must come to Hjördis or the others.

Dagny. Yes, yes, I will go with him. You are thoughtful even for Hjördis; thank you for that, Sigurd.

Sigurd. Go, go, Dagny!

Dagny. I am going; but we need not fear for Hjördis —she has a suit of golden armour in her chamber, and can defend herself.

Sigurd. So I think. But go now; be your father's guide, and watch over them all and—over Gunnar's wife!

Dagny. Trust to me. Farewell, till we meet again! (*Goes out.*)

Sigurd. This is the first time, foster-brother, that I have not taken up arms when you were in danger. (*Listens.*) I hear cries and sword-blows—they are at the house already. (*Turns to go, but stops suddenly and starts back in amazement.*) Hjördis! Is she come here?

(HjÖRDIS *enters hastily, dressed in a short scarlet kirtle and golden armour; helmet, coat of mail, arm-pieces and greaves; her hair is flying loose; on her back a quiver is slung, and she carries a small shield at her belt; in her hand is the bow with the bowstring of her own hair. She keeps looking behind her, as if in fear of something that followed her; goes close to* SIGURD, *catches him by the arm, and whispers to him:*)

Hjördis. Sigurd, Sigurd, can you see it?

Sigurd. What? Where?

Hjördis. The wolf—just behind me! It does not move—it glares at me with two red eyes!—It is my familiar, Sigurd! It has appeared to me three times; that means that I shall surely die to-night!

Sigurd. Hjördis! Hjördis!

Hjördis. Now he has disappeared into the ground! I have had my warning.

Sigurd. You are ill; come into shelter!

Hjördis. No, I will wait here; I have not much more time!

Sigurd. What has come over you?

Hjördis. What has come over me? I cannot tell; but what you said to-day was true, that Gunnar and Dagny stand between us. We must get away from them and from life; then we shall be together.

*C 552

Sigurd. We? Ah, you mean—!

Hjördis (with exaltation). I have known no real home since the day you took another woman to wife. It was a wicked deed you did then! There is only one gift a man may not give to his dearest friend—and that is, the woman he loves; for if he does that, he breaks the thread of fate that the Norn has spun, and two lives are ruined. There is a voice within me that tells me surely that my destiny was that my strong soul should encourage and support you when things went ill with you; and that yours was to let me find, in one man's love, all that was bravest and best in manhood. For this I know, Sigurd, that if our lives had been united you would have become the most renowned man, and I the happiest woman, in the world!

Sigurd. Such regrets are useless now. Do you suppose I can see any happiness in the life that lies before me? To be by Dagny's side every day, and to pretend a love that my heart shrinks from. However, it must be so; it cannot be altered.

Hjördis (with growing excitement). It shall be! We will both leave this life! Do you see this bowstring? I shall hit surely with this, for I have sung the goodliest spells of magic over it! *(Stretches the bow and fits an arrow to it.)* Listen! Listen, how the wind howls! It is the last ride of the dead men; my spells have called them hither. We shall follow in their train!

Sigurd (recoiling). Hjördis, Hjördis—I am afraid of you!

Hjördis (without heeding him). No power can alter our fate now! After all, it is better so, than if we had been married in this life; better than sitting in your house weaving linen and wool, and bearing children to you—ugh!

Sigurd. Stop, stop! Your magic arts have over-wrought your mind; your soul has sickened under them. *(In alarm.)* Ah, look—look! Gunnar's house —it is burning!

Hjördis. Let it burn! Let it burn! The mansions of the clouds are better than Gunnar's wooden halls!

Sigurd. But Egil, your son—they are killing him!

Hjördis. Let him die—and then my shame will die with him!

Sigurd. And Gunnar—they are taking your husband's life!

Hjördis. What matter to me! I shall follow a better husband home to-night! Yes, Sigurd, it must be so. This country holds no happiness for me. The White God is coming northwards; I will not stay to meet him. The old gods are not as mighty as they were; they are asleep, or sit like shadows of themselves; we will wrest their power from them. Out of this life, Sigurd; I will set you on the throne of heaven, and sit beside you there! (*The storm rages wildly.*) Listen, listen! There come our companions! Do you see the black horses flying by—one for you and one for me! (*Raises her bow and shoots him.*) Now to your last journey!

Sigurd. A goodly shot, Hjördis! (*Falls.*)

Hjördis (*in triumph, while she rushes towards him*). Sigurd, my brother—now we belong to one another!

Sigurd. Now less than ever. Here our ways part—for I am a Christian.

Hjördis (*dismayed*). You! Oh, no, no!

Sigurd. The White God is my god. King Athelstan taught me to know Him—it is to Him I am going now.

Hjördis (*in despair*). And I—! (*Lets her bow fall.*) Alas, alas!

Sigurd. My life has been oppressed with sorrow since the hour I tore you out of my heart and gave you to Gunnar. Thanks, Hjördis—now my heart is light and free! (*Dies.*)

Hjördis (*quietly*). Dead! And I have made shipwreck of my life! (*The storm increases. She cries in a wild outburst:*) There they come! My witchcraft has brought them! No, no—I will not go with them! I will not ride without Sigurd! It is no use—they see me; they laugh and beckon to me; they are spurring their horses! (*Rushes to the edge of the cliff.*) They are upon

me—and no shelter, nowhere to hide! Yes, perhaps
in the depths of the sea! (*Throws herself down.*)

(ÖRNULF, DAGNY, GUNNAR *carrying* EGIL, *come in
one by one from the right, followed by* SIGURD'S *men.*)

Örnulf (*turning to the grave-mound*). Now I can sleep
in peace; for you are not unavenged, my sons!

Dagny. Father, father—I am wellnigh dead with fear!
The ways are red with blood; and the storm!—listen,
listen!

Gunnar (*with* EGIL *in his arms*). Let me come in peace
and shelter my child!

Örnulf. Gunnar!

Gunnar. Yes, Örnulf, my house is burnt and my men
all slain. I am in your power—do what you will with
me!

Örnulf. That rests with Sigurd. But come into
shelter; it is not safe out here!

Dagny. Yes—in, in! (*Goes towards the boat-shed, sees*
SIGURD'S *dead body, and shrieks.*) Sigurd, my husband!
—they have killed him! (*Throws herself down beside
him.*)

Örnulf. Sigurd!

Gunnar (*setting* EGIL *down*). Sigurd killed!

Dagny (*looking wildly at them as they stand by the corpse*).
No, no, it is not true!—he must be alive still. (*Sees
the bow.*) Ah, what is that! (*Gets up.*)

Örnulf. Daughter, it is as you said at first—Sigurd
is slain.

Gunnar (*as if seized by a sudden thought*). And Hjördis!—Has Hjördis been here?

Dagny (*in a low voice, meaningly*). I do not know; but
this I know, that her bow has been here.

Gunnar. Ah, I feared it!

Dagny. Hush, hush! (*To herself.*) How bitterly she
must have hated him!

Gunnar (*in a low voice*). Killed him—the night before
the duel; at last she loved me, then.

(*All start suddenly as they hear, hurtling through the air
the last ride of the dead warriors.*)

Egil (in terror). Father! Look, look!

Gunnar. What is it?

Egil. Up there—all those black horses—!

Gunnar. It is only the clouds—

Örnulf. No, it is the last ride of the dead.

Egil (with a shriek). Mother is with them!

Dagny. Merciful gods!

Gunnar. Child, what are you saying?

Egil. There—in front—on the black horse! Father! father! *(Clings to his father in terror. A short pause; then the storm passes over, the clouds part, and the moon shines out over all the scene.)*

Gunnar (quietly and sadly). Now we know she is dead.

Örnulf. Yes, Gunnar—and it was she rather than you that was the object of my vengeance. Our meeting has cost us both dear; there is my hand—let there be peace and forgiveness between us.

Gunnar. Thanks, Örnulf! And now, to the ships. I am for Iceland with you!

Örnulf. Yes, to Iceland—and long shall this journey be remembered:

> Long remembered shall these heroes
> Be, in all our northern land;
> And our children's tongues shall honour
> Those that sleep upon this strand.

GHOSTS

A Domestic Drama in Three Acts

DRAMATIS PERSONÆ

Mrs. Alving (a widow).
Oswald Alving (her son, an artist).
Manders (the Pastor of the parish).
Engstrand (a carpenter).
Regina Engstrand (his daughter, in Mrs. Alving's
    service).

*The action takes place at Mrs Alving's house on one of the larger
fjords of western Norway.*

ACT I

(SCENE.—*A large room looking upon a garden. A door in the left-hand wall, and two in the right. In the middle of the room, a round table with chairs set about it, and books, magazines and newspapers upon it. In the foreground on the left, a window, by which is a small sofa with a work-table in front of it. At the back the room opens into a conservatory rather smaller than the room. From the right-hand side of this a door leads to the garden. Through the large panes of glass that form the outer wall of the conservatory, a gloomy fjord landscape can be discerned, half obscured by steady rain.*

ENGSTRAND *is standing close up to the garden door. His left leg is slightly deformed, and he wears a boot with a clump of wood under the sole.* REGINA, *with an empty garden-syringe in her hand, is trying to prevent his coming in.*)

Regina (*below her breath*). What is it you want? Stay where you are. The rain is dripping off you.

Engstrand. God's good rain, my girl.

Regina. The Devil's own rain, that's what it is!

Engstrand. Lord, how you talk, Regina. (*Takes a few limping steps forward.*) What I wanted to tell you was this—

Regina. Don't clump about like that, stupid! The young master is lying asleep upstairs.

Engstrand. Asleep still? In the middle of the day?

Regina. Well, it's no business of yours.

Engstrand. I was out on the spree last night—

Regina. I don't doubt it.

Engstrand. Yes, we are poor weak mortals, my girl—

Regina. We are indeed.

Engstrand. —and the temptations of the world are manifold, you know—but, for all that, here I was at my work at half-past five this morning.

Regina. Yes, yes, but make yourself scarce now. I am not going to stand here as if I had a *rendez-vous* with you.

Engstrand. As if you had a what?

Regina. I am not going to have any one find you here; so now you know, and you can go.

Engstrand (*coming a few steps nearer*). Not a bit of it! Not before we have had a little chat. This afternoon I shall have finished my job down at the school house, and I shall be off home to town by to-night's boat.

Regina (*mutters*). Pleasant journey to you!

Engstrand. Thanks, my girl. To-morrow is the opening of the Orphanage, and I expect there will be a fine kick-up here and plenty of good strong drink, don't you know. And no one shall say of Jacob Engstrand that he can't hold off when temptation comes in his way.

Regina. Oho!

Engstrand. Yes, because there will be a lot of fine folk here to-morrow. Parson Manders is expected from town, too.

Regina. What is more, he's coming to-day.

Engstrand. There you are! And I'm going to be precious careful he doesn't have anything to say against me, do you see?

Regina. Oh, that's your game, is it?

Engstrand. What do you mean?

Regina (*with a significant look at him*). What is it you want to humbug Mr. Manders out of, this time?

Engstrand. Sh! Sh! Are you crazy? Do you suppose *I* would want to humbug Mr. Manders? No, no— Mr. Manders has always been too kind a friend for me to do that. But what I wanted to talk to you about, was my going back home to-night.

Regina. The sooner you go, the better I shall be pleased.

Engstrand. Yes, only I want to take you with me, Regina.

Regina (open-mouthed). You want to take me—? What did you say?

Engstrand. I want to take you home with me, I said.

Regina (contemptuously). You will never get me home with you.

Engstrand. Ah, we shall see about that.

Regina. Yes, you can be quite certain we *shall* see about that. I, who have been brought up by a lady like Mrs. Alving?—I, who have been treated almost as if I were her own child?—do you suppose I am going home with *you?*—to such a house as yours? Not likely!

Engstrand. What the devil do you mean? Are you setting yourself up against your father, you hussy?

Regina (mutters, without looking at him). You have often told me I was none of yours.

Engstrand. Bah!—why do you want to pay any attention to that?

Regina. Haven't you many and many a time abused me and called me a —? For shame!

Engstrand. I'll swear I never used such an ugly word.

Regina. Oh, it doesn't matter what word you used.

Engstrand. Besides, that was only when I was a bit fuddled—hm! Temptations are manifold in this world, Regina.

Regina. Ugh!

Engstrand. And it was when your mother was in a nasty temper. I had to find some way of getting my knife into her, my girl. She was always so precious genteel. (*Mimicking her.*) "Let go, Jacob! Let me be! Please to remember that I was three years with the Alvings at Rosenvold, and they were people who went to Court!" (*Laughs.*) Bless my soul, she never could forget that Captain Alving got a Court appointment while she was in service here.

Regina. Poor mother—you worried her into her grave pretty soon.

Engstrand (*shrugging his shoulders*). Of course, of course; I have got to take the blame for everything.

Regina (*beneath her breath, as she turns away*). Ugh— that leg, too !

Engstrand. What are you saying, my girl ?

Regina. Pied de mouton.

Engstrand. Is that English ?

Regina. Yes.

Engstrand. You have had a good education out here, and no mistake; and it may stand you in good stead now, Regina.

Regina (*after a short silence*). And what was it you wanted me to come to town for ?

Engstrand. Need you ask why a father wants his only child ? Ain't I a poor lonely widower ?

Regina. Oh, don't come to me with that tale. Why do you want me to go ?

Engstrand. Well, I must tell you I am thinking of taking up a new line now.

Regina (*whistles*). You have tried that so often—but it has always proved a fool's errand.

Engstrand. Ah, but this time you will just see, Regina ! Strike me dead if—

Regina (*stamping her foot*). Stop swearing !

Engstrand. Sh ! Sh !—you're quite right, my girl, quite right ! What I wanted to say was only this, that I have put by a tidy penny out of what I have made by working at this new Orphanage up here.

Regina. Have you ? All the better for you.

Engstrand. What is there for a man to spend his money on, out here in the country ?

Regina. Well, what then ?

Engstrand. Well, you see, I thought of putting the money into something that would pay. I thought of some kind of an eating-house for seafaring folk—

Regina. Heavens !

Engstrand. Oh, a high-class eating-house, of course,— not a pigsty for common sailors. Damn it, no; it would be a place ships' captains and first mates would come to; really good sort of people, you know.

Regina. And what should I—?

Engstrand. You would help there. But only to make a show, you know. You wouldn't find it hard work, I can promise you, my girl. You should do exactly as you liked.

Regina. Oh, yes, quite so!

Engstrand. But we must have some women in the house; that is as clear as daylight. Because in the evening we must make the place a little attractive— some singing and dancing, and that sort of thing. Remember they are seafolk—wayfarers on the waters of life! (*Coming nearer to her.*) Now don't be a fool and stand in your own way, Regina. What good are you going to do here? Will this education, that your mistress has paid for, be of any use? You are to look after the children in the new Home, I hear. Is that the sort of work for you? Are you so frightfully anxious to go and wear out your health and strength for the sake of these dirty brats?

Regina. No, if things were to go as I want them to, then—. Well, it may happen; who knows? It may happen!

Engstrand. What may happen?

Regina. Never you mind. Is it much that you have put by, up here?

Engstrand. Taking it all round, I should say about forty or fifty pounds.

Regina. That's not so bad.

Engstrand. It's enough to make a start with, my girl.

Regina. Don't you mean to give me any of the money?

Engstrand. No, I'm hanged if I do.

Regina. Don't you mean to send me as much as a dress-length of stuff, just for once?

Engstrand. Come and live in the town with me and you shall have plenty of dresses.

Regina. Pooh!—I can get that much for myself, if I have a mind to.

Engstrand. But it's far better to have a father's guiding hand, Regina. Just now I can get a nice house in Little Harbour Street. They don't want much money down for it—and we could make it like a sort of seamen's home, don't you know.

Regina. But I have no intention of living with you! I have nothing whatever to do with you. So now, be off!

Engstrand. You wouldn't be living with me long, my girl. No such luck—not if you knew how to play your cards. Such a fine wench as you have grown this last year or two—

Regina. Well—?

Engstrand. It wouldn't be very long before some first mate came along—or perhaps a captain.

Regina. I don't mean to marry a man of that sort. Sailors have no *savoir-vivre*.

Engstrand. What haven't they got?

Regina. I know what sailors are, I tell you. They aren't the sort of people to marry.

Engstrand. Well, don't bother about marrying them. You can make it pay just as well. (*More confidentially.*) That fellow—the Englishman—the one with the yacht— he gave seventy pounds, he did; and she wasn't a bit prettier than you.

Regina (*advancing towards him*). Get out!

Engstrand (*stepping back*). Here! here!—you're not going to hit me, I suppose?

Regina. Yes! If you talk like that of mother, I will hit you. Get out, I tell you! (*Pushes him up to the garden door.*) And don't bang the doors. Young Mr. Alving—

Engstrand. Is asleep—I know. It's funny how anxious you are about young Mr. Alving. (*In a lower tone.*) Oho! is it possible that it is *he* that—?

Regina. Get out, and be quick about it! Your wits are wandering, my good man. No, don't go that way; Mr. Manders is just coming along. Be off down the kitchen stairs.

Engstrand (*moving towards the right*). Yes, yes—all right. But have a bit of a chat with him that's coming along. He's the chap to tell you what a child owes to its father. For I am your father, anyway, you know. I can prove it by the Register. (*He goes out through the farther door which* REGINA *has opened. She shuts it after him, looks hastily at herself in the mirror, fans herself with her handkerchief and sets her collar straight; then busies herself with the flowers.* MANDERS *enters the conservatory through the garden door. He wears an overcoat, carries an umbrella, and has a small travelling-bag slung over his shoulder on a strap.*)

Manders. Good morning, Miss Engstrand.

Regina (turning round with a look of pleased surprise). Oh, Mr. Manders, good morning. The boat is in, then?

Manders. Just in. (*Comes into the room.*) It is most tiresome, this rain every day.

Regina (following him in). It's a splendid rain for the farmers, Mr. Manders.

Manders. Yes, you are quite right. We town-folk think so little about that. (*Begins to take off his overcoat.*)

Regina. Oh, let me help you. That's it. Why, how wet it is! I will hang it up in the hall. Give me your umbrella, too; I will leave it open, so that it will dry.

(*She goes out with the things by the farther door on the right.* MANDERS *lays his bag and his hat down on a chair.* REGINA *re-enters.*)

Manders. Ah, it's very pleasant to get indoors. Well, is everything going on well here?

Regina. Yes, thanks.

Manders. Properly busy, though, I expect, getting ready for to-morrow?

Regina. Oh, yes, there is plenty to do.

Manders. And Mrs. Alving is at home, I hope?

Regina. Yes, she is. She has just gone upstairs to take the young master his chocolate.

Manders. Tell me—I heard down at the pier that Oswald had come back.

Regina. Yes, he came the day before yesterday. We didn't expect him till to-day.

Manders. Strong and well, I hope?

Regina. Yes, thank you, well enough. But dreadfully tired after his journey. He came straight from Paris without a stop—I mean, he came all the way without breaking his journey. I fancy he is having a sleep now, so we must talk a little bit more quietly, if you don't mind.

Manders. All right, we will be very quiet.

Regina (*while she moves an armchair up to the table*). Please sit down, Mr. Manders, and make yourself at home. (*He sits down; she puts a footstool under his feet.*) There! Is that comfortable?

Manders. Thank you, thank you. That is most comfortable. (*Looks at her.*) I'll tell you what, Miss Engstrand, I certainly think you have grown since I saw you last.

Regina. Do you think so? Mrs. Alving says, too, that I have developed.

Manders. Developed? Well, perhaps a little—just suitably. (*A short pause.*)

Regina. Shall I tell Mrs. Alving you are here?

Manders. Thanks, there is no hurry, my dear child.— Now tell me, Regina my dear, how has your father been getting on here?

Regina. Thank you, Mr. Manders, he is getting on pretty well.

Manders. He came to see me, the last time he was in town.

Regina. Did he? He is always so glad when he can have a chat with you.

Manders. And I suppose you have seen him pretty regularly every day?

Regina. I? Oh, yes, I do—whenever I have time, that is to say.

Manders. Your father has not a very strong character, Miss Engstrand. He sadly needs a guiding hand.

Regina. Yes, I can quite believe that.

Manders. He needs someone with him that he can cling to, someone whose judgment he can rely on. He acknowledged that freely himself, the last time he came up to see me.

Regina. Yes, he has said something of the same sort to me. But I don't know whether Mrs. Alving could do without me—most of all just now, when we have the new Orphanage to see about. And I should be dreadfully unwilling to leave Mrs. Alving, too; she has always been so good to me.

Manders. But a daughter's duty, my good child—. Naturally we should have to get your mistress' consent first.

Regina. Still I don't know whether it would be quite the thing, at my age, to keep house for a single man.

Manders. What!! My dear Miss Engstrand, it is your own father we are speaking of!

Regina. Yes, I dare say, but still—. Now, if it were in a good house and with a real gentleman—

Manders. But, my dear Regina—

Regina. —one whom I could feel an affection for, and really feel in the position of a daughter to—

Manders. Come, come—my dear good child—

Regina. I should like very much to live in town. Out here it is terribly lonely; and you know yourself, Mr. Manders, what it is to be alone in the world. And, though I say it, I really am both capable and willing. Don't you know any place that would be suitable for me, Mr. Manders?

Manders. I? No, indeed I don't.

Regina. But, dear Mr. Manders—at any rate don't forget me, in case—

Manders (getting up). No, I won't forget you, Miss Engstrand.

Regina. Because, if I—

Manders. Perhaps you will be so kind as to let Mrs. Alving know I am here?

Regina. I will fetch her at once, Mr. Manders. (*Goes out to the left. * MANDERS *walks up and down the room once or twice, stands for a moment at the farther end of the room with his hands behind his back and looks out into the garden. Then he comes back to the table, takes up a book*

*and looks at the title page, gives a start, and looks at some
of the others.)*

Manders. Hm!—Really!

(MRS. ALVING *comes in by the door on the left. She is
followed by* REGINA, *who goes out again at once
through the nearer door on the right.)*

Mrs. Alving (*holding out her hand*). I am very glad
to see you, Mr. Manders.

Manders. How do you do, Mrs. Alving. Here I am,
as I promised.

Mrs. Alving. Always punctual!

Manders. Indeed, I was hard put to it to get away.
What with vestry meetings and committees—

Mrs. Alving. It was all the kinder of you to come in
such good time; we can settle our business before dinner.
But where is your luggage?

Manders (*quickly*). My things are down at the village
shop. I am going to sleep there to-night.

Mrs. Alving (*repressing a smile*). Can't I really persuade you to stay the night here this time?

Manders. No, no; many thanks all the same; I will
put up there, as usual. It is so handy for getting on
board the boat again.

Mrs. Alving. Of course you shall do as you please.
But it seems to me quite another thing, now we are two
old people—

Manders. Ha! ha! You will have your joke! And
it's natural you should be in high spirits to-day—first
of all there is the great event to-morrow, and also you
have got Oswald home.

Mrs. Alving. Yes, am I not a lucky woman? It is
more than two years since he was home last, and he has
promised to stay the whole winter with me.

Manders. Has he, really? That is very nice and filial
of him; because there must be many more attractions
in his life in Rome or in Paris, I should think.

Mrs. Alving. Yes, but he has his mother here, you see.
Bless the dear boy, he has got a corner in his heart for
his mother still.

Manders. Oh, it would be very sad if absence and pre-occupation with such a thing as Art were to dull the natural affections.

Mrs. Alving. It would, indeed.   But there is no fear of that with him, I am glad to say.   I am quite curious to see if you recognise him again.   He will be down directly; he is just lying down for a little on the sofa upstairs. But do sit down, my dear friend.

Manders. Thank you.   You are sure I am not disturbing you?

Mrs. Alving. Of course not. (*She sits down at the table.*)

Manders. Good.   Then I will show you—. (*He goes to the chair where his bag is lying and takes a packet of papers from it; then sits down at the opposite side of the table and looks for a clear space to put the papers down.*) Now first of all, here is—(*breaks off*).   Tell me, Mrs. Alving, what are these books doing here?

Mrs. Alving. These books?   I am reading them.

Manders. Do you read this sort of thing?

Mrs. Alving. Certainly I do.

Manders. Do you feel any the better or the happier for reading books of this kind?

Mrs. Alving. I think it makes me, as it were, more self-reliant.

Manders. That is remarkable.   But why?

Mrs. Alving. Well, they give me an explanation or a confirmation of lots of different ideas that have come into my own mind.   But what surprises me, Mr. Manders, is that, properly speaking, there is nothing at all new in these books.   There is nothing more in them than what most people think and believe.   The only thing is, that most people either take no account of it or won't admit it to themselves.

Manders. But, good heavens, do you seriously think that most people—?

Mrs. Alving. Yes, indeed, I do.

Manders. But not here in the country at any rate? Not here amongst people like ourselves?

Mrs. Alving. Yes, amongst people like ourselves too.

Manders. Well, really, I must say—!

Mrs. Alving. But what is the particular objection that you have to these books?

Manders. What objection? You surely don't suppose that I take any particular interest in such productions?

Mrs. Alving. In fact, you don't know anything about what you are denouncing?

Manders. I have read quite enough about these books to disapprove of them.

Mrs. Alving. Yes, but your own opinion—

Manders. My dear Mrs. Alving, there are many occasions in life when one has to rely on the opinion of others. That is the way in this world, and it is quite right that it should be so. What would become of society, otherwise?

Mrs. Alving. Well, you may be right.

Manders. Apart from that, naturally I don't deny that literature of this kind may have a considerable attraction. And I cannot blame you, either, for wishing to make yourself acquainted with the intellectual tendencies which I am told are at work in the wider world in which you have allowed your son to wander for so long. But—

Mrs. Alving. But—?

Manders (lowering his voice). But one doesn't talk about it, Mrs. Alving. One certainly is not called upon to account to every one for what one reads or thinks in the privacy of one's own room.

Mrs. Alving. Certainly not. I quite agree with you.

Manders. Just think of the consideration you owe to this Orphanage, which you decided to build at a time when your thoughts on such subjects were very different from what they are now—as far as I am able to judge.

Mrs. Alving. Yes, I freely admit that. But it was about the Orphanage—

Manders. It was about the Orphanage we were going

to talk; quite so. Well—walk warily, dear Mrs. Alving!
And now let us turn to the business in hand. (*Opens an
envelope and takes out some papers.*) You see these?

Mrs. Alving. The deeds?

Manders. Yes, the whole lot—and everything in order.
I can tell you it has been no easy matter to get them in
time. I had positively to put pressure on the authorities; they are almost painfully conscientious when it is
a question of settling property. But here they are at
last. (*Turns over the papers.*) Here is the deed of con-
veyance of that part of the Rosenvold estate known as
the Solvik property, together with the buildings newly
erected thereon—the school, the masters' houses and the
chapel. And here is the legal sanction for the statutes
of the institution. Here, you see—(*reads*) "Statutes
for the Captain Alving Orphanage."

Mrs. Alving (*after a long look at the papers*). That seems
all in order.

Manders. I thought "Captain" was the better title
to use, rather than your husband's Court title of "Cham-
berlain." "Captain" seems less ostentatious.

Mrs. Alving. Yes, yes; just as you think best.

Manders. And here is the certificate for the investment
of the capital in the bank, the interest being earmarked
for the current expenses of the Orphanage.

Mrs. Alving. Many thanks; but I think it will be
most convenient if you will kindly take charge of them.

Manders. With pleasure. I think it will be best to
leave the money in the bank for the present. The
interest is not very high, it is true; four per cent at six
months' call. Later on, if we can find some good mortgage—of course it must be a first mortgage and on unex-
ceptionable security—we can consider the matter further.

Mrs. Alving. Yes, yes, my dear Mr. Manders, you
know best about all that.

Manders. I will keep my eye on it, anyway. But
there is one thing in connection with it that I have often
meant to ask you about.

Mrs. Alving. What is that?

Manders. Shall we insure the buildings, or not?

Mrs. Alving. Of course we must insure them.

Manders. Ah, but wait a moment, dear lady. Let us look into the matter a little more closely.

Mrs. Alving. Everything of mine is insured—the house and its contents, my livestock—everything.

Manders. Naturally. They are your own property. I do exactly the same, of course. But this, you see, is quite a different case. The Orphanage is, so to speak, dedicated to higher uses.

Mrs. Alving. Certainly, but—

Manders. As far as I am personally concerned, I can conscientiously say that I don't see the smallest objection to our insuring ourselves against all risks.

Mrs. Alving. That is exactly what I think.

Manders. But what about the opinion of the people hereabouts?

Mrs. Alving. Their opinion—?

Manders. Is there any considerable body of opinion here—opinion of some account, I mean—that might take exception to it?

Mrs. Alving. What, exactly, do you mean by opinion of some account?

Manders. Well, I was thinking particularly of persons of such independent and influential position that one could hardly refuse to attach weight to their opinion.

Mrs. Alving. There are a certain number of such people here, who might perhaps take exception to it if we—

Manders. That's just it, you see. In town there are lots of them. All my fellow-clergymen's congregations, for instance! It would be so extremely easy for them to interpret it as meaning that neither you nor I had a proper reliance on Divine protection.

Mrs. Alving. But as far as you are concerned, my dear friend, you have at all events the consciousness that—

Manders. Yes I know I know: my own mind is quite

easy about it, it is true. But we should not be able to
prevent a wrong and injurious interpretation of our
action. And that sort of thing, moreover, might very
easily end in exercising a hampering influence on the
work of the Orphanage.

Mrs. Alving. Oh, well, if that is likely to be the effect
of it—

Manders. Nor can I entirely overlook the difficult—
indeed, I may say, painful—position I might possibly be
placed in. In the best circles in town the matter of this
Orphanage is attracting a great deal of attention.
Indeed the Orphanang is to some extent built for the
benefit of the town, too, and it is to be hoped that it may
result in the lowering of our poor-rate by a considerable
amount. But as I have been your adviser in the matter
and have taken charge of the business side of it, I should
be afraid that it would be I that spiteful persons would
attack first of all—

Mrs. Alving. Yes, you ought not to expose yourself to
that.

Manders. Not to mention the attacks that would undoubtedly be made upon me in certain newspapers and
reviews—

Mrs. Alving. Say no more about it, dear Mr. Manders;
that quite decides it.

Manders. Then you don't wish it to be insured?

Mrs. Alving. No, we will give up the idea.

Manders (leaning back in his chair). But suppose,
now, that some accident happened?—one can never tell
—would you be prepared to make good the damage?

Mrs. Alving. No; I tell you quite plainly I would not
do so under any circumstances.

Manders. Still, you know, Mrs. Alving—after all, it is
a serious responsibility that we are taking upon ourselves.

Mrs. Alving. But do you think we can do otherwise?

Manders. No, that's just it. We really can't do otherwise. We ought not to expose ourselves to a mistaken
judgment; and we have no right to do anything that will
scandalise the community.

Mrs. Alving. You ought not to, as a clergyman, at any rate.

Manders. And, what is more, I certainly think that we may count upon our enterprise being attended by good fortune—indeed, that it will be under a special protection.

Mrs. Alving. Let us hope so, Mr. Manders.

Manders. Then we will leave it alone?

Mrs. Alving. Certainly.

Manders. Very good. As you wish. (*Makes a note.*) No insurance, then.

Mrs. Alving. It's a funny thing that you should just have happened to speak about that to-day—

Manders. I have often meant to ask you about it—

Mrs. Alving. —because yesterday we very nearly had a fire up there.

Manders. Do you mean it?

Mrs. Alving. Oh, as a matter of fact it was nothing of any consequence. Some shavings in the carpenter's shop caught fire.

Manders. Where Engstrand works?

Mrs. Alving. Yes. They say he is often so careless with matches.

Manders. He has so many things on his mind, poor fellow—so many anxieties. Heaven be thanked, I am told he is really making an effort to live a blameless life.

Mrs. Alving. Really? Who told you so?

Manders. He assured me himself that it is so. He's a good workman, too.

Mrs. Alving. Oh, yes, when he is sober.

Manders. Ah, that sad weakness of his! But the pain in his poor leg often drives him to it, he tells me. The last time he was in town, I was really quite touched by him. He came to my house and thanked me so gratefully for getting him work here, where he could have the chance of being with Regina.

Mrs. Alving. He doesn't see very much of her.

Manders. But he assured me that he saw her every day.

Mrs. Alving. Oh well, perhaps he does.

Manders. He feels so strongly that he needs some one who can keep a hold on him when temptations assail him. That is the most winning thing about Jacob Engstrand; he comes to one like a helpless child and accuses himself and confesses his frailty. The last time he came and had a talk with me—. Suppose now, Mrs. Alving, that it were really a necessity of his existence to have Regina at home with him again—

Mrs. Alving (standing up suddenly). Regina!

Manders. —you ought not to set yourself against him.

Mrs. Alving. Indeed, I set myself very definitely against that. And, besides, you know Regina is to have a post in the Orphanage.

Manders. But consider, after all he is her father—

Mrs. Alving. I know best what sort of a father he has been to her. No, she shall never go to him with my consent.

Manders (getting up). My dear lady, don't judge so hastily. It is very sad how you misjudge poor Engstrand. One would really think you were afraid—

Mrs. Alving (more calmly). That is not the question. I have taken Regina into my charge, and in my charge she remains. (*Listens.*) Hush, dear Mr. Manders, don't say any more about it. (*Her face brightens with pleasure.*) Listen! Oswald is coming downstairs. We will only think about him now.

(OSWALD ALVING, *in a light overcoat, hat in hand and smoking a big meerschaum pipe, comes in by the door on the left.*)

Oswald (standing in the doorway). Oh, I beg your pardon, I thought you were in the office. (*Comes in.*) Good morning, Mr. Manders.

Manders (staring at him). Well! It's most extraordinary—

Mrs. Alving. Yes, what do you think of him, Mr. Manders?

Manders. I—I— no, can it possibly be—?

Oswald. Yes, it really is the prodigal son, Mr. Manders,

Manders. Oh, my dear young friend—

Oswald. Well, the son come home, then.

Mrs. Alving. Oswald is thinking of the time when you were so opposed to the idea of his being a painter.

Manders. We are only fallible, and many steps seem to us hazardous at first, that afterwards—(*grasps his hand*). Welcome, welcome! Really, my dear Oswald —may I still call you Oswald?

Oswald. What else would you think of calling me?

Manders. Thank you. What I mean, my dear Oswald, is that you must not imagine that I have any unqualified disapproval of the artist's life. I admit that there are many who, even in that career, can keep the inner man free from harm.

Oswald. Let us hope so.

Mrs. Alving (beaming with pleasure). I know one who has kept both the inner and the outer man free from harm. Just take a look at him, Mr. Manders.

Oswald (walks across the room). Yes, yes, mother dear, of course.

Manders. Undoubtedly—no one can deny it. And I hear you have begun to make a name for yourself. I have often seen mention of you in the papers—and extremely favourable mention, too. Although, I must admit, latterly I have not seen your name so often.

Oswald (going towards the conservatory). I haven't done so much painting just lately.

Mrs. Alving. An artist must take a rest sometimes, like other people.

Manders. Of course, of course. At those times the artist is preparing and strengthening himself for a greater effort.

Oswald. Yes. Mother, will dinner soon be ready?

Mrs. Alving. In half an hour. He has a fine appetite, thank goodness.

Manders. And a liking for tobacco, too.

Oswald. I found father's pipe in the room upstairs, and—

Manders. Ah, that is what it was!

Mrs. Alving. What?

Manders. When Oswald came in at that door with the pipe in his mouth, I thought for the moment it was his father in the flesh.

Oswald. Really?

Mrs. Alving. How can you say so! Oswald takes after me.

Manders. Yes, but there is an expression about the corners of his mouth—something about the lips—that reminds me so exactly of Mr. Alving—especially when he smokes.

Mrs. Alving. I don't think so at all. To my mind, Oswald has much more of a clergyman's mouth.

Manders. Well, yes—a good many of my colleagues in the church have a similar expression.

Mrs. Alving. But put your pipe down, my dear boy. I don't allow any smoking in here.

Oswald (puts down his pipe). All right, I only wanted to try it, because I smoked it once when I was a child.

Mrs. Alving. You?

Oswald. Yes; it was when I was quite a little chap. And I can remember going upstairs to father's room one evening when he was in very good spirits.

Mrs. Alving. Oh, you can't remember anything about those days.

Oswald. Yes, I remember plainly that he took me on his knee and let me smoke his pipe. " Smoke, my boy," he said, "have a good smoke, boy!" And I smoked as hard as I could, until I felt I was turning quite pale and the perspiration was standing in great drops on my forehead. Then he laughed—such a hearty laugh—

Manders. It was an extremely odd thing to do.

Mrs. Alving. Dear Mr. Manders, Oswald only dreamt it.

Oswald. No indeed, mother, it was no dream. Because—don't you remember—you came into the room and carried me off to the nursery, where I was sick, and I saw that you were crying. Did father often play such tricks?

Manders. In his young days he was full of fun—

Oswald. And, for all that, he did so much with his life—so much that was good and useful, I mean—short as his life was.

Manders. Yes, my dear Oswald Alving, you have inherited the name of a man who undoubtedly was both energetic and worthy. Let us hope it will be a spur to your energies—

Oswald. It ought to be, certainly.

Manders. In any case it was nice of you to come home for the day that is to honour his memory.

Oswald. I could do no less for my father.

Mrs. Alving. And to let me keep him so long here—that's the nicest part of what he has done.

Manders. Yes, I hear you are going to spend the winter at home.

Oswald. I am here for an indefinite time, Mr. Manders. —Oh, it's good to be at home again!

Mrs. Alving (beaming). Yes, isn't it?

Manders (looking sympathetically at him). You went out into the world very young, my dear Oswald.

Oswald. I did. Sometimes I wonder if I wasn't too young.

Mrs. Alving. Not a bit of it. It is the best thing for an active boy, and especially for an only child. It's a pity when they are kept at home with their parents and get spoilt.

Manders. That is a very debatable question, Mrs. Alving. A child's own home is, and always must be, his proper place.

Oswald. There I agree entirely with Mr. Manders.

Manders. Take the case of your own son. Oh yes, we can talk about it before him. What has the result been in his case? He is six or seven and twenty, and has never yet had the opportunity of learning what a well-regulated home means.

Oswald. Excuse me, Mr. Manders, you are quite wrong there.

Manders. Indeed? I imagined that your life abroad had practically been spent entirely in artistic circles.

Oswald. So it has.

Manders. And chiefly amongst the younger artists.

Oswald. Certainly.

Manders. But I imagined that those gentry, as a rule, had not the means necessary for family life and the support of a home.

Oswald. There are a considerable number of them who have not the means to marry, Mr. Manders.

Manders. That is exactly my point.

Oswald. But they can have a home of their own, all the same; a good many of them have. And they are very well-regulated and very comfortable homes, too.

(MRS. ALVING, *who has listened to him attentively, nods assent, but says nothing.*)

Manders. Oh, but I am not talking of bachelor establishments. By a home I mean family life—the life a man lives with his wife and children.

Oswald. Exactly, or with his children and his children's mother.

Manders (starts and clasps his hands). Good heavens!

Oswald. What is the matter?

Manders. Lives with—with—his children's mother!

Oswald. Well, would you rather he should repudiate his children's mother?

Manders. Then what you are speaking of are those unprincipled conditions known as irregular unions!

Oswald. I have never noticed anything particularly unprincipled about these people's lives.

Manders. But do you mean to say that it is possible for a man of any sort of bringing up, and a young woman, to reconcile themselves to such a way of living—and to make no secret of it, either!

Oswald. What else are they to do? A poor artist, and a poor girl—it costs a good deal to get married. What else are they to do?

Manders. What are they to do? Well, Mr. Alving, I will tell you what they ought to do. They ought to keep away from each other from the very beginning—that is what they ought to do!

Oswald. That advice wouldn't have much effect upon hot-blooded young folk who are in love.

Mrs. Alving. No, indeed it wouldn't.

Manders (persistently). And to think that the authorities tolerate such things! That they are allowed to go on, openly! (*Turns to* MRS. ALVING.) Had I so little reason, then, to be sadly concerned about your son? In circles where open immorality is rampant—where, one may say, it is honoured—

Oswald. Let me tell you this, Mr. Manders. I have been a constant Sunday guest at one or two of these " irregular " households—

Manders. On Sunday, too!

Oswald. Yes, that is the day of leisure. But never have I heard one objectionable word there, still less have I ever seen anything that could be called immoral. No; but do you know when and where I *have* met with immorality in artists' circles?

Manders. No, thank heaven, I don't!

Oswald. Well, then, I shall have the pleasure of telling you. I have met with it when some one or other of your model husbands and fathers have come out there to have a bit of a look round on their own account, and have done the artists the honour of looking them up in their humble quarters. Then we had a chance of learning something, I can tell you. These gentlemen were able to instruct us about places and things that we had never so much as dreamt of.

Manders. What? Do you want me to believe that honourable men when they get away from home will—

Oswald. Have you never, when these same honourable men come home again, heard them deliver themselves on the subject of the prevalence of immorality abroad?

Manders. Yes, of course, but—

Mrs. Alving. I have heard them, too.

Oswald. Well, you can take their word for it, unhesitatingly. Some of them are experts in the matter. (*Putting his hands to his head.*) To think that the

glorious freedom of the beautiful life over there should
be so besmirched!

Mrs. Alving. You mustn't get too heated, Oswald; you
gain nothing by that.

Oswald. No, you are quite right, mother. Besides, it
isn't good for me. It's because I am so infernally tired,
you know. I will go out and take a turn before dinner.
I beg your pardon, Mr. Manders. It is impossible for
you to realise the feeling; but it takes me that way
(*Goes out by the farther door on the right.*)

Mrs. Alving. My poor boy!

Manders. You may well say so. This is what it has
brought him to! (MRS. ALVING *looks at him, but does
not speak.*) He called himself the prodigal son. It's
only too true, alas—only too true! (MRS. ALVING *looks
steadily at him.*) And what do you say to all this?

Mrs. Alving. I say that Oswald was right in every
single word he said.

Manders. Right? Right? To hold such principles
as that?

Mrs. Alving. In my loneliness here I have come to
just the same opinions as he, Mr. Manders. But I have
never presumed to venture upon such topics in conver-
sation. Now there is no need; my boy shall speak for me.

Manders. You deserve the deepest pity, Mrs. Alving.
It is my duty to say an earnest word to you. It is no
longer your business man and adviser, no longer your old
friend and your dead husband's old friend, that stands
before you now. It is your priest that stands before
you, just as he did once at the most critical moment of
your life.

Mrs. Alving. And what is it that my priest has to say
to me?

Manders. First of all I must stir your memory. The
moment is well chosen. To-morrow is the tenth anni-
versary of your husband's death; to-morrow the memorial to the departed will be unveiled; to-morrow I shall
speak to the whole assembly that will be met together.
But to-day I want to speak to you alone.

Mrs. Alving. Very well, Mr. Manders, speak!

Manders. Have you forgotten that after barely a year of married life you were standing at the very edge of a precipice?—that you forsook your house and home?—that you ran away from your husband—yes, Mrs. Alving, ran away, ran away—and refused to return to him in spite of his requests and entreaties?

Mrs. Alving. Have you forgotten how unspeakably unhappy I was during that first year?

Manders. To crave for happiness in this world is simply to be possessed by a spirit of revolt. What right have we to happiness? No! we must do our duty, Mrs. Alving. And your duty was to cleave to the man you had chosen and to whom you were bound by a sacred bond.

Mrs. Alving. You know quite well what sort of a life my husband was living at that time—what excesses he was guilty of.

Manders. I know only too well what rumour used to say of him; and I should be the last person to approve of his conduct as a young man, supposing that rumour spoke the truth. But it is not a wife's part to be her husband's judge. You should have considered it your bounden duty humbly to have borne the cross that a higher will had laid upon you. But, instead of that, you rebelliously cast off your cross, you deserted the man whose stumbling footsteps you should have supported, you did what was bound to imperil your good name and reputation, and came very near to imperilling the reputation of others into the bargain.

Mrs. Alving. Of others? Of one other, you mean.

Manders. It was the height of imprudence, your seeking refuge with me.

Mrs. Alving. With our priest? With our intimate friend?

Manders. All the more on that account. You should thank God that I possessed the necessary strength of mind—that I was able to turn you from your outrageous intention, and that it was vouchsafed to me to succeed in leading you back into the path of duty and back to your lawful husband.

Mrs. Alving. Yes, Mr. Manders, that certainly was your doing.

Manders. I was but the humble instrument of a higher power. And is it not true that my having been able to bring you again under the yoke of duty and obedience sowed the seeds of a rich blessing on all the rest of your life? Did things not turn out as I foretold to you? Did not your husband turn from straying in the wrong path, as a man should? Did he not, after that, live a life of love and good report with you all his days? Did he not become a benefactor to the neighbourhood? Did he not so raise you up to his level, so that by degrees you became his fellow-worker in all his undertakings— and a noble fellow-worker, too, I know, Mrs. Alving; that praise I will give you.—But now I come to the second serious false step in your life.

Mrs. Alving. What do you mean?

Manders. Just as once you forsook your duty as a wife, so, since then, you have forsaken your duty as a mother.

Mrs. Alving. Oh—!

Manders. You have been overmastered all your life by a disastrous spirit of wilfulness. All your impulses have led you towards what is undisciplined and lawless. You have never been willing to submit to any restraint. Anything in life that has seemed irksome to you, you have thrown aside recklessly and unscrupulously, as if it were a burden that you were free to rid yourself of if you would. It did not please you to be a wife any longer, and so you left your husband. Your duties as a mother were irksome to you, so you sent your child away among strangers.

Mrs. Alving. Yes, that is true; I did that.

Manders. And that is why you have become a stranger to him.

Mrs. Alving. No, no, I am not that!

Manders. You are; you must be. And what sort

of a son is it that you have got back? Think over it
seriously, Mrs. Alving. You erred grievously in your
husband's case—you acknowledge as much, by erecting
this memorial to him. Now you are bound to acknowledge how much you have erred in your son's case; possibly there may still be time to reclaim him from the
paths of wickedness. Turn over a new leaf, and set
yourself to reform what there may still be that is capable
of reformation in him. Because (*with uplifted fore-
finger*) in very truth, Mrs. Alving, you are a guilty
mother!—That is what I have thought it my duty to
say to you.

(*A short silence.*)

Mrs. Alving (*speaking slowly and with self-control*).
You have had your say, Mr. Manders, and to-
morrow you will be making a public speech in memory
of my husband. I shall not speak to-morrow. But
now I wish to speak to you for a little, just as you have
been speaking to me.

Manders. By all means; no doubt you wish to bring
forward some excuses for your behaviour—

Mrs. Alving. No. I only want to tell you something.

Manders. Well?

Mrs. Alving. In all that you said just now about me
and my husband, and about our life together after you
had, as you put it, led me back into the path of duty—
there was nothing that you knew at first hand. From
that moment you never again set foot in our house—
you, who had been our daily companion before that.

Manders. Remember that you and your husband
moved out of town immediately afterwards.

Mrs. Alving. Yes, and you never once came out here
to see us in my husband's lifetime. It was only the
business in connection with the Orphanage that obliged
you to come and see me.

Manders (*in a low and uncertain voice*). Helen—if that
is a reproach, I can only beg you to consider—

Mrs. Alving. —the respect you owed to your calling?
—yes. All the more as I was a wife who had tried to

run away from her husband. One can never be too careful to have nothing to do with such reckless women.

Manders. My dear—Mrs. Alving, you are exaggerating
dreadfully—

Mrs. Alving. Yes, yes,—very well. What I mean
is this, that when you condemn my conduct as a wife
you have nothing more to go upon than ordinary public
opinion.

Manders. I admit it. What then?

Mrs. Alving. Well—now, Mr. Manders, now I am
going to tell you the truth. I had sworn to myself that
you should know it one day—you, and you only!

Manders. And what may the truth be?

Mrs. Alving. The truth is this, that my husband died
just as great a profligate as he had been all his life.

Manders (feeling for a chair). What are you saying?

Mrs. Alving. After nineteen years of married life,
just as profligate—in his desires at all events—as he was
before you married us.

Manders. And can you talk of his youthful indiscre-
tions—his irregularities—his excesses, if you like—as a
profligate life!

Mrs. Alving. That was what the doctor who attended
him called it.

Manders. I don't understand what you mean.

Mrs. Alving. It is not necessary you should.

Manders. It makes my brain reel. To think that
your marriage—all the years of wedded life you spent
with your husband—were nothing but a hidden abyss
of misery.

Mrs. Alving. That and nothing else. Now you know.

Manders. This—this bewilders me. I can't understand
it! I can't grasp it! How in the world was it possible—?
How could such a state of things remain concealed?

Mrs. Alving. That was just what I had to fight for
incessantly, day after day. When Oswald was born,
I thought I saw a slight improvement. But it didn't
last long. And after that I had to fight doubly hard—
fight a desperate fight so that no one should know what

sort of a man my child's father was. You know quite
well what an attractive manner he had; it seemed as if
people could believe nothing but good of him. He was
one of those men whose mode of life seems to have no
effect upon their reputations. But at last, Mr. Manders—you must hear this too—at last something happened more abominable than everything else.

Manders. More abominable than what you have told
me?

Mrs. Alving. I had borne with it all, though I knew
only too well what he indulged in in secret, when he was
out of the house. But when it came to the point of the
scandal coming within our four walls—

Manders. Can you mean it? Here?

Mrs. Alving. Yes, here, in our own home. It was in
there (*pointing to the nearer door on the right*) in the dining-
room that I got the first hint of it. I had something to
do in there and the door was standing ajar. I heard our
maid come up from the garden with water for the flowers
in the conservatory.

Manders. Well—?

Mrs. Alving. Shortly afterwards I heard my husband
come in, too. I heard him say something to her in a low
voice. And then I heard—(*with a short laugh*)—oh, it
rings in my ears still, with its mixture of what was
heartbreaking and what was so ridiculous—I heard my
own servant whisper: " Let me go, Mr. Alving! Let
me be ! "

Manders. What unseemly levity on his part! But
surely nothing more than levity, Mrs. Alving, believe
me.

Mrs. Alving. I soon knew what to believe. My
husband had his will of the girl—and that intimacy had
consequences, Mr. Manders.

Manders (as if turned to stone). And all that in this
house! In this house!

Mrs. Alving. I have suffered a good deal in this house.
To keep him at home in the evening—and at night—I
have had to play the part of boon companion in his secret

drinking-bouts in his room up there. I have had to sit there alone with him, have had to hobnob and drink with him, have had to listen to his ribald senseless talk, have had to fight with brute force to get him to bed—

Manders (*trembling*). And you were able to endure all this!

Mrs. Alving. I had my little boy, and endured it for his sake. But when the crowning insult came—when my own servant—then I made up my mind that there should be an end of it. I took the upper hand in the house, absolutely—both with him and all the others. I had a weapon to use against him, you see; he didn't dare to speak. It was then that Oswald was sent away. He was about seven then, and was beginning to notice things and ask questions as children will. I could endure all that, my friend. It seemed to me that the child would be poisoned if he breathed the air of this polluted house. That was why I sent him away. And now you understand, too, why he never set foot here as long as his father was alive. No one knows what it meant to me.

Manders. You have indeed had a pitiable experience.

Mrs. Alving. I could never have gone through with it, if I had not had my work. Indeed, I can boast that I have worked. All the increase in the value of the property, all the improvements, all the useful arrangements that my husband got the honour and glory of— do you suppose that he troubled himself about any of them? He, who used to lie the whole day on the sofa reading old Official Lists! No, you may as well know that too. It was I that kept him up to the mark when he had his lucid intervals; it was I that had to bear the whole burden of it when he began his excesses again or took to whining about his miserable condition.

Manders. And this is the man you are building a memorial to!

Mrs. Alving. There you see the power of an uneasy conscience.

Manders. An uneasy conscience? What do you mean?

Mrs. Alving. I had always before me the fear that

it was impossible that the truth should not come out and be believed. That is why the Orphanage is to exist, to silence all rumours and clear away all doubt.

Manders. You certainly have not fallen short of the mark in that, Mrs. Alving.

Mrs. Alving. I had another very good reason. I did not wish Oswald, my own son, to inherit a penny that belonged to his father.

Manders. Then it is with Mr. Alving's property—

Mrs. Alving. Yes. The sums of money that, year after year, I have given towards this Orphanage, make up the amount of property—I have reckoned it carefully—which in the old days made Lieutenant Alving a catch.

Manders. I understand.

Mrs. Alving. That was my purchase money. I don't wish it to pass into Oswald's hands. My son shall have everything from me, I am determined.

(OSWALD *comes in by the farther door on the right. He has left his hat and coat outside.*)

Mrs. Alving. Back again, my own dear boy?

Oswald. Yes, what can one do outside in this everlasting rain? I hear dinner is nearly ready. That's good!

(REGINA *comes in from the dining-room, carrying a parcel.*)

Regina. This parcel has come for you, ma'am. (*Gives it to her.*)

Mrs. Alving (*glancing at* MANDERS). The ode to be sung to-morrow, I expect.

Manders. Hm—!

Regina. And dinner is ready.

Mrs. Alving. Good. We will come in a moment. I will just—(*begins to open the parcel*).

Regina (*to* OSWALD). Will you drink white or red wine, sir?

Oswald. Both, Miss Engstrand.

Regina. Bien—very good, Mr. Alving. (*Goes into the dining-room.*)

Oswald. I may as well help you to uncork it—. (*Fol-*

*lows her into the dining-room, leaving the door ajar after
him.*)

Mrs. Alving. Yes, I thought so.   Here is the ode, Mr
Manders.

Manders (clasping his hands). How shall I ever have the
courage to-morrow to speak the address that—

Mrs. Alving.   Oh, you will get through it.

*Manders (in a low voice, fearing to be heard in the dining-
room).*   Yes, we must raise no suspicions.

Mrs. Alving (quietly but firmly).   No; and then this long
dreadful comedy will be at an end.   After to-morrow, I
shall feel as if my dead husband had never lived in this
house.   There will be no one else here then but my boy
and his mother.

(*From the dining-room is heard the noise of a chair
falling; then* REGINA'S *voice is heard in a loud whisper:* Oswald!   Are you mad?   Let me go!)

Mrs. Alving (starting in horror). Oh—!

(*She stares wildly at the half-open door.* OSWALD *is
heard coughing and humming, then the sound of a
bottle being uncorked.*)

Manders (in an agitated manner). What's the matter?
What is it, Mrs. Alving?

Mrs. Alving (hoarsely). Ghosts.   The couple in the
conservatory—over again.

Manders. What are you saying! Regina—? Is
she—?

Mrs. Alving. Yes.   Come.   Not a word—!

(*Grips* MANDERS *by the arm and walks unsteadily with
him into the dining-room.*)

ACT II

(*The same scene. The landscape is still obscured by mist.* MANDERS *and* MRS. ALVING *come in from the dining-room.*)

Mrs. Alving (*calls into the dining-room from the doorway*). Aren't you coming in here, Oswald?

Oswald. No, thanks; I think I will go out for a bit.

Mrs. Alving. Yes, do; the weather is clearing a little. (*She shuts the dining-room door, then goes to the hall door and calls.*) Regina!

Regina (*from without*). Yes, ma'am?

Mrs. Alving. Go down into the laundry and help with the garlands.

Regina. Yes, ma'am.

(MRS. ALVING *satisfies herself that she has gone, then shuts the door.*)

Manders. I suppose he can't hear us?

Mrs. Alving. Not when the door is shut. Besides, he is going out.

Manders. I am still quite bewildered. I don't know how I managed to swallow a mouthful of your excellent dinner.

Mrs. Alving (*walking up and down, and trying to control her agitation*). Nor I. But what are we to do?

Manders. Yes, what are we to do? Upon my word I don't know; I am so completely unaccustomed to things of this kind.

Mrs. Alving. I am convinced that nothing serious has happened yet.

Manders. Heaven forbid! But it is most unseemly behaviour, for all that.

Mrs. Alving. It is nothing more than a foolish jest of Oswald's, you may be sure.

Manders. Well, of course, as I said, I am quite inexperienced in such matters; but it certainly seems to me—

Mrs. Alving. Out of the house she shall go—and at once. That part of it is as clear as daylight—

Manders. Yes, that is quite clear.

Mrs. Alving. But where is she to go? We should not be justified in—

Manders. Where to? Home to her father, of course.

Mrs. Alving. To whom, did you say?

Manders. To her—. No, of course Engstrand isn't—. But, great heavens, Mrs. Alving, how is such a thing possible? You surely may have been mistaken, in spite of everything.

Mrs. Alving. There was no chance of mistake, more's the pity. Joanna was obliged to confess it to me—and my husband couldn't deny it. So there was nothing else to do but to hush it up.

Manders. No, that was the only thing to do.

Mrs. Alving. The girl was sent away at once, and was given a tolerably liberal sum to hold her tongue. She looked after the rest herself when she got to town. She renewed an old acquaintance with the carpenter Engstrand; gave him a hint, I suppose, of how much money she had got, and told him some fairy tale about a foreigner who had been here in his yacht in the summer. So she and Engstrand were married in a great hurry. Why, you married them yourself!

Manders. I can't understand it—. I remember clearly Engstrand's coming to arrange about the marriage. He was full of contrition, and accused himself bitterly for the light conduct he and his fiancée had been guilty of.

Mrs. Alving. Of course he had to take the blame on himself.

Manders. But the deceitfulness of it! And with me, too! I positively would not have believed it of Jacob Engstrand. I shall most certainly give him a serious talking to.—And the immorality of such a marriage! Simply for the sake of the money—! What sum was it that the girl had?

Mrs. Alving. It was seventy pounds.

Manders. Just think of it—for a paltry seventy pounds to let yourself be bound in marriage to a fallen woman!

Mrs. Alving. What about myself, then?—I let myself be bound in marriage to a fallen man.

Manders. Heaven forgive you! what are you saying? A fallen man?

Mrs. Alving. Do you suppose my husband was any purer, when I went with him to the altar, than Joanna was when Engstrand agreed to marry her?

Manders. The two cases are as different as day from night—

Mrs. Alving. Not so very different, after all. It is true there was a great difference in the price paid, between a paltry seventy pounds and a whole fortune.

Manders. How can you compare such totally different things! I presume you consulted your own heart—and your relations.

Mrs. Alving (looking away from him). I thought you understood where what you call my heart had strayed to at that time.

Manders (in a constrained voice). If I had understood anything of the kind, I would not have been a daily guest in your husband's house.

Mrs. Alving. Well, at any rate this much is certain, that I didn't consult myself in the matter at all.

Manders. Still you consulted those nearest to you, as was only right—your mother, your two aunts.

Mrs. Alving. Yes, that is true. The three of them settled the whole matter for me. It seems incredible to me now, how clearly they made out that it would be sheer folly to reject such an offer. If my mother could only see what all that fine prospect has led to!

Manders. No one can be responsible for the result of it. Anyway there is this to be said, that the match was made in complete conformity with law and order.

Mrs. Alving (going to the window). Oh, law and order! I often think it is that that is at the bottom of all the misery in the world.

Manders. Mrs. Alving, it is very wicked of you to say that.

Mrs. Alving. That may be so; but I don't attach importance to those obligations and considerations any longer. I cannot! I must struggle for my freedom.

Manders. What do you mean?

Mrs. Alving (tapping on the window panes). I ought never to have concealed what sort of a life my husband led. But I had not the courage to do otherwise then—for my own sake, either. I was too much of a coward.

Manders. A coward?

Mrs. Alving. If others had known anything of what happened, they would have said: " Poor man, it is natural enough that he should go astray, when he has a wife that has run away from him."

Manders. They would have had a certain amount of justification for saying so.

Mrs. Alving (looking fixedly at him). If I had been the woman I ought, I would have taken Oswald into my confidence and said to him: " Listen, my son, your father was a dissolute man "—

Manders. Miserable woman—

Mrs. Alving. —and I would have told him all I have told you, from beginning to end.

Manders. I am almost shocked at you, Mrs. Alving.

Mrs. Alving. I know. I know quite well! I am shocked at myself when I think of it. *(Comes away from the window.)* I am coward enough for that.

Manders. Can you call it cowardice that you simply did your duty! Have you forgotten that a child should love and honour his father and mother?

Mrs. Alving. Don't let us talk in such general terms. Suppose we say: " Ought Oswald to love and honour Mr. Alving? "

Manders. You are a mother—isn't there a voice in your heart that forbids you to shatter your son's ideals?

Mrs. Alving. And what about the truth?

Manders. What about his ideals?

Mrs. Alving. Oh—ideals, ideals! If only I were not such a coward as I am!

Manders. Do not spurn ideals, Mrs. Alving—they have a way of avenging themselves cruelly. Take Oswald's own case, now. He hasn't many ideals, more's the pity. But this much I have seen, that his father is something of an ideal to him.

Mrs. Alving. You are right there.

Manders. And his conception of his father is what you inspired and encouraged by your letters.

Mrs. Alving. Yes, I was swayed by duty and consideration for others; that was why I lied to my son, year in and year out. Oh, what a coward—what a coward I have been!

Manders. You have built up a happy illusion in your son's mind, Mrs. Alving—and that is a thing you certainly ought not to undervalue.

Mrs. Alving. Ah, who knows if that is such a desirable thing after all!—But anyway I don't intend to put up with any goings on with Regina. I am not going to let him get the poor girl into trouble.

Manders. Good heavens, no—that would be a frightful thing!

Mrs. Alving. If only I knew whether he meant it seriously, and whether it would mean happiness for him—

Manders. In what way? I don't understand.

Mrs. Alving. But that is impossible; Regina is not equal to it, unfortunately.

Manders. I don't understand. What do you mean?

Mrs. Alving. If I were not such a miserable coward, I would say to him: " Marry her, or make any arrangement you like with her—only let there be no deceit in the matter."

Manders. Heaven forgive you! Are you actually suggesting anything so abominable, so unheard of, as a marriage between them!

Mrs. Alving. Unheard of, do you call it? Tell me honestly, Mr. Manders, don't you suppose there are plenty of married couples out here in the country that are just as nearly related as they are?

Manders. I am sure I don't understand you.

Mrs. Alving. Indeed you do.

Manders. I suppose you are thinking of cases where possibly—. It is only too true, unfortunately, that family life is not always as stainless as it should be. But as for the sort of thing you hint at—well, it's impossible to tell, at all events with any certainty. Here, on the other hand—for you, a mother, to be willing to allow your—

Mrs. Alving. But I am not willing to allow it. I would not allow it for anything in the world; that is just what I was saying.

Manders. No, because you are a coward, as you put it. But, supposing you were not a coward—! Great heavens—such a revolting union!

Mrs. Alving. Well, for the matter of that, we are all descended from a union of that description, so we are told. And who was it that was responsible for this state of things, Mr. Manders?

Manders. I can't discuss such questions with you, Mrs. Alving; you are by no means in the right frame of mind for that. But for you to dare to say that it is cowardly of you—!

Mrs. Alving. I will tell you what I mean by that. I am frightened and timid, because I am obsessed by the presence of ghosts that I never can get rid of.

Manders. The presence of what?

Mrs. Alving. Ghosts. When I heard Regina and Oswald in there, it was just like seeing ghosts before my eyes. I am half inclined to think we are all ghosts, Mr. Manders. It is not only what we have inherited from our fathers and mothers that exists again in us, but all sorts of old dead ideas and all kinds of old dead beliefs and things of that kind. They are not actually alive in us; but there they are dormant, all the same, and we can never be rid of them. Whenever I take up a news-paper and read it, I fancy I see ghosts creeping between the lines. There must be ghosts all over the world. They must be as countless as the grains of the sands, it seems to me. And we are so miserably afraid of the light, all of us.

Manders. Ah!—there we have the outcome of your reading. Fine fruit it has borne — this abominable, subversive, free-thinking literature!

Mrs. Alving. You are wrong there, my friend. You are the one who made me begin to think; and I owe you my best thanks for it.

Manders. I?

Mrs. Alving. Yes, by forcing me to submit to what you called my duty and my obligations; by praising as right and just what my whole soul revolted against, as it would against something abominable. That was what led me to examine your teachings critically. I only wanted to unravel one point in them; but as soon as I had got that unravelled, the whole fabric came to pieces. And then I realised that it was only machine-made.

Manders (softly, and with emotion). Is that all I accomplished by the hardest struggle of my life?

Mrs. Alving. Call it rather the most ignominious defeat of your life.

Manders. It was the greatest victory of my life, Helen; victory over myself.

Mrs. Alving. It was a wrong done to both of us.

Manders. A wrong?—wrong for me to entreat you as a wife to go back to your lawful husband, when you came to me half distracted and crying: " Here I am, take me! " Was that a wrong?

Mrs. Alving. I think it was.

Manders. We two do not understand one another.

Mrs. Alving. Not now, at all events.

Manders. Never—even in my most secret thoughts— have I for a moment regarded you as anything but the wife of another.

Mrs. Alving. Do you believe what you say?

Manders. Helen—!

Mrs. Alving. One so easily forgets one's own feelings.

Manders. Not I. I am the same as I always was.

Mrs. Alving. Yes, yes—don't let us talk any more about the old days. You are buried up to your eyes now in committees and all sorts of business; and I am here, fighting with ghosts both without and within me.

Manders. I can at all events help you to get the better of those without you. After all that I have been horrified to hear you from to-day, I cannot conscientiously allow a young defenceless girl to remain in your house.

Mrs. Alving. Don't you think it would be best if we could get her settled?—by some suitable marriage, I mean.

Manders. Undoubtedly. I think, in any case, it would have been desirable for her. Regina is at an age now that—well, I don't know much about these things, but—

Mrs. Alving. Regina developed very early.

Manders. Yes, didn't she. I fancy I remember thinking she was remarkably well developed, bodily, at the time I prepared her for Confirmation. But, for the time being, she must in any case go home. Under her father's care—no, but of course Engstrand is not—. To think that he, of all men, could so conceal the truth from me!

(*A knock is heard at the hall door.*)

Mrs. Alving. Who can that be? Come in!

(ENGSTRAND, *dressed in his Sunday clothes, appears in the doorway.*)

Engstrand. I humbly beg pardon, but—

Manders. Aha! Hm!—

Mrs. Alving. Oh, it's you, Engstrand!

Engstrand. There was none of the maids about, so I took the great liberty of knocking.

Mrs. Alving. That's all right. Come in. Do you want to speak to me?

Engstrand (*coming in*). No, thank you very much, ma'am. It was Mr. Manders I wanted to speak to for a moment.

Manders (*walking up and down*). Hm!—do you. You want to speak to me, do you?

Engstrand. Yes, sir, I wanted so very much to—

Manders (*stopping in front of him*). Well, may I ask what it is you want?

Engstrand. It's this way, Mr. Manders. We are being paid off now. And many thanks to you, Mrs. Alving. And now the work is quite finished, I thought it would be so nice and suitable if all of us, who have worked so honestly together all this time, were to finish up with a few prayers this evening.

Manders. Prayers? Up at the Orphanage?

Engstrand. Yes, sir, but if it isn't agreeable to you, then—

Manders. Oh, certainly—but—hm!—

Engstrand. I have made a practice of saying a few prayers there myself each evening—

Mrs. Alving. Have you?

Engstrand. Yes, ma'am, now and then—just as a little edification, so to speak. But I am only a poor common man, and haven't rightly the gift, alas—and so I thought that as Mr. Manders happened to be here, perhaps—

Manders. Look here, Engstrand. First of all I must ask you a question. Are you in a proper frame of mind for such a thing? Is your conscience free and untroubled?

Engstrand. Heaven have mercy on me a sinner! My conscience isn't worth our speaking about, Mr. Manders.

Manders. But it is just what we must speak about. What do you say to my question?

Engstrand. My conscience? Well—it's uneasy sometimes, of course.

Manders. Ah, you admit that at all events. Now will you tell me, without any concealment—what is your relationship to Regina?

Mrs. Alving (*hastily*). Mr. Manders!

Manders (*calming her*).—Leave it to me!

Engstrand. With Regina? Good Lord, how you frightened me! (*Looks at* MRS. ALVING.) There is nothing wrong with Regina, is there?

Manders. Let us hope not. What I want to know is, what is your relationship to her? You pass as her father, don't you?

Engstrand (*unsteadily*). Well—hm!—you know, sir, what happened between me and my poor Joanna.

Manders. No more distortion of the truth! Your late wife made a full confession to Mrs. Alving, before she left her service.

Engstrand. What!—do you mean to say—? Did she do that after all?

Manders. You see it has all come out, Engstrand.

Engstrand. Do you mean to say that she, who gave me her promise and solemn oath—

Manders. Did she take an oath?

Engstrand. Well, no—she only gave me her word, but as seriously as a woman could.

Manders. And all these years you have been hiding the truth from me—from me, who have had such complete and absolute faith in you.

Engstrand. I am sorry to say I have, sir.

Manders. Did I deserve that from you, Engstrand? Haven't I been always ready to help you in word and deed as far as lay in my power? Answer me! Is it not so?

Engstrand. Indeed there's many a time I should have been very badly off without you, sir.

Manders. And this is the way you repay me— by causing me to make false entries in the church registers, and afterwards keeping back from me for years the information which you owed it both to me and to your sense of the truth to divulge. Your conduct has been absolutely inexcusable, Engstrand, and from to-day everything is at an end between us.

Engstrand (*with a sigh*). Yes, I can see that's what it means.

Manders. Yes, because how can you possibly justify what you did?

Engstrand. Was the poor girl to go and increase her load of shame by talking about it? Just suppose, sir, for a moment that your reverence was in the same predicament as my poor Joanna—

Manders. I!

Engstrand. Good Lord, sir, I don't mean the same predicament. I mean, suppose there were something your reverence were ashamed of in the eyes of the world, so to speak. We men oughtn't to judge a poor woman too hardly, Mr. Manders.

Manders. But I am not doing so at all. It is you I am blaming.

Engstrand. Will your reverence grant me leave to ask you a small question?

Manders. Ask away.

Engstrand. Shouldn't you say it was right for a man to raise up the fallen?

Manders. Of course it is.

Engstrand. And isn't a man bound to keep his word of honour?

Manders. Certainly he is; but—

Engstrand. At the time when Joanna had her misfortune with this Englishman—or maybe he was an American or a Russian, as they call 'em—well, sir, then she came to town. Poor thing, she had refused me once or twice before; she only had eyes for good-looking men in those days, and I had this crooked leg then. Your reverence will remember how I had ventured up into a dancing-saloon where seafaring men were revelling in drunkenness and intoxication, as they say. And when I tried to exhort them to turn from their evil ways—

Mrs. Alving (coughs from the window). Ahem!

Manders. I know, Engstrand, I know—the rough brutes threw you downstairs. You have told me about that incident before. The affliction to your leg is a credit to you.

Engstrand. I don't want to claim credit for it, your reverence. But what I wanted to tell you was that she came then and confided in me with tears and gnashing of teeth. I can tell you, sir, it went to my heart to hear her.

Manders. Did it, indeed, Engstrand? Well, what then?

Engstrand. Well, then I said to her: " The American is roaming about on the high seas, he is. And you, Joanna," I said, " you have committed a sin and are a fallen woman. But here stands Jacob Engstrand," I said, " on two strong legs "—of course that was only speaking in a kind of metaphor, as it were, your reverence.

Manders. I quite understand. Go on.

Engstrand. Well, sir, that was how I rescued her and made her my lawful wife, so that no one should know how recklessly she had carried on with the stranger.

Manders. That was all very kindly done. The only thing I cannot justify was your bringing yourself to accept the money—

Engstrand. Money? I? Not a farthing.

Manders (to MRS. ALVING, *in a questioning tone*). But—

Engstrand. Ah, yes!—wait a bit; I remember now. Joanna did have a trifle of money, you are quite right. But I didn't want to know anything about that. " Fie," I said, " on the mammon of unrighteousness, it's the price of your sin; as for this tainted gold "——or notes, or whatever it was—" we will throw it back in the American's face," I said. But he had gone away and disappeared on the stormy seas, your reverence.

Manders. Was that how it was, my good fellow?

Engstrand. It was, sir. So then Joanna and I decided that the money should go towards the child's bringing-up, and that's what became of it; and I can give a faithful account of every single penny of it.

Manders. This alters the complexion of the affair very considerably.

Engstrand. That's how it was, your reverence. And I make bold to say that I have been a good father

to Regina—as far as was in my power—for I am a
poor erring mortal, alas!

Manders. There, there, my dear Engstrand—

Engstrand. Yes, I do make bold to say that I brought
up the child, and made my poor Joanna a loving and
careful husband, as the Bible says we ought. But it
never occurred to me to go to your reverence and claim
credit for it or boast about it because I had done one
good deed in this world. No; when Jacob Engstrand
does a thing like that, he holds his tongue about it.
Unfortunately it doesn't often happen, I know that only
too well. And whenever I do come to see your reverence, I never seem to have anything but trouble and
wickedness to talk about. Because, as I said just now—
and I say it again—conscience can be very hard on us
sometimes.

Manders. Give me your hand, Jacob Engstrand.

Engstrand. Oh, sir, I don't like—

Manders. No nonsense. (*Grasps his hand.*) That's
it!

Engstrand. And may I make bold humbly to beg
your reverence's pardon—

Manders. You? On the contrary it is for me to beg
your pardon—

Engstrand. Oh no, sir.

Manders. Yes, certainly it is, and I do it with my
whole heart. Forgive me for having so much misjudged
you. And I assure you that if I can do anything for you
to prove my sincere regret and my goodwill towards
you—

Engstrand. Do you mean it, sir?

Manders. It would give me the greatest pleasure.

Engstrand. As a matter of fact, sir, you could do it
now. I am thinking of using the honest money I have
put away out of my wages up here, in establishing a
sort of Sailors' Home in the town.

Mrs. Alving. You?

Engstrand. Yes, to be a sort of Refuge, as it were.
There are such manifold temptations lying in wait for

sailor men when they are roaming about on shore. But my idea is that in this house of mine they should have a sort of parental care looking after them.

Manders. What do you say to that, Mrs. Alving?

Engstrand. I haven't much to begin such a work with, I know; but Heaven might prosper it, and if I found any helping hand stretched out to me, then—

Manders. Quite so; we will talk over the matter further. Your project attracts me enormously. But in the meantime go back to the Orphanage and put everything tidy and light the lights, so that the occasion may seem a little solemn. And then we will spend a little edifying time together, my dear Engstrand, for now I am sure you are in a suitable frame of mind.

Engstrand. I believe I am, sir, truly. Good-bye, then, Mrs. Alving, and thank you for all your kindness; and take good care of Regina for me. (*Wipes a tear from his eye.*) Poor Joanna's child—it is an extraordinary thing, but she seems to have grown into my life and to hold me by the heartstrings. That's how I feel about it, truly. (*Bows, and goes out.*)

Manders. Now then, what do you think of him, Mrs Alving? That was quite another explanation that he gave us.

Mrs. Alving. It was, indeed.

Manders. There, you see how exceedingly careful we ought to be in condemning our fellow-men. But at the same time it gives one genuine pleasure to find that one was mistaken. Don't you think so?

Mrs. Alving. What I think is that you are, and always will remain, a big baby, Mr. Manders.

Manders. I?

Mrs. Alving (*laying her hands on his shoulders*). And I think that I should like very much to give you a good hug.

Manders (*drawing back hastily*). No, no, good gracious! What an idea!

Mrs. Alving (*with a smile*). Oh, you needn't be afraid of me.

Manders (*standing by the table*). You choose such an extravagant way of expressing yourself sometimes. Now I must get these papers together and put them in my bag. (*Does so.*) That's it. And now good-bye, for the present. Keep your eyes open when Oswald comes back. I will come back and see you again presently.

(*He takes his hat and goes out by the hall door.* MRS. ALVING *sighs, glances out of the window, puts one or two things tidy in the room and turns to go into the dining-room. She stops in the doorway with a stifled cry.*)

Mrs. Alving. Oswald, are you still sitting at table?

Oswald (*from the dining-room*). I am only finishing my cigar.

Mrs. Alving. I thought you had gone out for a little turn.

Oswald (*from within the room*). In weather like this? (*A glass is heard clinking.* MRS. ALVING *leaves the door open and sits down with her knitting on the couch by the window.*) Wasn't that Mr. Manders that went out just now?

Mrs. Alving. Yes, he has gone over to the Orphanage.

Oswald. Oh. (*The clink of a bottle on a glass is heard again.*)

Mrs. Alving (*with an uneasy expression.*) Oswald, dear, you should be careful with that liqueur. It is strong.

Oswald. It's a good protective against the damp.

Mrs. Alving. Wouldn't you rather come in here?

Oswald. You know you don't like smoking in there.

Mrs. Alving. You may smoke a cigar in here, certainly.

Oswald. All right; I will come in, then. Just one drop more. There! (*Comes in, smoking a cigar, and shuts the door after him. A short silence.*) Where has the parson gone?

Mrs. Alving. I told you he had gone over to the Orphanage.

Oswald. Oh, so you did.

Mrs. Alving. You shouldn't sit so long at table, Oswald.

Oswald (holding his cigar behind his back). But it's so nice and cosy, mother dear. (*Caresses her with one hand.*) Think what it means to me—to have come home; to sit at my mother's own table, in my mother's own room, and to enjoy the charming meals she gives me.

Mrs. Alving. My dear, dear boy!

Oswald (a little impatiently, as he walks up and down smoking.) And what else is there for me to do here? I have no occupation—

Mrs. Alving. No occupation?

Oswald. Not in this ghastly weather, when there isn't a blink of sunshine all day long. (*Walks up and down the floor.*) Not to be able to work, it's—!

Mrs. Alving. I don't believe you were wise to come home.

Oswald. Yes, mother; I had to.

Mrs. Alving. Because I would ten times rather give up the happiness of having you with me, sooner than that you should—

Oswald (standing still by the table). Tell me, mother—is it really such a great happiness for you to have me at home?

Mrs. Alving. Can you ask?

Oswald (crumpling up a newspaper). I should have thought it would have been pretty much the same to you whether I were here or away.

Mrs. Alving. Have you the heart to say that to your mother, Oswald?

Oswald. But you have been quite happy living without me so far.

Mrs. Alving. Yes, I have lived without you—that is true.

(*A silence. The dusk falls by degrees.* OSWALD *walks restlessly up and down. He has laid aside his cigar.*)

Oswald (stopping beside MRS. ALVING). Mother, may I sit on the couch beside you?

Mrs. Alving. Of course, my dear boy.

Oswald (sitting down). Now I must tell you something mother.

Mrs. Alving (anxiously). What?

Oswald (staring in front of him). I can't bear it any longer.

Mrs. Alving. Bear what? What do you mean?

Oswald (as before). I couldn't bring myself to write to you about it; and since I have been at home—

Mrs. Alving (catching him by the arm). Oswald, what is it?

Oswald. Both yesterday and to-day I have tried to push my thoughts away from me—to free myself from them. But I can't.

Mrs. Alving (getting up). You must speak plainly, Oswald!

Oswald (drawing her down to her seat again). Sit still, and I will try and tell you. I have made a great deal of the fatigue I felt after my journey—

Mrs. Alving. Well, what of that?

Oswald. But that isn't what is the matter. It is no ordinary fatigue—

Mrs. Alving (trying to get up). You are not ill, Oswald!

Oswald (pulling her down again). Sit still, mother. Do take it quietly. I am not exactly ill—not ill in the usual sense. *(Takes his head in his hands.)* Mother, it's my mind that has broken down—gone to pieces—I shall never be able to work any more! *(Buries his face in his hands and throws himself at her knees in an outburst of sobs.)*

Mrs. Alving (pale and trembling). Oswald! Look at me! No, no, it isn't true!

Oswald (looking up with a distracted expression). Never to be able to work any more! Never—never! A living death! Mother, can you imagine anything so horrible!

Mrs. Alving. My poor unhappy boy! How has this terrible thing happened?

Oswald (sitting up again). That is just what I cannot possibly understand. I have never lived recklessly, in any sense. You must believe that of me, mother! I have never done that.

Mrs. Alving. I haven't a doubt of it, Oswald.

Oswald. And yet this comes upon me all the same!—this terrible disaster!

Mrs. Alving. Oh, but it will all come right again, my dear precious boy. It is nothing but overwork. Believe me, that is so.

Oswald (*dully*). I thought so too, at first; but it isn't so.

Mrs. Alving. Tell me all about it.

Oswald. Yes, I will.

Mrs. Alving. When did you first feel anything?

Oswald. It was just after I had been home last time and had got back to Paris. I began to feel the most violent pains in my head—mostly at the back, I think. It was as if a tight band of iron was pressing on me from my neck upwards.

Mrs. Alving. And then?

Oswald. At first I thought it was nothing but the head-aches I always used to be so much troubled with while I was growing.

Mrs. Alving. Yes, yes—

Oswald. But it wasn't; I soon saw that. I couldn't work any longer. I would try and start some big new picture; but it seemed as if all my faculties had forsaken me, as if all my strength were paralysed. I couldn't manage to collect my thoughts; my head seemed to swim—everything went round and round. It was a horrible feeling! At last I sent for a doctor—and from him I learnt the truth.

Mrs. Alving. In what way, do you mean?

Oswald. He was one of the best doctors there. He made me describe what I felt, and then he began to ask me a whole heap of questions which seemed to me to have nothing to do with the matter. I couldn't see what he was driving at—

Mrs. Alving. Well?

Oswald. At last he said: "You have had the canker of disease in you practically from your birth"—the actual word he used was "*vermoulu.*"

E **552**

Mrs. Alving (anxiously). What did he mean by that?

Oswald. I couldn't understand, either—and I asked him for a clearer explanation, And then the old cynic said—(*clenching his fist*). Oh!—

Mrs. Alving. What did he say?

Oswald. He said: "The sins of the fathers are visited on the children."

Mrs. Alving (getting up slowly). The sins of the fathers— !

Oswald. I nearly struck him in the face—

Mrs. Alving (walking across the room). The sins of the fathers—!

Oswald (smiling sadly). Yes, just imagine! Naturally I assured him that what he thought was impossible. But do you think he paid any heed to me? No, he persisted in his opinion; and it was only when I got out your letters and translated to him all the passages that referred to my father—

Mrs. Alving. Well, and then?

Oswald. Well, then of course he had to admit that he was on the wrong tack; and then I learnt the truth—the incomprehensible truth! I ought to have had nothing to do with the joyous happy life I had lived with my comrades. It had been too much for my strength. So it was my own fault!

Mrs. Alving. No, no, Oswald! Don't believe that!

Oswald. There was no other explanation of it possible, he said. That is the most horrible part of it. My whole life incurably ruined—just because of my own imprudence. All that I wanted to do in the world—not to dare to think of it any more—not to be *able* to think of it! Oh! if only I could live my life over again—if only I could undo what I have done! (*Throws himself on his face on the couch.* MRS. ALVING *wrings her hands, and walks up and down silently fighting with herself.*)

Oswald (looks up after a while, raising himself on his elbows). If only it had been something I had inherited—something I could not help. But, instead of that, to have disgracefully, stupidly, thoughtlessly thrown away

one's happiness, one's health, everything in the world—
one's future, one's life—

Mrs. Alving. No, no, my darling boy; that is
impossible! (*Bending over him.*) Things are not so
desperate as you think.

Oswald. Ah, you don't know—. (*Springs up.*) And to
think, mother, that I should bring all this sorrow
upon you! Many a time I have almost wished and
hoped that you really did not care so very much for
me.

Mrs. Alving. I, Oswald? My only son! All that I
have in the world! The only thing I care about!

Oswald (*taking hold of her hands and kissing them*).
Yes, yes, I know that is so. When I am at home I know
that is true. And that is one of the hardest parts of
it to me. But now you know all about it; and now we
won't talk any more about it to-day. I can't stand
thinking about it long at a time. (*Walks across the
room.*) Let me have something to drink, mother!

Mrs. Alving. To drink? What do you want?

Oswald. Oh, anything you like. I suppose you have
got some punch in the house.

Mrs. Alving. Yes, but my dear Oswald—!

Oswald. Don't tell me I mustn't, mother. Do be
nice! I must have something to drown these gnawing
thoughts. (*Goes into the conservatory.*) And how—how
gloomy it is here! (MRS. ALVING *rings the bell.*) And
this incessant rain. It may go on week after week—a
whole month. Never a ray of sunshine. I don't remember
ever having seen the sun shine once when I have been
at home.

Mrs. Alving. Oswald—you are thinking of going away
from me!

Oswald. Hm!—(*sighs deeply*). I am not thinking about
anything. I *can't* think about anything! (*In a low
voice.*) I have to let that alone.

Regina (*coming from the dining-room*). Did you ring,
ma'am?

Mrs. Alving. Yes, let us have the lamp in.

Regina. In **a** moment, ma'am; it is all ready lit. *(Goes out.)*

Mrs. Alving (going up to OSWALD). Oswald, don't keep anything back from me.

Oswald. I don't, mother. *(Goes to the table.)* It seems to me I have told you a good lot.

(REGINA *brings the lamp and puts it upon the table.*)

Mrs. Alving. Regina, you might bring us a small bottle of champagne.

Regina. Yes, ma'am. *(Goes out.)*

Oswald (taking hold of his mother's face). That's right. I knew my mother wouldn't let her son go thirsty.

Mrs. Alving. My poor dear boy, how could I refuse you anything now?

Oswald (eagerly). Is that true, mother? Do you mean it?

Mrs. Alving. Mean what?

Oswald. That you couldn't deny me anything?

Mrs. Alving. My dear Oswald—

Oswald. Hush!

(REGINA *brings in a tray with a small bottle of champagne and two glasses, which she puts on the table.*)

Regina. Shall I open the bottle?

Oswald. No, thank you, I will do it.

(REGINA *goes out.*)

Mrs. Alving (sitting down at the table). What did you mean, when you asked if I could refuse you nothing?

Oswald (busy opening the bottle). Let us have a glass first—or two.

(*He draws the cork, fills one glass and is going to fill the other.*)

Mrs. Alving (holding her hand over the second glass). No, thanks—not for me.

Oswald. Oh, well, for me then! (*He empties his glass, fills it again and empties it; then sits down at the table.*)

Mrs. Alving (expectantly). Now, tell me.

Oswald (without looking at her). Tell me this; I thought you and Mr. Manders seemed so strange—so quiet—at dinner.

Mrs. Alving. Did you notice that?

Oswald. Yes. Ahem! (*After a short pause.*) Tell me—what do you think of Regina?

Mrs. Alving. What do I think of her?

Oswald. Yes, isn't she splendid?

Mrs. Alving. Dear Oswald, you don't know her as well as I do—

Oswald. What of that?

Mrs. Alving. Regina was too long at home, unfortunately. I ought to have taken her under my charge sooner.

Oswald. Yes, but isn't she splendid to look at, mother? (*Fills his glass.*)

Mrs. Alving. Regina has many serious faults—

Oswald. Yes, but what of that? (*Drinks.*)

Mrs. Alving. But I am fond of her, all the same; and I have made myself responsible for her. I wouldn't for the world she should come to any harm.

Oswald (*jumping up*). Mother, Regina is my only hope of salvation!

Mrs. Alving (*getting up*). What do you mean?

Oswald. I can't go on bearing all this agony of mind alone.

Mrs. Alving. Haven't you your mother to help you to bear it?

Oswald. Yes, I thought so; that was why I came home to you. But it is no use; I see that it isn't. I cannot spend my life here.

Mrs. Alving. Oswald!

Oswald. I must live a different sort of life, mother; so I shall have to go away from you. I don't want you watching it.

Mrs. Alving. My unhappy boy! But, Oswald, as long as you are ill like this—

Oswald. If it was only a matter of feeling ill, I would stay with you, mother. You are the best friend I have in the world.

Mrs. Alving. Yes, I am that, Oswald, am I not?

Oswald (*walking restlessly about*). But all this torment

—the regret, the remorse—and the deadly fear. Oh—this horrible fear!

Mrs. Alving (following him). Fear? Fear of what? What do you mean?

Oswald. Oh, don't ask me any more about it. I don't know what it is. I can't put it into words. (MRS. ALVING *crosses the room and rings the bell.*) What do you want?

Mrs. Alving. I want my boy to be happy, that's what I want. He mustn't brood over anything. (*To* REGINA, *who has come to the door.*) More champagne—a large bottle.

Oswald. Mother!

Mrs. Alving. Do you think we country people don't know how to live?

Oswald. Isn't she splendid to look at? What a figure! And the picture of health!

Mrs. Alving (sitting down at the table). Sit down, Oswald, and let us have a quiet talk.

Oswald (sitting down). You don't know, mother, that I owe Regina a little reparation.

Mrs. Alving. You!

Oswald. Oh, it was only a little thoughtlessness—call it what you like. Something quite innocent, anyway. The last time I was home—

Mrs. Alving. Yes?

Oswald. —she used often to ask me questions about Paris, and I told her one thing and another about the life there. And I remember saying one day: " Wouldn't you like to go there yourself? "

Mrs. Alving. Well?

Oswald. I saw her blush, and she said: " Yes, I should like to very much." " All right," I said, " I daresay it might be managed "—or something of that sort.

Mrs. Alving. And then?

Oswald. I naturally had forgotten all about it; but the day before yesterday I happened to ask her if she was glad I was to be so long at home—

Mrs. Alving. Well?

Oswald. —and she looked so queerly at me, and asked: " But what is to become of my trip to Paris?"

Mrs. Alving. Her trip!

Oswald. And then I got it out of her that she had taken the thing seriously, and had been thinking about me all the time, and had set herself to learn French—

Mrs. Alving. So that was why—

Oswald. Mother—when I saw this fine, splendid, handsome girl standing there in front of me—I had never paid any attention to her before then—but now, when she stood there as if with open arms ready for me to take her to myself—

Mrs. Alving. Oswald!

Oswald. —then I realised that my salvation lay in her, for I saw the joy of life in her.

Mrs. Alving (starting back). The joy of life—? Is there salvation in that?

Regina (coming in from the dining-room with a bottle of champagne). Excuse me for being so long; but I had to go to the cellar. *(Puts the bottle down on the table.)*

Oswald. Bring another glass, too.

Regina (looking at him in astonishment). The mistress's glass is there, sir.

Oswald. Yes, but fetch one for yourself, Regina. (REGINA *starts, and gives a quick shy glance at* MRS. ALVING.) Well?

Regina (in a low and hesitating voice). Do you wish me to, ma'am?

Mrs. Alving. Fetch the glass, Regina. (REGINA *goes into the dining-room.*)

Oswald (looking after her). Have you noticed how well she walks?—so firmly and confidently!

Mrs. Alving. It cannot be, Oswald.

Oswald. It is settled. You must see that. It is no use forbidding it. (REGINA *comes in with a glass, which she holds in her hand.*) Sit down, Regina. (REGINA *looks questioningly at* MRS. ALVING.)

Mrs. Alving. Sit down. (REGINA *sits down on a chair*

near the dining-room door, still holding the glass in her hand.) Oswald, what was it you were saying about the joy of life?

Oswald. Ah, mother—the joy of life! You don't know very much about that at home here. I shall never realise it here.

Mrs. Alving. Not even when you are with me?

Oswald. Never at home. But you can't understand that.

Mrs. Alving. Yes, indeed I almost think I do understand you—now.

Oswald. That—and the joy of work. They are really the same thing at bottom. But you don't know anything about that either.

Mrs. Alving. Perhaps you are right. Tell me some more about it, Oswald.

Oswald. Well, all I mean is that here people are brought up to believe that work is a curse and a punishment for sin, and that life is a state of wretchedness and that the sooner we can get out of it the better.

Mrs. Alving. A vale of tears, yes. And we quite conscientiously make it so.

Oswald. But the people over there will have none of that. There is no one there who really believes doctrines of that kind any longer. Over there the mere fact of being alive is thought to be a matter for exultant happiness. Mother, have you noticed that everything I have painted has turned upon the joy of life?—always upon the joy of life, unfailingly. There is light there, and sunshine, and a holiday feeling—and people's faces beaming with happiness. That is why I am afraid to stay at home here with you.

Mrs. Alving. Afraid? What are you afraid of here, with me?

Oswald. I am afraid that all these feelings that are so strong in me would degenerate into something ugly here.

Mrs. Alving (looking steadily at him). Do you think that is what would happen?

Oswald. I am certain it would. Even if one lived the same life at home here, as over there—it would never really be the same life.

Mrs. Alving (who has listened anxiously to him, gets up with a thoughtful expression and says:) Now I see clearly how it all happened.

Oswald. What do you see?

Mrs. Alving. I see it now for the first time. And now I can speak.

Oswald (getting up). Mother, I don't understand you.

Regina (who has got up also). Perhaps I had better go.

Mrs. Alving. No, stay here. Now I can speak. Now, my son, you shall know the whole truth. Oswald! Regina!

Oswald. Hush!—here is the parson—

(MANDERS *comes in by the hall door.*)

Manders. Well, my friends, we have been spending an edifying time over there.

Oswald. So have we.

Manders. Engstrand must have help with his Sailors' Home. Regina must go home with him and give him her assistance.

Regina. No, thank you, Mr. Manders.

Manders (perceiving her for the first time). What—? You in here?—and with a wineglass in your hand!

Regina (putting down the glass hastily). I beg your pardon—!

Oswald. Regina is going away with me, Mr. Manders.

Manders. Going away! With you!

Oswald. Yes, as my wife—if she insists on that.

Manders. But, good heavens—!

Regina. It is not my fault, Mr. Manders.

Oswald. Or else she stays here if I stay.

Regina (involuntarily). Here!

Manders. I am amazed at you, Mrs. Alving.

Mrs. Alving. Neither of those things will happen, for now I can speak openly.

Manders. But you won't do that! No, no, no!

Mrs. Alving. Yes, I can and I will. And without destroying any one's ideals.

*E 552

Oswald. Mother, what is it that is being concealed from me?

Regina (*listening*). Mrs. Alving! Listen! They are shouting outside.

     (*Goes into the conservatory and looks out.*)

Oswald (*going to the window on the left*). What can be the matter? Where does that glare come from?

Regina (*calls out*). The Orphanage is on fire!

Mrs. Alving (*going to the window*). On fire?

Manders. On fire? Impossible. I was there just a moment ago.

Oswald. Where is my hat? Oh, never mind that. Father's Orphanage—!

     (*Runs out through the garden door.*)

Mrs. Alving. My shawl, Regina! The whole place is in flames.

Manders. How terrible! Mrs. Alving, that fire is a judgment on this house of sin!

Mrs. Alving. Quite so. Come, Regina.

     (*She and* REGINA *hurry out.*)

Manders (*clasping his hands*). And no insurance!

     (*Follows them out.*)

ACT III

(*The same scene. All the doors are standing open. The lamp is still burning on the table. It is dark outside, except for a faint glimmer of light seen through the windows at the back.* MRS. ALVING, *with a shawl over her head, is standing in the conservatory, looking out.* REGINA, *also wrapped in a shawl, is standing a little behind her.*)

Mrs. Alving. Everything burnt—down to the ground.

Regina. It is burning still in the basement.

Mrs. Alving. I can't think why Oswald doesn't come back. There is no chance of saving anything.

Regina. Shall I go and take his hat to him?

Mrs. Alving. Hasn't he even got his hat?

Regina (pointing to the hall). No, there it is, hanging up.

Mrs. Alving. Never mind. He is sure to come back soon. I will go and see what he is doing. (*Goes out by the garden door.* MANDERS *comes in from the hall.*)

Manders. Isn't Mrs. Alving here?

Regina. She has just this moment gone down into the garden.

Manders. I have never spent such a terrible night in my life.

Regina. Isn't it a shocking misfortune, sir!

Manders. Oh, don't speak about it. I scarcely dare to think about it.

Regina. But how can it have happened?

Manders. Don't ask me, Miss Engstrand! How should I know? Are you going to suggest too—? Isn't it enough that your father—?

Regina. What has he done?

Manders. He has nearly driven me crazy.

Engstrand (coming in from the hall). Mr. Manders—!

Manders (turning round with a start). Have you even followed me here!

Engstrand. Yes, God help us all—! Great heavens! What a dreadful thing, your reverence!

Manders (walking up and down). Oh dear, oh dear!

Regina. What do you mean?

Engstrand. Our little prayer-meeting was the cause of it all, don't you see? (*Aside, to* REGINA.) Now we've got the old fool, my girl. (*Aloud.*) And to think it is my fault that Mr. Manders should be the cause of such a thing!

Manders. I assure you, Engstrand—

Engstrand. But there was no one else carrying a light there except you, sir.

Manders (standing still). Yes, so you say. But I have no clear recollection of having had a light in my hand.

Engstrand. But I saw quite distinctly your reverence

take a candle and snuff it with your fingers and throw away the burning bit of wick among the shavings.

Manders. Did you see that?

Engstrand. Yes, distinctly.

Manders. I can't understand it at all. It is never my habit to snuff a candle with my fingers.

Engstrand. Yes, it wasn't like you to do that, sir. But who would have thought it could be such a dangerous thing to do?

Manders (*walking restlessly backwards and forwards*). Oh, don't ask me!

Engstrand (*following him about*). And you hadn't insured it either, had you, sir?

Manders. No, no, no; you heard me say so.

Engstrand. You hadn't insured it—and then went and set light to the whole place! Good Lord, what bad luck!

Manders (*wiping the perspiration from his forehead*). You may well say so, Engstrand.

Engstrand. And that it should happen to a charitable institution that would have been of service both to the town and the country, so to speak! The newspapers won't be very kind to your reverence, I expect.

Manders. No, that is just what I am thinking of. It is almost the worst part of the whole thing. The spiteful attacks and accusations—it is horrible to think of!

Mrs. Alving (*coming in from the garden*). I can't get him away from the fire.

Manders. Oh, there you are, Mrs. Alving.

Mrs. Alving. You will escape having to make your inaugural address now, at all events, Mr. Manders.

Manders. Oh, I would so gladly have—

Mrs. Alving (*in a dull voice*). It is just as well it has happened. This Orphanage would never have come to any good.

Manders. Don't you think so?

Mrs. Alving. Do you?

Manders. But it is none the less an extraordinary piece of ill luck.

Mrs. Alving. We will discuss it simply as a business matter.—Are you waiting for Mr. Manders, Engstrand?

Engstrand (at the hall door). Yes, I am.

Mrs. Alving. Sit down then, while you are waiting.

Engstrand. Thank you, I would rather stand.

Mrs. Alving (to MANDERS). I suppose you are going by the boat?

Manders. Yes. It goes in about an hour.

Mrs. Alving. Please take all the documents back with you. I don't want to hear another word about the matter. I have something else to think about now—

Manders. Mrs. Alving—

Mrs. Alving. Later on I will send you a power of attorney to deal with it exactly as you please.

Manders. I shall be most happy to undertake that. I am afraid the original intention of the bequest will have to be entirely altered now.

Mrs. Alving. Of course.

Manders. Provisionally, I should suggest this way of disposing of it. Make over the Solvik property to the parish. The land is undoubtedly not without a certain value; it will always be useful for some purpose or another. And as for the interest on the remaining capital that is on deposit in the bank, possibly I might make suitable use of that in support of some undertaking that promises to be of use to the town.

Mrs. Alving. Do exactly as you please. The whole thing is a matter of indifference to me now.

Engstrand. You will think of my Sailors' Home, Mr. Manders?

Manders. Yes, certainly, that is a suggestion. But we must consider the matter carefully.

Engstrand (aside). Consider!—devil take it! Oh Lord.

Manders (sighing). And unfortunately I can't tell how much longer I may have anything to do with the matter—whether public opinion may not force me to retire from it altogether. That depends entirely upon the result of the enquiry into the cause of the fire.

Mrs. Alving. What do you say?

Manders. And one cannot in any way reckon upon the result beforehand.

Engstrand (going nearer to him). Yes, indeed one can; because here stand I, Jacob Engstrand.

Manders. Quite so, but—

Engstrand (lowering his voice). And Jacob Engstrand isn't the man to desert a worthy benefactor in the hour of need, as the saying is.

Manders. Yes, but, my dear fellow—how—?

Engstrand. You might say Jacob Engstrand is an angel of salvation, so to speak, your reverence.

Manders. No, no, I couldn't possibly accept that.

Engstrand. That's how it will be, all the same. I know some one who has taken the blame for some one else on his shoulders before now, I do.

Manders. Jacob! *(Grasps his hand.)* You are one in a thousand! You shall have assistance in the matter of your Sailors' Home, you may rely upon that.

(Engstrand tries to thank him, but is prevented by emotion.)

Manders (hanging his wallet over his shoulder). Now we must be off. We will travel together.

Engstrand (by the dining-room door, says aside to Regina). Come with me, you hussy! You shall be as cosy as the yolk in an egg!

Regina (tossing her head). Merci!

(She goes out into the hall and brings back Manders' luggage.)

Manders. Good-bye, Mrs. Alving! And may the spirit of order and of what is lawful speedily enter into this house.

Mrs. Alving. Good-bye, Mr. Manders.

(She goes into the conservatory, as she sees Oswald coming in by the garden door.)

Engstrand (as he and Regina are helping Manders on with his coat). Good-bye, my child. And if anything should happen to you, you know where Jacob Engstrand is to be found. *(Lowering his voice.)* Little Harbour

Street, ahem—! (*To* MRS. ALVING *and* OSWALD.) And my house for poor seafaring men shall be called the "Alving Home," it shall. And, if I can carry out my own ideas about it, I shall make bold to hope that it may be worthy of bearing the late Mr. Alving's name.

Manders (*at the door*). Ahem—ahem! Come along, my dear Engstrand. Good-bye—good-bye!

(*He and* ENGSTRAND *go out by the hall door.*)

Oswald (*going to the table*). What house was he speaking about?

Mrs. Alving. I believe it is some sort of a Home that he and Mr. Manders want to start.

Oswald. It will be burnt up just like this one.

Mrs. Alving. What makes you think that?

Oswald. Everything will be burnt up; nothing will be left that is in memory of my father. Here am I being burnt up, too.

(REGINA *looks at him in alarm.*)

Mrs. Alving. Oswald! You should not have stayed so long over there, my poor boy.

Oswald (*sitting down at the table*). I almost believe you are right.

Mrs. Alving. Let me dry your face, Oswald; you are all wet. (*Wipes his face with her handkerchief.*)

Oswald (*looking straight before him, with no expression in his eyes*). Thank you, mother.

Mrs. Alving. And aren't you tired, Oswald? Don't you want to go to sleep?

Oswald (*uneasily*). No, no—not to sleep! I never sleep; I only pretend to. (*Gloomily.*) That will come soon enough.

Mrs. Alving (*looking at him anxiously*). Anyhow you are really ill, my darling boy.

Regina (*intently*). Is Mr. Alving ill?

Oswald (*impatiently*). And do shut all the doors! This deadly fear—

Mrs. Alving. Shut the doors, Regina. (REGINA *shuts the doors and remains standing by the hall door.* MRS. ALVING *takes off her shawl;* REGINA *does the same.* MRS.

ALVING *draws up a chair near to* OSWALD'S *and sits down
beside him.*) That's it! Now I will sit beside you—

Oswald. Yes, do. And Regina must stay in here too.
Regina must always be near me. You must give me a
helping hand, you know, Regina. Won't you do that?

Regina. I don't understand—

Mrs. Alving. A helping hand?

Oswald. Yes—when there is need for it.

Mrs. Alving. Oswald, have you not your mother to
give you a helping hand?

Oswald. You? (*Smiles.*) No, mother, you will never give
me the kind of helping hand I mean. (*Laughs grimly.*)
You! Ha, ha! (*Looks gravely at her.*) After all, you have
the best right. (*Impetuously.*) Why don't you call
me by my Christian name, Regina? Why don't you say
Oswald?

Regina (*in a low voice*). I did not think Mrs. Alving
would like it.

Mrs. Alving. It will not be long before you have the
right to do it. Sit down here now beside us, too. (RE-
GINA *sits down quietly and hesitatingly at the other side of
the table.*) And now, my poor tortured boy, I am
going to take the burden off your mind—

Oswald. You, mother?

Mrs. Alving. —all that you call remorse and regret
and self-reproach.

Oswald. And you think you can do that?

Mrs. Alving. Yes, now I can, Oswald. A little while
ago you were talking about the joy of life, and what you
said seemed to shed a new light upon everything in my
whole life.

Oswald (*shaking his head*). I don't in the least understand what you mean.

Mrs. Alving. You should have known your father
in his young days in the army. He was full of the joy
of life, I can tell you.

Oswald. Yes, I know.

Mrs. Alving. It gave me a holiday feeling only to look
at him, full of irrepressible energy and exuberant spirits.

Oswald. What then?

Mrs. Alving. Well, then this boy, full of the joy of life—for he was just like a boy, then—had to make his home in a second-rate town which had none of the joy of life to offer him, but only dissipations. He had to come out here and live an aimless life; he had only an official post. He had no work worth devoting his whole mind to; he had nothing more than official routine to attend to. He had not a single companion capable of appreciating what the joy of life meant; nothing but idlers and tipplers—

Oswald. Mother—!

Mrs. Alving. And so the inevitable happened!

Oswald. What was the inevitable?

Mrs. Alving. You said yourself this evening what would happen in your case if you stayed at home.

Oswald. Do you mean by that, that father—?

Mrs. Alving. Your poor father never found any outlet for the overmastering joy of life that was in him. And I brought no holiday spirit into his home, either.

Oswald. You didn't, either?

Mrs. Alving. I had been taught about duty, and the sort of thing that I believed in so long here. Everything seemed to turn upon duty—my duty, or his duty—and I am afraid I made your poor father's home unbearable to him, Oswald.

Oswald. Why did you never say anything about it to me in your letters?

Mrs. Alving. I never looked at it as a thing I could speak of to you, who were his son.

Oswald. What way did you look at it, then?

Mrs. Alving. I only saw the one fact, that your father was a lost man before ever you were born.

Oswald (in a choking voice). Ah—! (*He gets up and goes to the window.*)

Mrs. Alving. And then I had the one thought in my mind, day and night, that Regina in fact had as good a right in this house—as my own boy had.

Oswald (turns round suddenly). Regina—?

Regina (gets up and asks in choking tones). I—?

Mrs. Alving. Yes, now you both know it.

Oswald. Regina!

Regina (to herself). So mother was one of that sort too.

Mrs. Alving. Your mother had many good qualities, Regina.

Regina. Yes, but she was one of that sort too, all the same. I have even thought so myself, sometimes, but—. Then, if you please, Mrs. Alving, may I have permission to leave at once?

Mrs. Alving. Do you really wish to, Regina?

Regina. Yes, indeed, I certainly wish to.

Mrs. Alving. Of course you shall do as you like, but—

Oswald (going up to REGINA). Leave now? This is your home.

Regina. Merci, Mr. Alving—oh, of course I may say Oswald now, but that is not the way I thought it would become allowable.

Mrs. Alving. Regina, I have not been open with you—

Regina. No, I can't say you have! If I had known Oswald was ill—. And now that there can never be anything serious between us—. No, I really can't stay here in the country and wear myself out looking after invalids.

Oswald. Not even for the sake of one who has so near a claim on you?

Regina. No, indeed I can't. A poor girl must make some use of her youth, otherwise she may easily find herself out in the cold before she knows where she is. And I have got the joy of life in me too, Mrs. Alving!

Mrs. Alving. Yes, unfortunately; but don't throw yourself away, Regina.

Regina. Oh, what's going to happen will happen. If Oswald takes after his father, it is just as likely I take after my mother, I expect.—May I ask, Mrs. Alving, whether Mr. Manders knows this about me?

Mrs. Alving. Mr. Manders knows everything.

Regina (putting on her shawl). Oh, well then, the best

thing I can do is to get away by the boat as soon as I can.
Mr. Manders is such a nice gentleman to deal with; and
it certainly seems to me that I have just as much right
to some of that money as he—as that horrid carpenter.

Mrs. Alving. You are quite welcome to it, Regina.

Regina (looking at her fixedly). You might as well
have brought me up like a gentleman's daughter; it
would have been more suitable. (*Tosses her head.*)
Oh, well—never mind! (*With a bitter glance at the un-
opened bottle.*) I daresay some day I shall be drinking
champagne with gentlefolk, after all.

Mrs. Alving. If ever you need a home, Regina, come
to me.

Regina. No, thank you, Mrs. Alving. Mr. Manders
takes an interest in me, I know. And if things should
go very badly with me, I know one house at any rate
where I shall feel at home.

Mrs. Alving. Where is that?

Regina. In the " Alving Home."

Mrs. Alving. Regina—I can see quite well—you are
going to your ruin!

Regina. Pooh!—good-bye.

(*She bows to them and goes out through the hall.*)

Oswald (standing by the window and looking out). Has
she gone?

Mrs. Alving. Yes.

Oswald (muttering to himself). I think it's all wrong.

*Mrs. Alving (going up to him from behind and putting
her hands on his shoulders).* Oswald, my dear boy—has
it been a great shock to you?

Oswald (turning his face towards her). All this about
father, do you mean?

Mrs. Alving. Yes, about your unhappy father. I am
so afraid it may have been too much for you.

Oswald. What makes you think that? Naturally it
has taken me entirely by surprise; but, after all, I don't
know that it matters much to me.

Mrs. Alving (drawing back her hands). Doesn't matter!
—that your father's life was such a terrible failure!

Oswald. Of course I can feel sympathy for him, just as I would for anyone else, but—

Mrs. Alving. No more than that! For your own father!

Oswald (*impatiently*). Father—father! I never knew anything of my father. I don't remember anything else about him except that he once made me sick.

Mrs. Alving. It is dreadful to think of!—But surely a child should feel some affection for his father, whatever happens?

Oswald. When the child has nothing to thank his father for? When he has never known him? Do you really cling to that antiquated superstition—you, who are so broad-minded in other things?

Mrs. Alving. You call it nothing but a superstition!

Oswald. Yes, and you can see that for yourself quite well, mother. It is one of those beliefs that are put into circulation in the world, and—

Mrs. Alving. Ghosts of beliefs!

Oswald (*walking across the room*). Yes, you might call them ghosts.

Mrs. Alving (*with an outburst of feeling*). Oswald—then you don't love me either!

Oswald. You I know, at any rate—

Mrs. Alving. You know me, yes; but is that all?

Oswald. And I know how fond you are of me, and I ought to be grateful to you for that. Besides, you can be so tremendously useful to me, now that I am ill.

Mrs. Alving. Yes, can't I, Oswald! I could almost bless your illness, as it has driven you home to me. For I see quite well that you are not my very own yet; you must be won.

Oswald (*impatiently*). Yes, yes, yes; all that is just a way of talking. You must remember I am a sick man, mother. I can't concern myself much with anyone else; I have enough to do, thinking about myself.

Mrs. Alving (*gently*). I will be very good and patient.

Oswald. And cheerful too, mother!

Mrs. Alving. Yes, my dear boy, you are quite right.

(*Goes up to him.*)   Now have I taken away all your remorse and self-reproach?

Oswald. Yes, you have done that. But who will take
away the fear?

Mrs. Alving. The fear?

Oswald (crossing the room). Regina would have done it
for one kind word.

Mrs. Alving. I don't understand you. What fear
do you mean—and what has Regina to do with it?

Oswald. Is it very late, mother?

Mrs. Alving. It is early morning. (*Looks out through
the conservatory windows.*) The dawn is breaking already
on the heights. And the sky is clear, Oswald. In a
little while you will see the sun .

Oswald. I am glad of that. After all, there may be
many things yet for me to be glad of and to live for—

Mrs. Alving. I should hope so!

Oswald. Even if I am not able to work—

Mrs. Alving. You will soon find you are able to work
again now, my dear boy. You have no longer all those
painful depressing thoughts to brood over.

Oswald. No, it is a good thing that you have been
able to rid me of those fancies. If only, now, I
could overcome this one thing—. (*Sits down on the
couch.*) Let us have a little chat, mother.

Mrs. Alving. Yes, let us. (*Pushes an armchair near
to the couch and sits down beside him.*)

Oswald. The sun is rising—and you know all about it;
so I don't feel the fear any longer.

Mrs. Alving. I know all about what?

Oswald (without listening to her). Mother, isn't it the
case that you said this evening there was nothing in
the world you would not do for me if I asked you?

Mrs. Alving. Yes, certainly I said so.

Oswald. And will you be as good as your word,
mother?

Mrs. Alving. You may rely upon that, my own dear
boy. I have nothing else to live for, but you.

Oswald. Yes, yes; well, listen to me, mother. You

are very strong-minded, I know. I want you to sit quite quiet when you hear what I am going to tell you.

Mrs. Alving. But what is this dreadful thing—?

Oswald. You mustn't scream. Do you hear? Will you promise me that? We are going to sit and talk it over quite quietly. Will you promise me that, mother?

Mrs. Alving. Yes, yes, I promise—only tell me what it is.

Oswald. Well, then, you must know that this fatigue of mine—and my not being able to think about my work —all that is not really the illness itself—

Mrs. Alving. What is the illness itself?

Oswald. What I am suffering from is hereditary; it— (*touches his forehead, and speaks very quietly*)—it lies here.

Mrs. Alving (*almost speechless*). Oswald! No—no!

Oswald. Don't scream; I can't stand it. Yes, I tell you, it lies here, waiting. And any time, any moment, it may break out.

Mrs. Alving. How horrible—!

Oswald. Do keep quiet. That is the state I am in—

Mrs. Alving (*springing up*). It isn't true, Oswald! It is impossible! It can't be that!

Oswald. I had one attack while I was abroad. It passed off quickly. But when I learnt the condition I had been in, then this dreadful haunting fear took possession of me.

Mrs. Alving. That was the fear, then—

Oswald. Yes, it is so indescribably horrible, you know. If only it had been an ordinary mortal disease—. I am not so much afraid of dying; though, of course, I should like to live as long as I can.

Mrs. Alving. Yes, yes, Oswald, you must!

Oswald. But this is so appallingly horrible. To become like a helpless child again—to have to be fed, to have to be—. Oh, it's unspeakable!

Mrs. Alving. My child has his mother to tend him.

Oswald (*jumping up*). No, never; that is just what I won't endure! I dare not think what it would mean to linger on like that for years—to get old and grey like that. And you might die before I did. (*Sits down in* MRS. ALVING'S *chair*.) Because it doesn't necessarily have a fatal end quickly, the doctor said. He called it a kind of softening of the brain—or something of that sort. (*Smiles mournfully.*) I think that expression sounds so nice. It always makes me think of cherry-coloured velvet curtains—something that is soft to stroke.

Mrs. Alving (with a scream). Oswald!

Oswald (jumps up and walks about the room). And now you have taken Regina from me! If I had only had her. She would have given me a helping hand, I know.

Mrs. Alving (going up to him). What do you mean, my darling boy? Is there any help in the world I would not be willing to give you?

Oswald. When I had recovered from the attack I had abroad, the doctor told me that when it recurred—and it will recur—there would be no more hope.

Mrs. Alving. And he was heartless enough to—

Oswald. I insisted on knowing. I told him I had arrangements to make—. (*Smiles cunningly.*) And so I had. (*Takes a small box from his inner breast-pocket.*) Mother, do you see this?

Mrs. Alving. What is it?

Oswald. Morphia powders.

Mrs. Alving (looking at him in terror). Oswald—my boy!

Oswald. I have twelve of them saved up—

Mrs. Alving (snatching at it). Give me the box, Oswald!

Oswald. Not yet, mother. (*Puts it back in his pocket.*)

Mrs. Alving. I shall never get over this!

Oswald. You must. If I had had Regina here now, I would have told her quietly how things stand with me—and asked her to give me this last helping hand. She would have helped me, I am certain.

Mrs. Alving. Never!

Oswald. If this horrible thing had come upon me and she had seen me lying helpless, like a baby, past help, past saving, past hope—with no chance of recovering—

Mrs. Alving. Never in the world would Regina have done it.

Oswald. Regina would have done it. Regina was so splendidly light-hearted. And she would **very** soon have tired of looking after an invalid like me.

Mrs. Alving. Then thank heaven Regina is not here!

Oswald. Well, now you have got to give me that helping hand, mother.

Mrs. Alving (with a loud scream). I?

Oswald. Who has a better right than you?

Mrs. Alving. I? Your mother?

Oswald. Just for that reason.

Mrs. Alving. I, who gave you your life?

Oswald. I never asked you for life. And what kind of a life was it that you gave me? I don't want it! You shall take it back!

Mrs. Alving. Help! Help! *(Runs into the hall.)*

Oswald (following her). Don't leave me! Where are you going?

Mrs. Alving (in the hall). To fetch the doctor to you, Oswald! Let me out!

Oswald (going into the hall). You shan't go out. And no one shall come in. *(Turns the key in the lock.)*

Mrs. Alving (coming in again). Oswald! Oswald!—my child!

Oswald (following her). Have you a mother's heart—and can bear to see me suffering this unspeakable terror?

Mrs. Alving (controlling herself, after a moment's silence). There is my hand on it.

Oswald. Will you—?

Mrs. Alving. If it becomes necessary. But it shan't become necessary. No, no—it is impossible it should!

Oswald. Let us hope so. And let us live together as long as we can. Thank you, mother.

(He sits down in the armchair, which Mrs. Alving *had moved beside the couch. Day is breaking; the lamp is still burning on the table.)*

Mrs. Alving (coming cautiously nearer). Do you feel calmer now?

Oswald. Yes.

Mrs. Alving (bending over him). It has only been a dreadful fancy of yours, Oswald. Nothing but fancy. All this upset has been bad for you. But now you will get some rest, at home with your own mother, my darling boy. You shall have everything you want, just as you did when you were a little child.—There, now. The attack is over. You see how easily it passed off! I knew it would.—And look, Oswald, what a lovely day we are going to have! Brilliant sunshine. Now you will be able to see your home properly. *(She goes to the table and puts out the lamp. It is sunrise. The glaciers and peaks in the distance are seen bathed in bright morning light.)*

Oswald (who has been sitting motionless in the armchair, with his back to the scene outside, suddenly says:) Mother, give me the sun.

Mrs. Alving (standing at the table, and looking at him in amazement). What do you say?

Oswald (repeats in a dull, toneless voice). The sun—the sun.

Mrs. Alving (going up to him). Oswald, what is the matter with you? *(OSWALD seems to shrink up in the chair; all his muscles relax; his face loses its expression, and his eyes stare stupidly. MRS. ALVING is trembling with terror.)* What is it! *(Screams.)* Oswald! What is the matter with you! *(Throws herself on her knees beside him and shakes him.)* Oswald! Oswald! Look at me! Don't you know me!

Oswald (in an expressionless voice, as before). The sun—the sun.

Mrs. Alving (jumps up despairingly, beats her head with her hands, and screams). I can't bear it! *(Whispers as though paralysed with fear.)* I can't bear it! Never! *(Suddenly.)* Where has he got it? *(Passes her hand quickly over his coat.)* Here! *(Draws back a little way and cries:)* No, no, no!—Yes!—no, no! *(She stands a few steps from him, her hands thrust into her hair, and stares at him in speechless terror.)*

Oswald (sitting motionless, as before). The sun—the sun.

AN ENEMY OF THE PEOPLE
A Play in Five Acts

DRAMATIS PERSONÆ

Dr. Thomas Stockmann, Medical Officer of the Municipal Baths.

Mrs. Stockmann, his wife.

Petra, their daughter, a teacher.

Ejlif
Morten } their sons (aged 13 and 10 respectively).

Peter Stockmann, the Doctor's elder brother; Mayor of the Town and Chief Constable, Chairman of the Baths Committee, etc., etc.

Morten Kiil, a tanner (Mrs. Stockmann's adoptive father).

Hovstad, editor of the " People's Messenger."

Billing, sub-editor.

Captain Horster.

Aslaksen, a printer.

Men of various conditions and occupations, some few women, and a troop of schoolboys—the audience at a public meeting.

The action takes place in a coast town in southern Norway.

ACT I

(SCENE.—DR. STOCKMANN'S *sitting-room. It is evening.
The room is plainly but neatly appointed and furnished.
In the right-hand wall are two doors; the farther leads out
to the hall, the nearer to the doctor's study. In the left-
hand wall, opposite the door leading to the hall, is a door
leading to the other rooms occupied by the family. In the
middle of the same wall stands the stove, and, further forward, a couch with a looking-glass hanging over it and an
oval table in front of it. On the table, a lighted lamp, with
a lampshade. At the back of the room, an open door leads
to the dining-room.* BILLING *is seen sitting at the dining
table, on which a lamp is burning. He has a napkin
tucked under his chin, and* MRS. STOCKMANN *is standing
by the table handing him a large plate-full of roast beef. The
other places at the table are empty, and the table somewhat in disorder, a meal having evidently recently been
finished.*)

Mrs. Stockmann. You see, if you come an hour late,
Mr. Billing, you have to put up with cold meat.

Billing (as he eats). It is uncommonly good, thank
you—remarkably good.

Mrs. Stockmann. My husband makes such a point
of having his meals punctually, you know—

Billing. That doesn't affect me a bit. Indeed, I
almost think I enjoy a meal all the better when I can
sit down and eat all by myself and undisturbed.

Mrs. Stockmann. Oh well, as long as you are enjoying
it—. (*Turns to the hall door, listening.*) I expect that is
Mr. Hovstad coming too.

Billing. Very likely.

(PETER STOCKMANN *comes in. He wears an overcoat
and his official hat, and carries a stick.*)

Peter Stockmann. Good evening, Katherine.

Mrs. Stockmann (coming forward into the sitting-room).
Ah, good evening—is it you? How good of you to
come up and see us!

Peter Stockmann. I happened to be passing, and so—
(*looks into the dining-room*). But you have company
with you, I see.

Mrs. Stockmann (a little embarrassed). Oh, no—it was
quite by chance he came in. (*Hurriedly.*) Won't you
come in and have something, too?

Peter Stockmann. I? No, thank you. Good gracious
—hot meat at night! Not with my digestion.

Mrs. Stockmann. Oh, but just once in a way—

Peter Stockmann. No, no, my dear lady; I stick to
my tea and bread and butter. It is much more wholesome in the long run—and a little more economical,
too.

Mrs. Stockmann (smiling). Now you mustn't think that
Thomas and I are spendthrifts.

Peter Stockmann. Not you, my dear; I would never
think that of you. (*Points to the Doctor's study.*) Is he
not at home?

Mrs. Stockmann. No, he went out for a little turn after
supper—he and the boys.

Peter Stockmann. I doubt if that is a wise thing to do.
(*Listens.*) I fancy I hear him coming now.

Mrs. Stockmann. No, I don't think it is he. (*A knock
is heard at the door.*) Come in! (HOVSTAD *comes in from
the hall.*) Oh, it is you, Mr. Hovstad!

Hovstad. Yes, I hope you will forgive me, but I was
delayed at the printers. Good evening, Mr. Mayor.

Peter Stockmann (bowing a little distantly). Good evening. You have come on business, no doubt.

Hovstad. Partly. It's about an article for the paper.

Peter Stockmann. So I imagined. I hear my brother
has become a prolific contributor to the " People's Messenger."

Hovstad. Yes, he is good enough to write in the " People's Messenger " when he has any home truths to tell.

Mrs. Stockmann (*to* HOVSTAD). But won't you—?
(*Points to the dining-room.*)

Peter Stockmann. Quite so, quite so. I don't blame him in the least, as a writer, for addressing himself to the quarters where he will find the readiest sympathy. And, besides that, I personally have no reason to bear any ill will to your paper, Mr. Hovstad.

Hovstad. I quite agree with you.

Peter Stockmann. Taking one thing with another, there is an excellent spirit of toleration in the town—an admirable municipal spirit. And it all springs from the fact of our having a great common interest to unite us—an interest that is in an equally high degree the concern of every right-minded citizen—

Hovstad. The Baths, yes.

Peter Stockmann. Exactly—our fine, new, handsome Baths. Mark my words, Mr. Hovstad—the Baths will become the focus of our municipal life! Not a doubt of it!

Mrs. Stockmann. That is just what Thomas says.

Peter Stockmann. Think how extraordinarily the place has developed within the last year or two! Money has been flowing in, and there is some life and some business doing in the town. Houses and landed property are rising in value every day.

Hovstad. And unemployment is diminishing.

Peter Stockmann. Yes, that is another thing. The burden of the poor rates has been lightened, to the great relief of the propertied classes; and that relief will be even greater if only we get a really good summer this year, and lots of visitors—plenty of invalids, who will make the Baths talked about.

Hovstad. And there is a good prospect of that, I hear.

Peter Stockmann. It looks very promising. Enquiries about apartments and that sort of thing are reaching us every day.

Hovstad. Well, the doctor's article will come in very suitably.

Peter Stockmann. Has he been writing something just lately?

Hovstad. This is something he wrote in the winter; a recommendation of the Baths—an account of the excellent sanitary conditions here. But I held the article over, temporarily.

Peter Stockmann. Ah,—some little difficulty about it, I suppose?

Hovstad. No, not at all; I thought it would be better to wait till the spring, because it is just at this time that people begin to think seriously about their summer quarters.

Peter Stockmann. Quite right; you were perfectly right, Mr. Hovstad.

Hovstad. Yes, Thomas is really indefatigable when it is a question of the Baths.

Peter Stockmann. Well—remember, he is the Medical Officer to the Baths.

Hovstad. Yes, and what is more, they owe their existence to him.

Peter Stockmann. To him? Indeed! It is true I have heard from time to time that some people are of that opinion. At the same time I must say I imagined that I took a modest part in the enterprise.

Mrs. Stockmann. Yes, that is what Thomas is always saying.

Hovstad. But who denies it, Mr. Stockmann? You set the thing going and made a practical concern of it; we all know that. I only meant that the idea of it came first from the doctor.

Peter Stockmann. Oh, ideas—yes! My brother has had plenty of them in his time—unfortunately. But when it is a question of putting an idea into practical shape, you have to apply to a man of different mettle, Mr. Hovstad. And I certainly should have thought that in this house at least—

Mrs. Stockmann. My dear Peter—

Hovstad. How can you think that—?

Mrs. Stockmann. Won't you go in and have something,

Mr. Hovstad? My husband is sure to be back directly.

Hovstad. Thank you, perhaps just a morsel. (*Goes into the dining-room.*)

Peter Stockmann (*lowering his voice a little*). It is a curious thing that these farmers' sons never seem to lose their want of tact.

Mrs. Stockmann. Surely it is not worth bothering about! Cannot you and Thomas share the credit as brothers?

Peter Stockmann. I should have thought so; but apparently some people are not satisfied with a share.

Mrs. Stockmann. What nonsense! You and Thomas get on so capitally together. (*Listens.*) There he is at last, I think. (*Goes out and opens the door leading to the hall.*)

Dr. Stockmann (*laughing and talking outside*). Look here—here is another guest for you, Katherine. Isn't that jolly! Come in, Captain Horster; hang your coat up on this peg. Ah, you don't wear an overcoat. Just think, Katherine; I met him in the street and could hardly persuade him to come up! (CAPTAIN HORSTER *comes into the room and greets* MRS. STOCKMANN. *He is followed by* DR. STOCKMANN.) Come along in, boys. They are ravenously hungry again, you know. Come along, Captain Horster; you must have a slice of beef. (*Pushes* HORSTER *into the dining-room.* EJLIF *and* MORTEN *go in after them.*)

Mrs. Stockmann. But, Thomas, don't you see—?

Dr. Stockmann (*turning in the doorway*). Oh, is it you, Peter? (*Shakes hands with him.*) Now that is very delightful.

Peter Stockmann. Unfortunately I must go in a moment—

Dr. Stockmann. Rubbish! There is some toddy just coming in. You haven't forgotten the toddy, Katherine?

Mrs. Stockmann. Of course not; the water is boiling now. (*Goes into the dining-room.*)

Peter Stockmann. Toddy too!

F 552

Dr. Stockmann. Yes, sit down and we will have it comfortably.

Peter Stockmann. Thanks, I never care about an evening's drinking.

Dr. Stockmann. But this isn't an evening's drinking.

Peter Stockmann. It seems to me—. (*Looks towards the dining-room.*) It is extraordinary how they can put away all that food.

Dr. Stockmann (*rubbing his hands*). Yes, isn't it splendid to see young people eat? They have always got an appetite, you know! That's as it should be. Lots of food—to build up their strength! They are the people who are going to stir up the fermenting forces of the future, Peter.

Peter Stockmann. May I ask what they will find here to " stir up," as you put it?

Dr. Stockmann. Ah, you must ask the young people that—when the times comes. We shan't be able to see it, of course. That stands to reason—two old fogies, like us—

Peter Stockmann. Really, really! I must say that is an extremely odd expression to—

Dr. Stockmann. Oh, you mustn't take me too literally, Peter. I am so heartily happy and contented, you know. I think it is such an extraordinary piece of good fortune to be in the middle of all this growing, germinating life. It is a splendid time to live in! It is as if a whole new world were being created around one.

Peter Stockmann. Do you really think so?

Dr. Stockmann. Ah, naturally you can't appreciate it as keenly as I. You have lived all your life in these surroundings, and your impressions have got blunted. But I, who have been buried all these years in my little corner up north, almost without ever seeing a stranger who might bring new ideas with him—well, in my case it has just the same effect as if I had been transported into the middle of a crowded city.

Peter Stockmann. Oh, a city—!

Dr. Stockmann. I know, I know; it is all cramped

enough here, compared with many other places. But there is life here—there is promise—there are innumerable things to work for and fight for; and that is the main thing. (*Calls.*) Katherine, hasn't the postman been here?

Mrs. Stockmann (*from the dining-room*). No.

Dr. Stockmann. And then to be comfortably off, Peter! That is something one learns to value, when one has been on the brink of starvation, as we have.

Peter Stockmann. Oh, surely—

Dr. Stockmann. Indeed I can assure you we have often been very hard put to it, up there. And now to be able to live like a lord! To-day, for instance, we had roast beef for dinner—and, what is more, for supper too. Won't you come and have a little bit? Or let me show it you, at any rate? Come here—

Peter Stockmann. No, no—not for worlds!

Dr. Stockmann. Well, but just come here then. Do you see, we have got a table-cover?

Peter Stockmann. Yes, I noticed it.

Dr. Stockmann. And we have got a lamp-shade too. Do you see? All out of Katherine's savings! It makes the room so cosy. Don't you think so? Just stand here for a moment—no, no, not there—just here, that's it! Look now, when you get the light on it altogether— I really think it looks very nice, doesn't it?

Peter Stockmann. Oh, if you can afford luxuries of this kind—

Dr. Stockmann. Yes, I can afford it now. Katherine tells me I earn almost as much as we spend.

Peter Stockmann. Almost—yes!

Dr. Stockmann. But a scientific man must live in a little bit of style. I am quite sure an ordinary civil servant spends more in a year than I do.

Peter Stockmann. I daresay. A civil servant—a man in a well-paid position—

Dr. Stockmann. Well, any ordinary merchant, then! A man in that position spends two or three times as much as—

Peter Stockmann. It just depends on circumstances.

Dr. Stockmann. At all events I assure you I don't waste money unprofitably. But I can't find it in my heart to deny myself the pleasure of entertaining my friends. I need that sort of thing, you know. I have lived for so long shut out of it all, that it is a necessity of life to me to mix with young, eager, ambitious men, men of liberal and active minds; and that describes every one of those fellows who are enjoying their supper in there. I wish you knew more of Hovstad—

Peter Stockmann. By the way, Hovstad was telling me he was going to print another article of yours.

Dr. Stockmann. An article of mine?

Peter Stockmann. Yes, about the Baths. An article you wrote in the winter.

Dr. Stockmann. Oh, that one! No, I don't intend that to appear just for the present.

Peter Stockmann. Why not? It seems to me that this would be the most opportune moment.

Dr. Stockmann. Yes, very likely—under normal conditions. (*Crosses the room.*)

Peter Stockmann (*following him with his eyes*). Is there anything abnormal about the present conditions?

Dr. Stockmann (*standing still*). To tell you the truth, Peter, I can't say just at this moment—at all events not to-night. There may be much that is very abnormal about the present conditions—and it is possible there may be nothing abnormal about them at all. It is quite possible it may be merely my imagination.

Peter Stockmann. I must say it all sounds most mysterious. Is there something going on that I am to be kept in ignorance of? I should have imagined that I, as Chairman of the governing body of the Baths—

Dr. Stockmann. And I should have imagined that I—. Oh, come, don't let us fly out at one another, Peter.

Peter Stockmann. Heaven forbid! I am not in the habit of flying out at people, as you call it. But I am entitled to request most emphatically that all arrangements shall be made in a business-like manner, through the proper channels, and shall be dealt with by the legally constituted authorities. I can allow no going behind our backs by any roundabout means.

Dr. Stockmann. Have I ever at any time tried to go behind your backs!

Peter Stockmann. You have an ingrained tendency to take your own way, at all events; and that is almost equally inadmissible in a well ordered community. The individual ought undoubtedly to acquiesce in subordinating himself to the community—or, to speak more accurately, to the authorities who have the care of the community's welfare.

Dr. Stockmann. Very likely. But what the deuce has all this got to do with me?

Peter Stockmann. That is exactly what you never appear to be willing to learn, my dear Thomas. But, mark my words, some day you will have to suffer for it —sooner or later. Now I have told you. Good-bye.

Dr. Stockmann. Have you taken leave of your senses? You are on the wrong scent altogether.

Peter Stockmann. I am not usually that. You must excuse me now if I— (*calls into the dining-room*). Good night, Katherine. Good night, gentlemen. (*Goes out.*)

Mrs. Stockmann (*coming from the dining-room*). Has he gone?

Dr. Stockmann. Yes, and in such a bad temper.

Mrs. Stockmann. But, dear Thomas, what have you been doing to him again?

Dr. Stockmann. Nothing at all. And, anyhow, he can't oblige me to make my report before the proper time.

Mrs. Stockmann. What have you got to make a report to him about?

Dr. Stockmann. Hm! Leave that to me, Katherine.— It is an extraordinary thing that the postman doesn't come.

(HOVSTAD, BILLING *and* HORSTER *have got up from the table and come into the sitting-room.* EJLIF *and* MORTEN *come in after them.*)

Billing (*stretching himself*). Ah!—one feels a new man after a meal like that.

Hovstad. The mayor wasn't in a very sweet temper to-night, then.

Dr. Stockmann. It is his stomach; he has a wretched digestion.

Hovstad. I rather think it was us two of the " People's Messenger " that he couldn't digest.

Mrs. Stockmann. I thought you came out of it pretty well with him.

Hovstad. Oh yes; but it isn't anything more than a sort of truce.

Billing. That is just what it is! That word sums up the situation.

Dr. Stockmann. We must remember that Peter is a lonely man, poor chap. He has no home comforts of any kind; nothing but everlasting business. And all that infernal weak tea wash that he pours into himself! Now then, my boys, bring chairs up to the table. Aren't we going to have that toddy, Katherine?

Mrs. Stockmann (going into the dining-room). I am just getting it.

Dr. Stockmann. Sit down here on the couch beside me, Captain Horster. We so seldom see you—. Please sit down, my friends. (*They sit down at the table.* MRS. STOCKMANN *brings a tray, with a spirit-lamp, glasses, bottles, etc., upon it.*)

Mrs. Stockmann. There you are! This is arrack, and this is rum, and this one is the brandy. Now every one must help themselves.

Dr. Stockmann (taking a glass). We will. (*They all mix themselves some toddy.*) And let us have the cigars. Ejlif, you know where the box is. And you, Morten, can fetch my pipe. (*The two boys go into the room on the right.*) I have a suspicion that Ejlif pockets a cigar now and then!—but I take no notice of it. (*Calls out.*) And my smoking-cap too, Morten. Katherine, you can tell him where I left it. Ah, he has got it. (*The boys bring the various things.*) Now, my friends. I stick to my pipe, you know. This one has seen plenty of bad weather with me up north. (*Touches glasses with them.*)

Your good health! Ah, it is good to be sitting snug and warm here.

Mrs. Stockmann (who sits knitting). Do you sail soon, Captain Horster?

Horster. I expect to be ready to sail next week.

Mrs. Stockmann. I suppose you are going to America.

Horster. Yes, that is the plan.

Mrs. Stockmann. Then you won't be able to take part in the coming election.

Horster. Is there going to be an election?

Billing. Didn't you know?

Horster. No, I don't mix myself up with those things.

Billing. But do you not take an interest in public affairs?

Horster. No, I don't know anything about politics.

Billing. All the same, one ought to vote, at any rate.

Horster. Even if one doesn't know anything about what is going on?

Billing. Doesn't know! What do you mean by that? A community is like a ship; every one ought to be prepared to take the helm.

Horster. May be that is all very well on shore; but on board ship it wouldn't work.

Hovstad. It is astonishing how little most sailors care about what goes on on shore.

Billing. Very extraordinary.

Dr. Stockmann. Sailors are like birds of passage; they feel equally at home in any latitude. And that is only an additional reason for our being all the more keen, Hovstad. Is there to be anything of public interest in to-morrow's " Messenger "?

Hovstad. Nothing about municipal affairs. But the day after to-morrow I was thinking of printing your article—

Dr. Stockmann. Ah, devil take it — my article! Look here, that must wait a bit.

Hovstad. Really? We had just got convenient space for it, and I thought it was just the opportune moment—

Dr. Stockmann. Yes, yes, very likely you are right;

but it must wait all the same. I will explain to you
later. (PETRA *comes in from the hall, in hat and
cloak and with a bundle of exercise books under her arm.*)

Petra. Good evening.

Dr. Stockmann. Good evening, Petra; come along.
(*Mutual greetings;* PETRA *takes off her things and puts
them down on a chair by the door.*)

Petra. And you have all been sitting here enjoying
yourselves, while I have been out slaving!

Dr. Stockmann. Well, come and enjoy yourself too!

Billing. May I mix a glass for you?

Petra (*coming to the table*). Thanks, I would rather
do it; you always mix it too strong. But I forgot,
father—I have a letter for you. (*Goes to the chair where
she has laid her things.*)

Dr. Stockmann. A letter? From whom?

Petra (*looking in her coat pocket*). The postman gave it
to me just as I was going out—

Dr. Stockmann (*getting up and going to her*). And you
only give it to me now!

Petra. I really had not time to run up again. There
it is!

Dr. Stockmann (*seizing the letter*). Let's see, let's see,
child! (*Looks at the address.*) Yes, that's all right!

Mrs. Stockmann. Is it the one you have been expecting
so anxiously, Thomas?

Dr. Stockmann. Yes, it is. I must go to my room now
and—. Where shall I get a light, Katherine? Is there
no lamp in my room again?

Mrs. Stockmann. Yes, your lamp is all ready lit on
your desk.

Dr. Stockmann. Good, good. Excuse me for a moment—.
(*Goes into his study.*)

Petra. What do you suppose it is, mother?

Mrs. Stockmann. I don't know; for the last day or
two he has always been asking if the postman has not been.

Billing. Probably some country patient.

Petra. Poor old dad!—he will overwork himself soon.
(*Mixes a glass for herself.*) There, that will taste good!

Hovstad. Have you been teaching in the evening school again to-day?

Petra (sipping from her glass). Two hours.

Billing. And four hours of school in the morning—

Petra. Five hours.

Mrs. Stockmann. And you have still got exercises to correct, I see.

Petra. A whole heap, yes.

Horster. You are pretty full up with work, too, it seems to me.

Petra. Yes—but that is good. One is so delightfully tired after it.

Billing. Do you like that?

Petra. Yes, because one sleeps so well then.

Morten. You must be dreadfully wicked, Petra.

Petra. Wicked?

Morten. Yes, because you work so much. Mr. Rörlund says work is a punishment for our sins.

Ejlif. Pooh, what a duffer you are, to believe a thing like that!

Mrs. Stockmann. Come, come, Ejlif!

Billing (laughing). That's capital!

Hovstad. Don't you want to work as hard as that, Morten?

Morten. No, indeed I don't.

Hovstad. What do you want to be, then?

Morten. I should like best to be a Viking.

Ejlif. You would have to be a pagan then.

Morten. Well, I could become a pagan, couldn't I?

Billing. I agree with you, Morten! My sentiments, exactly.

Mrs. Stockmann (signalling to him). I am sure that is not true, Mr. Billing.

Billing. Yes, I swear it is! I am a pagan, and I am proud of it. Believe me, before long we shall all be pagans.

Morten. And then shall be allowed to do anything we like?

Billing. Well, you see, Morten—.

Mrs. Stockmann. You must go to your room now, boys; I am sure you have some lessons to learn for to-morrow.

Ejlif. I should like so much to stay a little longer—

Mrs. Stockmann. No, no; away you go, both of you. (*The boys say good night and go into the room on the left.*)

Hovstad. Do you really think it can do the boys any harm to hear such things?

Mrs. Stockmann. I don't know; but I don't like it.

Petra. But you know, mother, I think you really are wrong about it.

Mrs. Stockmann. Maybe, but I don't like it—not in our own home.

Petra. There is so much falsehood both at home and at school. At home one must not speak, and at school we have to stand and tell lies to the children.

Horster. Tell lies?

Petra. Yes, don't you suppose we have to teach them all sorts of things that we don't believe?

Billing. That is perfectly true.

Petra. If only I had the means I would start a school of my own, and it would be conducted on very different lines.

Billing. Oh, bother the means—!

Horster. Well if you are thinking of that, Miss Stockmann, I shall be delighted to provide you with a school-room. The great big old house my father left me is standing almost empty; there is an immense dining-room downstairs—

Petra (*laughing*). Thank you very much; but I am afraid nothing will come of it.

Hovstad. No, Miss Petra is much more likely to take to journalism, I expect. By the way, have you had time to do anything with that English story you promised to translate for us?

Petra. No, not yet; but you shall have it in good time.

(DR. STOCKMANN *comes in from his room with an open letter in his hand.*)

Dr. Stockmann (waving the letter). Well, now the town will have something new to talk about, I can tell you!

Billing. Something new?

Mrs. Stockmann. What is this?

Dr. Stockmann. A great discovery, Katherine.

Hovstad. Really?

Mrs. Stockmann. A discovery of yours?

Dr. Stockmann. A discovery of mine. (*Walks up and down.*) Just let them come saying, as usual, that it is all fancy and a crazy man's imagination! But they will be careful what they say this time, I can tell you!

Petra. But, father, tell us what it is.

Dr. Stockmann. Yes, yes—only give me time, and you shall know all about it. If only I had Peter here now! It just shows how we men can go about forming our judgments, when in reality we are as blind as any moles—

Hovstad. What are you driving at, Doctor?

Dr. Stockmann (standing still by the table). Isn't it the universal opinion that our town is a healthy spot?

Hovstad. Certainly.

Dr. Stockmann. Quite an unusually healthy spot, in fact—a place that deserves to be recommended in the warmest possible manner either for invalids or for people who are well—

Mrs. Stockmann. Yes, but my dear Thomas—

Dr. Stockmann. And we have been recommending it and praising it—I have written and written, both in the " Messenger " and in pamphlets—

Hovstad. Well, what then?

Dr. Stockmann. And the Baths—we have called them the " main artery of the town's life-blood," the " nerve-centre of our town," and the devil knows what else—

Billing. " The town's pulsating heart " was the expression I once used on an important occasion—

Dr. Stockmann. Quite so. Well, do you know what they really are, these great, splendid, much praised Baths, that have cost so much money—do you know what they are?

Hovstad. No, what are they?

Mrs. Stockmann. Yes, what are they?

Dr. Stockmann. The whole place is a pesthouse!

Petra. The Baths, father?

Mrs. Stockmann (at the same time). Our Baths!

Hovstad. But, Doctor—

Billing. Absolutely incredible!

Dr. Stockmann. The whole Bath establishment is a whited, poisoned sepulchre, I tell you—the gravest possible danger to the public health! All the nastiness up at Mölledal, all that stinking filth, is infecting the water in the conduit-pipes leading to the reservoir; and the same cursed, filthy poison oozes out on the shore too—

Horster. Where the bathing-place is?

Dr. Stockmann. Just there.

Hovstad. How do you come to be so certain of all this, Doctor?

Dr. Stockmann. I have investigated the matter most conscientiously. For a long time past I have suspected something of the kind. Last year we had some very strange cases of illness among the visitors—typhoid cases, and cases of gastric fever—

Mrs. Stockmann. Yes, that is quite true.

Dr. Stockmann. At the time, we supposed the visitors had been infected before they came; but later on, in the winter, I began to have a different opinion; and so I set myself to examine the water, as well as I could.

Mrs. Stockmann. Then that is what you have been so busy with?

Dr. Stockmann. Indeed I have been busy, Katherine. But here I had none of the necessary scientific apparatus; so I sent samples, both of the drinking-water and of the sea-water, up to the University, to have an accurate analysis made by a chemist.

Hovstad. And have you got that?

Dr. Stockmann (showing him the letter). Here it is! It proves the presence of decomposing organic matter in the water—it is full of infusoria. The water is absolutely dangerous to use, either internally or externally.

Mrs. Stockmann. What a mercy you discovered it in time.

Dr. Stockmann. You may well say so.

Hovstad. And what do you propose to do now, Doctor?

Dr. Stockmann. To see the matter put right—naturally.

Hovstad. Can that be done?

Dr. Stockmann. It must be done. Otherwise the Baths will be absolutely useless and wasted. But we need not anticipate that; I have a very clear idea what we shall have to do.

Mrs. Stockmann. But why have you kept this all so secret, dear?

Dr. Stockmann. Do you suppose I was going to run about the town gossiping about it, before I had absolute proof? No, thank you. I am not such a fool.

Petra. Still, you might have told us—

Dr. Stockmann. Not a living soul. But to-morrow you may run round to the old Badger—

Mrs. Stockmann. Oh, Thomas! Thomas!

Dr. Stockmann. Well, to your grandfather, then. The old boy will have something to be astonished at! I know he thinks I am cracked—and there are lots of other people think so too, I have noticed. But now these good folks shall see—they shall just see—! (*Walks about, rubbing his hands.*) There will be a nice upset in the town, Katherine; you can't imagine what it will be. All the conduit-pipes will have to be relaid.

Hovstad (getting up). All the conduit-pipes—?

Dr. Stockmann. Yes, of course. The intake is too low down; it will have to be lifted to a position much higher up.

Petra. Then you were right after all.

Dr. Stockmann. Ah, you remember, Petra—I wrote opposing the plans before the work was begun. But at that time no one would listen to me. Well, I am goiug to let them have it, now! Of course I have prepared a report for the Baths Committee; I have had it ready for a week, and was only waiting for this to come. (*Shows the letter.*) Now it shall go off at once. (*Goes into his room and comes back with some papers.*) Look at that! Four closely written sheets!—and the letter shall go with them. Give me a bit of paper, Katherine—something to wrap them up in. That will do! Now give it to—to—(*stamps his foot*)—what the deuce is her name? —give it to the maid, and tell her to take it at once to the Mayor.

(*Mrs. Stockmann takes the packet and goes out through the dining-room.*)

Petra. What do you think uncle Peter will say, father?

Dr. Stockmann. What is there for him to say? I should think he would be very glad that such an important truth has been brought to light.

Hovstad. Will you let me print a short note about your discovery in the " Messenger ? "

Dr. Stockmann. I shall be very much obliged if you will.

Hovstad. It is very desirable that the public should be informed of it without delay.

Dr. Stockmann. Certainly.

Mrs. Stockmann (*coming back*). She has just gone with it.

Billing. Upon my soul, Doctor, you are going to be the foremost man in the town!

Dr. Stockmann (*walking about happily*). Nonsense! As a matter of fact I have done nothing more than my duty. I have only made a lucky find—that's all. Still, all the same—

Billing. Hovstad, don't you think the town ought to give Dr. Stockmann some sort of testimonial?

Hovstad. I will suggest it, anyway.

Billing. And I will speak to Aslaksen about it.

Dr. Stockmann. No, my good friends, don't let us have any of that nonsense. I won't hear of anything of the kind. And if the Baths Committee should think of voting me an increase of salary, I will not accept it. Do you hear, Katherine?—I won't accept it.

Mrs. Stockmann. You are quite right, Thomas.

Petra (lifting her glass). Your health, father!

Hovstad and Billing. Your health, Doctor! Good health!

Horster (touches glasses with DR. STOCKMANN). I hope it will bring you nothing but good luck.

Dr. Stockmann. Thank you, thank you, my dear fellows! I feel tremendously happy! It is a splendid thing for a man to be able to feel that he has done a service to his native town and to his fellow-citizens. Hurrah, Katherine! *(He puts his arms round her and whirls her round and round, while she protests with laughing cries. They all laugh, clap their hands, and cheer the* DOCTOR. *The boys put their heads in at the door to see what is going on.)*

ACT II

(SCENE—The same. The door into the dining-room is shut. It is morning. MRS. STOCKMANN, *with a sealed letter in her hand, comes in from the dining-room, goes to the door of the* DOCTOR'S *study, and peeps in.)*

Mrs. Stockmann. Are you in, Thomas?

Dr. Stockmann (from within his room). Yes, I have just come in. *(Comes into the room.)* What is it?

Mrs. Stockmann. A letter from your brother.

Dr. Stockmann. Aha, let us see! *(Opens the letter and reads:)* "I return herewith the manuscript you sent me"—*(reads on in a low murmur)* Hm!—

Mrs. Stockmann. What does he say?

Dr. Stockmann (putting the papers in his pocket). Oh, he only writes that he will come up here himself about midday.

Mrs. Stockmann. Well, try and remember to be at home this time.

Dr. Stockmann. That will be all right; I have got through all my morning visits.

Mrs. Stockmann. I am extremely curious to know how he takes it.

Dr. Stockmann. You will see he won't like it's having been I, and not he, that made the discovery.

Mrs. Stockmann. Aren't you a little nervous about that?

Dr. Stockmann. Oh, he really will be pleased enough, you know. But, at the same time, Peter is so confoundedly afraid of anyone's doing any service to the town except himself.

Mrs. Stockmann. I will tell you what, Thomas—you should be good natured, and share the credit of this with him. Couldn't you make out that it was he who set you on the scent of this discovery?

Dr. Stockmann. I am quite willing. If only I can get the thing set right. I—

(MORTEN KIIL *puts his head in through the door leading from the hall, looks round in an enquiring manner, and chuckles.*)

Morten Kiil (*slyly*). Is it—is it true?

Mrs. Stockmann (*going to the door*). Father!—is it you?

Dr. Stockmann. Ah, Mr. Kiil—good morning, good morning!

Mrs. Stockmann. But come along in.

Morten Kiil. If it is true, I will; if not, I am off.

Dr. Stockmann. If what is true?

Morten Kiil. This tale about the water supply. Is it true?

Dr. Stockmann. Certainly it is true. But how did you come to hear it?

Morten Kiil (*coming in*). Petra ran in on her way to the school—

Dr. Stockmann. Did she?

Morten Kiil. Yes; and she declares that—. I thought she was only making a fool of me, but it isn't like Petra to do that.

Dr. Stockmann. Of course not. How could you imagine such a thing!

Morten Kiil. Oh well, it is better never to trust anybody; you may find you have been made a fool of before you know where you are. But it is really true, all the same?

Dr. Stockmann. You can depend upon it that it is true. Won't you sit down? (*Settles him on the couch.*) Isn't it a real bit of luck for the town—

Morten Kiil (*suppressing his laughter*). A bit of luck for the town?

Dr. Stockmann. Yes, that I made the discovery in good time.

Morten Kiil (*as before*). Yes, yes, yes!—But I should never have thought you the sort of man to pull your own brother's leg like this!

Dr. Stockmann. Pull his leg!

Mrs. Stockmann. Really, father dear—

Morten Kiil (*resting his hands and his chin on the handle of his stick and winking slyly at the* DOCTOR). Let me see, what was the story? Some kind of beast that had got into the water-pipes, wasn't it?

Dr. Stockmann. Infusoria—yes.

Morten Kiil. And a lot of these beasts had got in, according to Petra—a tremendous lot.

Dr. Stockmann. Certainly; hundreds of thousands of them, probably.

Morten Kiil. But no one can see them—isn't that so?

Dr. Stockmann. Yes; you can't see them.

Morten Kiil (*with a quiet chuckle*). Damme—it's the finest story I have ever heard!

Dr. Stockmann. What do you mean?

Morten Kiil. But you will never get the Mayor to believe a thing like that.

Dr. Stockmann. We shall see.

Morten Kiil. Do you think he will be fool enough to—?

Dr. Stockmann. I hope the whole town will be fools enough.

Morten Kiil. The whole town! Well, it wouldn't be a bad thing. It would just serve them right, and teach them a lesson. They think themselves so much cleverer than we old fellows. They hounded me out of the council; they did, I tell you—they hounded me out. Now they shall pay for it. You pull their legs, too, Thomas!

Dr. Stockmann. Really, I—

Morten Kiil. You pull their legs! (*Gets up.*) If you can work it so that the Mayor and his friends all swallow the same bait, I will give ten pounds to a charity— like a shot!

Dr. Stockmann. That is very kind of you.

Morten Kiil. Yes, I haven't got much money to throw away, I can tell you; but if you can work this, I will give five pounds to a charity at Christmas.

(HOVSTAD *comes in by the hall door.*)

Hovstad. Good morning! (*Stops.*) Oh, I beg your pardon—

Dr. Stockmann. Not at all; come in.

Morten Kiil (*with another chuckle*). Oho!—is he in this too?

Hovstad. What do you mean?

Dr. Stockmann. Certainly he is.

Morten Kiil. I might have known it! It must get into the papers. You know how to do it, Thomas! Set your wits to work. Now I must go.

Dr. Stockmann. Won't you stay a little while?

Morten Kiil. No, I must be off now. You keep up this game for all it is worth; you won't repent it, I'm damned if you will!

(*He goes out;* MRS. STOCKMANN *follows him into the hall.*)

Dr. Stockmann (*laughing*). Just imagine—the old chap doesn't believe a word of all this about the water supply.

Hovstad. Oh that was it, then?

Dr. Stockmann. Yes, that was what we were talking about. Perhaps it is the same thing that brings you here?

Hovstad. Yes, it is. Can you spare me a few minutes, Doctor?

Dr. Stockmann. As long as you like, my dear fellow.

Hovstad. Have you heard from the Mayor yet?

Dr. Stockmann. Not yet. He is coming here later.

Hovstad. I have given the matter a great deal of thought since last night.

Dr. Stockmann. Well?

Hovstad. From your point of view, as a doctor and a man of science, this affair of the water-supply is an isolated matter. I mean, you do not realise that it involves a great many other things.

Dr. Stockmann. How, do you mean?—Let us sit down, my dear fellow. No, sit here on the couch. (HOVSTAD *sits down on the couch,* DR. STOCKMANN *on a chair on the other side of the table.*) Now then. You mean that—?

Hovstad. You said yesterday that the pollution of the water was due to impurities in the soil.

Dr. Stockmann. Yes, unquestionably it is due to that poisonous morass up at Mölledal.

Hovstad. Begging your pardon, doctor, I fancy it is due to quite another morass altogether.

Dr. Stockmann. What morass?

Hovstad. The morass that the whole life of our town is built on and is rotting in.

Dr. Stockmann. What the deuce are you driving at, Hovstad?

Hovstad. The whole of the town's interests have, little by little, got into the hands of a pack of officials.

Dr. Stockmann. Oh, come!—they are not all officials.

Hovstad. No, but those that are not officials are at any rate the officials' friends and adherents; it is the wealthy folk, the old families in the town, that have got us entirely in their hands.

Dr. Stockmann. Yes, but after all they are men of ability and knowledge.

Hovstad. Did they show any ability or knowledge when they laid the conduit-pipes where they are now?

Dr. Stockmann. No, of course that was a great piece of stupidity on their part. But that is going to be set right now.

Hovstad. Do you think that will be all such plain sailing?

Dr. Stockmann. Plain sailing or no, it has got to be done, anyway.

Hovstad. Yes, provided the press takes up the question.

Dr. Stockmann. I don't think that will be necessary, my dear fellow, I am certain my brother—

Hovstad. Excuse me, doctor; I feel bound to tell you I am inclined to take the matter up.

Dr. Stockmann. In the paper?

Hovstad. Yes. When I took over the " People's Messenger " my idea was to break up this ring of self-opinionated old fossils who had got hold of all the influence.

Dr. Stockmann. But you know you told me yourself what the result had been; you nearly ruined your paper.

Hovstad. Yes, at the time we were obliged to climb down a peg or two, it is quite true; because there was a danger of the whole project of the Baths coming to nothing if they failed us. But now the scheme has been carried through, and we can dispense with these grand gentlemen.

Dr. Stockmann. Dispense with them, yes; but we owe them a great debt of gratitude.

Hovstad. That shall be recognised ungrudgingly. But a journalist of my democratic tendencies cannot let such an opportunity as this slip. The bubble of official infallibility must be pricked. This superstition must be destroyed, like any other.

Dr. Stockmann. I am whole-heartedly with you in that, Mr. Hovstad; if it is a superstition, away with it!

Hovstad. I should be very reluctant to bring the Mayor into it, because he is your brother. But I am sure you will agree with me that truth should be the first consideration.

Dr. Stockmann. That goes without saying. (*With sudden emphasis.*) Yes, but—but—

Hovstad. You must not misjudge me. I am neither more self-interested nor more ambitious than most men.

Dr. Stockmann. My dear fellow—who suggests anything of the kind?

Hovstad. I am of humble origin, as you know; and that has given me opportunities of knowing what is the most crying need in the humbler ranks of life. It is that they should be allowed some part in the direction of public affairs, Doctor. That is what will develop their faculties and intelligence and self respect—

Dr. Stockmann. I quite appreciate that.

Hovstad. Yes—and in my opinion a journalist incurs a heavy responsibility if he neglects a favourable opportunity of emancipating the masses—the humble and oppressed. I know well enough that in exalted circles I shall be called an agitator, and all that sort of thing; but they may call what they like. If only my conscience doesn't reproach me, then—

Dr. Stockmann. Quite right! Quite right, Mr. Hovstad. But all the same—devil take it! (*A knock is heard at the door.*) Come in!

(ASLAKSEN *appears at the door. He is poorly but decently dressed, in black, with a slightly crumpled white neckcloth; he wears gloves and has a felt hat in his hand.*)

Aslaksen (*bowing*). Excuse my taking the liberty, Doctor—

Dr. Stockmann (*getting up*). Ah, it is you, Aslaksen!

Aslaksen. Yes, Doctor.

Hovstad (*standing up*). Is it me you want, Aslaksen?

Aslaksen. No; I didn't know I should find you here. No, it was the Doctor I—

Dr. Stockmann. I am quite at your service. What is it?

Aslaksen. Is what I heard from Mr. Billing true, sir—that you mean to improve our water-supply?

Dr. Stockmann. Yes, for the Baths.

Aslaksen. Quite so, I understand. Well, I have come to say that I will back that up by every means in my power.

Hovstad (to the DOCTOR). You see!

Dr. Stockmann. I shall be very grateful to you, but—

Aslaksen. Because it may be no bad thing to have us small tradesmen at your back. We form, as it were, a compact majority in the town—if we choose. And it is always a good thing to have the majority with you, Doctor.

Dr. Stockmann. That is undeniably true; but I confess I don't see why such unusual precautions should be necessary in this case. It seems to me that such a plain, straightforward thing—

Aslaksen. Oh, it may be very desirable, all the same. I know our local authorities so well; officials are not generally very ready to act on proposals that come from other people. That is why I think it would not be at all amiss if we made a little demonstration.

Hovstad. That's right.

Dr. Stockmann. Demonstration, did you say? What on earth are you going to make a demonstration about?

Aslaksen. We shall proceed with the greatest moderation, Doctor. Moderation is always my aim; it is the greatest virtue in a citizen—at least, I think so.

Dr. Stockmann. It is well known to be a characteristic of yours, Mr. Aslaksen.

Aslaksen. Yes, I think I may pride myself on that. And this matter of the water-supply is of the greatest importance to us small tradesmen. The Baths promise to be a regular gold-mine for the town. We shall all make our living out of them, especially those of us who are householders. That is why we will back up the project as strongly as possible. And as I am at present Chairman of the Householders' Association—

Dr. Stockmann. Yes—?

Aslaksen. And, what is more, local secretary of the Temperance Society—you know, sir, I suppose, that I am a worker in the temperance cause?

Dr. Stockmann. Of course, of course.

Aslaksen. Well, you can understand that I come into contact with a great many people. And as I have the reputation of a temperate and law-abiding citizen— like yourself, Doctor—I have a certain influence in the town, a little bit of power, if I may be allowed to say so.

Dr. Stockmann. I know that quite well, Mr. Aslaksen.

Aslaksen. So you see it would be an easy matter for me to set on foot some testimonial, if necessary.

Dr. Stockmann. A testimonial?

Aslaksen. Yes, some kind of an address of thanks from the townsmen for your share in a matter of such importance to the community. I need scarcely say that it would have to be drawn up with the greatest regard to moderation, so as not to offend the authorities—who, after all, have the reins in their hands. If we pay strict attention to that, no one can take it amiss, I should think!

Hovstad. Well, and even supposing they didn't like it—

Aslaksen. No, no, no; there must be no discourtesy to the authorities, Mr. Hovstad. It is no use falling foul of those upon whom our welfare so closely depends. I have done that in my time, and no good ever comes of it. But no one can take exception to a reasonable and frank expression of a citizen's views.

Dr. Stockmann (shaking him by the hand). I can't tell you, dear Mr. Aslaksen, how extremely pleased I am to find such hearty support among my fellow-citizens. I am delighted—delighted! Now, you will take a small glass of sherry, eh?

Aslaksen. No, thank you; I never drink alcohol of that kind.

Dr. Stockmann. Well, what do you say to a glass of beer, then?

Aslaksen. Nor that either, thank you, Doctor. I never drink anything as early as this. I am going into town now to talk this over with one or two householders, and prepare the ground.

Dr. Stockmann. It is tremendously kind of you, Mr. Aslaksen; but I really cannot understand the necessity for all these precautions. It seems to me that the thing should go of itself.

Aslaksen. The authorities are somewhat slow to move, Doctor. Far be it from me to seem to blame them—

Hovstad. We are going to stir them up in the paper to-morrow, Aslaksen.

Aslaksen. But not violently, I trust, Mr. Hovstad. Proceed with moderation, or you will do nothing with them. You may take my advice; I have gathered my experience in the school of life. Well, I must say good-bye, Doctor. You know now that we small tradesmen are at your back at all events, like a solid wall. You have the compact majority on your side, Doctor.

Dr. Stockmann. I am very much obliged, dear Mr. Aslaksen. (*Shakes hands with him.*) Good-bye, good-bye.

Aslaksen. Are you going my way, towards the printing-office, Mr. Hovstad?

Hovstad. I will come later; I have something to settle up first.

Aslaksen. Very well. (*Bows and goes out;* STOCKMANN *follows him into the hall.*)

Hovstad (*as* STOCKMANN *comes in again*). Well, what do you think of that, Doctor? Don't you think it is high time we stirred a little life into all this slackness and vacillation and cowardice?

Dr. Stockmann. Are you referring to Aslaksen?

Hovstad. Yes, I am. He is one of those who are floundering in a bog—decent enough fellow though he may be, otherwise. And most of the people here are in just the same case—see-sawing and edging first to one side and then to the other, so overcome with caution and scruple that they never dare to take any decided step.

Dr. Stockmann. Yes, but Aslaksen seemed to me so thoroughly well-intentioned.

Hovstad. There is one thing I esteem higher than that;

and that is for a man to be self-reliant and sure of himself.

Dr. Stockmann. I think you are perfectly right there.

Hovstad. That is why I want to seize this opportunity, and try if I cannot manage to put a little virility into these well-intentioned people for once. The idol of Authority must be shattered in this town. This gross and inexcusable blunder about the water-supply must be brought home to the mind of every municipal voter.

Dr. Stockmann. Very well; if you are of opinion that it is for the good of the community, so be it. But not until I have had a talk with my brother.

Hovstad. Anyway, I will get a leading article ready; and if the Mayor refuses to take the matter up—

Dr. Stockmann. How can you suppose such a thing possible?

Hovstad. It is conceivable. And in that case—

Dr. Stockmann. In that case I promise you—. Look here, in that case you may print my report—every word of it.

Hovstad. May I? Have I your word for it?

Dr. Stockmann (giving him the MS.). Here it is; take it with you. It can do no harm for you to read it through, and you can give it me back later on.

Hovstad. Good, good! That is what I will do. And now good-bye, Doctor.

Dr. Stockmann. Good-bye, good-bye. You will see everything will run quite smoothly, Mr. Hovstad— quite smoothly.

Hovstad. Hm!—we shall see. *(Bows and goes out.)*

Dr. Stockmann (opens the dining-room door and looks in). Katherine! Oh, you are back, Petra?

Petra (coming in). Yes, I have just come from the school.

Mrs. Stockmann (coming in). Has he not been here yet?

Dr. Stockmann. Peter? No. But I have had a long talk with Hovstad. He is quite excited about my discovery. I find it has a much wider bearing than I at first imagined. And he has put his paper at my disposal if necessity should arise.

Mrs. Stockmann. Do you think it will?

Dr. Stockmann. Not for a moment. But at all events it makes me feel proud to know that I have the liberal-minded independent press on my side. Yes, and— just imagine—I have had a visit from the Chairman of the Householders' Association!

Mrs. Stockmann. Oh! What did he want?

Dr. Stockmann. To offer me his support too. They will support me in a body if it should be necessary. Katherine—do you know what I have got behind me?

Mrs. Stockmann. Behind you? No, what have you got behind you?

Dr. Stockmann. The compact majority.

Mrs. Stockmann. Really? Is that a good thing for you Thomas?

Dr. Stockmann. I should think it was a good thing. (*Walks up and down rubbing his hands.*) By Jove, it's a fine thing to feel this bond of brotherhood between oneself and one's fellow citizens!

Petra. And to be able to do so much that is good and useful, father!

Dr. Stockmann. And for one's own native town into the bargain, my child!

Mrs. Stockmann. That was a ring at the bell.

Dr. Stockmann. It must be he, then. (*A knock is heard at the door.*) Come in!

Peter Stockmann (*comes in from the hall*). Good morning.

Dr. Stockmann. Glad to see you, Peter!

Mrs. Stockmann. Good morning, Peter. How are you?

Peter Stockmann. So so, thank you. (*To* DR. STOCKMANN.) I received from you yesterday, after office hours, a report dealing with the condition of the water at the Baths.

Dr. Stockmann. Yes. Have you read it?

Peter Stockmann. Yes, I have.

Dr. Stockmann. And what have you to say to it?

Peter Stockmann (with a sidelong glance). Hm!—

Mrs. Stockmann. Come along, Petra. (*She and* Petra *go into the room on the left.*)

Peter Stockmann (after a pause). Was it necessary to make all these investigations behind my back?

Dr. Stockmann. Yes, because until I was absolutely certain about it—

Peter Stockmann. Then you mean that you are absolutely certain now?

Dr. Stockmann. Surely you are convinced of that.

Peter Stockmann. Is it your intention to bring this document before the Baths Committee as a sort of official communication?

Dr. Stockmann. Certainly. Something must be done in the matter—and that quickly.

Peter Stockmann. As usual, you employ violent expressions in your report. You say, amongst other things, that what we offer visitors in our Baths is a permanent supply of poison.

Dr. Stockmann. Well, can you describe it any other way, Peter? Just think—water that is poisonous, whether you drink it or bathe in it! And this we offer to the poor sick folk who come to us trustfully and pay us at an exorbitant rate to be made well again!

Peter Stockmann. And your reasoning leads you to this conclusion, that we must build a sewer to draw off the alleged impurities from Mölledal and must relay the water-conduits.

Dr. Stockmann. Yes. Do you see any other way out of it? I don't.

Peter Stockmann. I made a pretext this morning to go and see the town engineer, and, as if only half seriously, broached the subject of these proposals as a thing we might perhaps have to take under consideration some time later on.

Dr. Stockmann. Some time later on!

Peter Stockmann. He smiled at what he considered to be my extravagance, naturally. Have you taken the trouble to consider what your proposed alterations would cost? According to the information I obtained, the expenses would probably mount up to fifteen or twenty thousand pounds.

Dr. Stockmann. Would it cost so much?

Peter Stockmann. Yes; and the worst part of it would be that the work would take at least two years.

Dr. Stockmann. Two years? Two whole years?

Peter Stockmann. At least. And what are we to do with the Baths in the meantime? Close them? Indeed we should be obliged to. And do you suppose any one would come near the place after it had got about that the water was dangerous?

Dr. Stockmann. Yes but, Peter, that is what it is.

Peter Stockmann. And all this at this juncture— just as the Baths are beginning to be known. There are other towns in the neighbourhood with qualifications to attract visitors for bathing purposes. Don't you suppose they would immediately strain every nerve to divert the entire stream of strangers to themselves? Unquestionably they would; and then where should we be? We should probably have to abandon the whole thing, which has cost us so much money—and then you would have ruined your native town.

Dr. Stockmann. I—should have ruined—!

Peter Stockmann. It is simply and solely through the Baths that the town has before it any future worth mentioning. You know that just as well as I.

Dr. Stockmann. But what do you think ought to be done, then?

Peter Stockmann. Your report has not convinced me that the condition of the water at the Baths is as bad as you represent it to be.

Dr. Stockmann. I tell you it is even worse!—or at all events it will be in summer, when the warm weather comes.

Peter Stockmann. As I said, I believe you exaggerate the matter considerably. A capable physician ought to know what measures to take—he ought to be capable of preventing injurious influences or of remedying them if they become obviously persistent.

Dr. Stockmann. Well? What more?

Peter Stockmann. The water supply for the Baths is now an established fact, and in consequence must be treated as such. But probably the Committee, at its discretion, will not be disinclined to consider the question of how far it might be possible to introduce certain improvements consistently with a reasonable expenditure.

Dr. Stockmann. And do you suppose that I will have anything to do with such a piece of trickery as that?

Peter Stockmann. Trickery!!

Dr. Stockmann. Yes, it would be a trick—a fraud, a lie, a downright crime towards the public, towards the whole community!

Peter Stockmann. I have not, as I remarked before, been able to convince myself that there is actually any imminent danger.

Dr. Stockmann. You have! It is impossible that you should not be convinced. I know I have represented the facts absolutely truthfully and fairly. And you know it very well, Peter, only you won't acknowledge it. It was owing to your action that both the Baths and the water-conduits were built where they are; and that is what you won't acknowledge—that damnable blunder of yours. Pooh!—do you suppose I don't see through you?

Peter Stockmann. And even if that were true? If I perhaps guard my reputation somewhat anxiously, it is in the interests of the town. Without moral authority I am powerless to direct public affairs as seems, to my judgment, to be best for the common good. And on that account—and for various other reasons too—it appears to me to be a matter of importance that your report should not be delivered to the Committee. In the interests of the public, you must withhold it. Then, later on, I will raise the question and we will do our best, privately; but nothing of this unfortunate affair—

not a single word of it—must come to the ears of the public.

Dr. Stockmann. I am afraid you will not be able to prevent that now, my dear Peter.

Peter Stockmann. It must and shall be prevented.

Dr. Stockmann. It is no use, I tell you. There are too many people that know about it.

Peter Stockmann. That know about it? Who? Surely you don't mean those fellows on the "People's Messenger"?

Dr. Stockmann. Yes, they know. The liberal-minded independent press is going to see that you do your duty.

Peter Stockmann (after a short pause). You are an extraordinarily independent man, Thomas. Have you given no thought to the consequences this may have for yourself?

Dr. Stockmann. Consequences?—for me?

Peter Stockmann. For you and yours, yes.

Dr. Stockmann. What the deuce do you mean?

Peter Stockmann. I believe I have always behaved in a brotherly way to you—have always been ready to oblige or to help you?

Dr. Stockmann. Yes, you have, and I am grateful to you for it.

Peter Stockmann. There is no need. Indeed, to some extent I was forced to do so—for my own sake. I always hoped that, if I helped to improve your financial position, I should be able to keep some check on you.

Dr. Stockmann. What!! Then it was only for your own sake—!

Peter Stockmann. Up to a certain point, yes. It is painful for a man in an official position to have his nearest relative compromising himself time after time.

Dr. Stockmann. And do you consider that I do that?

Peter Stockmann. Yes, unfortunately, you do, without even being aware of it. You have a restless, pugnacious, rebellious disposition. And then there is that disastrous propensity of yours to want to write about every sort of possible and impossible thing. The moment an idea comes into your head, you must needs go and write a newspaper article or a whole pamphlet about it.

Dr. Stockmann. Well, but is it not the duty of a citizen to let the public share in any new ideas he may have?

Peter Stockmann. Oh, the public doesn't require any new ideas. The public is best served by the good, old-established ideas it already has.

Dr. Stockmann. And that is your honest opinion?

Peter Stockmann. Yes, and for once I must talk frankly to you. Hitherto I have tried to avoid doing so, because I know how irritable you are; but now I must tell you the truth, Thomas. You have no conception what an amount of harm you do yourself by your impetuosity. You complain of the authorities, you even complain of the government—you are always pulling them to pieces; you insist that you have been neglected and persecuted. But what else can such a cantankerous man as you expect?

Dr. Stockmann. What next! Cantankerous, am I?

Peter Stockmann. Yes, Thomas, you are an extremely cantankerous man to work with—I know that to my cost. You disregard everything that you ought to have consideration for. You seem completely to forget that it is me you have to thank for your appointment here as medical officer to the Baths—

Dr. Stockmann. I was entitled to it as a matter of course!—I and nobody else! I was the first person to see that the town could be made into a flourishing watering-place, and I was the only one who saw it at that time. I had to fight single-handed in support of the idea for many years; and I wrote and wrote—

Peter Stockmann. Undoubtedly. But things were not ripe for the scheme then—though, of course, you could not judge of that in your out-of-the-way corner up north. But as soon as the opportune moment came I—and the others—took the matter into our hands—

Dr. Stockmann. Yes, and made this mess of all my beautiful plan. It is pretty obvious now what clever fellows you were!

Peter Stockmann. To my mind the whole thing only seems to mean that you are seeking another outlet for your combativeness. You want to pick a quarrel with your superiors—an old habit of yours. You cannot put up with any authority over you. You look askance at anyone who occupies a superior official position; you regard him as a personal enemy, and then any stick is good enough to beat him with. But now I have called your attention to the fact that the town's interests are at stake—and, incidentally, my own too. And therefore I must tell you, Thomas, that you will find me inexorable with regard to what I am about to require you to do.

Dr. Stockmann. And what is that?

Peter Stockmann. As you have been so indiscreet as to speak of this delicate matter to outsiders, despite the fact that you ought to have treated it as entirely official and confidential, it is obviously impossible to hush it up now. All sorts of rumours will get about directly, and everybody who has a grudge against us will take care to embellish these rumours. So it will be necessary for you to refute them publicly.

Dr. Stockmann. I? How? I don't understand.

Peter Stockmann. What we shall expect is that, after making further investigations, you will come to the conclusion that the matter is not by any means as dangerous or as critical as you imagined in the first instance.

Dr. Stockmann. Oho!—so that is what you expect!

Peter Stockmann. And, what is more, we shall expect you to make public profession of your confidence in the Committee and in their readiness to consider fully and conscientiously what steps may be necessary to remedy any possible defects.

Dr. Stockmann. But you will never be able to do that by patching and tinkering at it—never! Take my word for it, Peter; I mean what I say, as deliberately and emphatically as possible.

Peter Stockmann. As an officer under the Committee, you have no right to any individual opinion.

Dr. Stockmann (amazed). No right?

Peter Stockmann. In your official capacity, no. As a private person, it is quite another matter. But as a subordinate member of the staff of the Baths, you have no right to express any opinion which runs contrary to that of your superiors.

Dr. Stockmann. This is too much! I, a doctor, a man of science, have no right to—!

Peter Stockmann. The matter in hand is not simply a scientific one. It is a complicated matter, and has its economic as well as its technical side.

Dr. Stockmann. I don't care what it is! I intend to be free to express my opinion on any subject under the sun.

Peter Stockmann. As you please—but not on any subject concerning the Baths. That we forbid.

Dr. Stockmann (shouting). You forbid—! You! A pack of—

Peter Stockmann. I forbid it—I, your chief; and if I forbid it, you have to obey.

Dr. Stockmann (controlling himself). Peter—if you were not my brother—

Petra (throwing open the door). Father, you shan't stand this!

Mrs. Stockmann (coming in after her). Petra, Petra!

Peter Stockmann. Oh, so you have been eavesdropping.

Mrs. Stockmann. You were talking so loud, we couldn't help—

Petra. Yes, I was listening,

Peter Stockmann. Well, after all, I am very glad—

Dr. Stockmann (going up to him). You were saying something about forbidding and obeying?

Peter Stockmann. You obliged me to take that tone with you.

Dr. Stockmann. And so I am to give myself the lie, publicly?

Peter Stockmann. We consider it absolutely necessary that you should make some such public statement as I have asked for.

Dr. Stockmann. And if I do not—obey?

Peter Stockmann. Then we shall publish a statement ourselves to reassure the public.

Dr. Stockmann. Very well; but in that case I shall use my pen against you. I stick to what I have said; I will show that I am right and that you are wrong. And what will you do then?

Peter Stockmann. Then I shall not be able to prevent your being dismissed.

Dr. Stockmann. What—?

Petra. Father—dismissed!

Mrs. Stockmann. Dismissed!

Peter Stockmann. Dismissed from the staff of the Baths. I shall be obliged to propose that you shall immediately be given notice, and shall not be allowed any further participation in the Baths' affairs.

Dr. Stockmann. You would dare to do that!

Peter Stockmann. It is you that are playing the daring game.

Petra. Uncle, that is a shameful way to treat a man like father!

Mrs. Stockmann. Do hold your tongue, Petra!

Peter Stockmann (*looking at* PETRA). Oh, so we volunteer our opinions already, do we? Of course. (*To* MRS. STOCKMANN.) Katherine, I imagine you are the most sensible person in this house. Use any influence you may have over your husband, and make him see what this will entail for his family as well as—

Dr. Stockmann. My family is my own concern and nobody else's!

Peter Stockmann. —for his own family, as I was saying, as well as for the town he lives in.

Dr. Stockmann. It is I who have the real good of the town at heart! I want to lay bare the defects that sooner or later must come to the light of day. I will show whether I love my native town.

Peter Stockmann. You, who in your blind obstinacy want to cut off the most important source of the town's welfare?

Dr. Stockmann. The source is poisoned, man! Are you mad? We are making our living by retailing filth and corruption! The whole of our flourishing municipal life derives its sustenance from a lie!

Peter Stockmann. All imagination—or something even worse. The man who can throw out such offensive insinuations about his native town must be an enemy to our community.

Dr. Stockmann (going up to him). Do you dare to—!

Mrs. Stockmann (throwing herself between them). Thomas!

Petra (catching her father by the arm). Don't lose your temper, father!

Peter Stockmann. I will not expose myself to violence. Now you have had a warning; so reflect on what you owe to yourself and your family. Good-bye. *(Goes out.)*

Dr. Stockmann (walking up and down). Am I to put up with such treatment as this? In my own house, Katherine! What do you think of that?

Mrs. Stockmann. Indeed it is both shameful and absurd, Thomas—

Petra. If only I could give uncle a piece of my mind—

Dr. Stockmann. It is my own fault. I ought to have flown out at him long ago!—shown my teeth!— bitten! To hear him call me an enemy to our community! Me! I shall not take that lying down, upon my soul!

Mrs. Stockmann. But, dear Thomas, your brother has power on his side—

Dr. Stockmann. Yes, but I have right on mine, I tell you.

Mrs. Stockmann. Oh yes, right—right. What is the use of having right on your side if you have not got might?

Petra. Oh, mother!—how can you say such a thing!

Dr. Stockmann. Do you imagine that in a free country it is no use having right on your side? You are absurd, Katherine. Besides, haven't I got the liberal-minded, independent press to lead the way, and the compact majority behind me? That is might enough, I should think!

Mrs. Stockmann. But, good heavens, Thomas, you don't mean to—?

Dr. Stockmann. Don't mean to what?

Mrs. Stockmann. To set yourself up in opposition to your brother.

Dr. Stockmann. In God's name, what else do you suppose I should do but take my stand on right and truth?

Petra. Yes, I was just going to say that.

Mrs. Stockmann. But it won't do you any earthly good. If they won't do it, they won't.

Dr. Stockmann. Oho, Katherine! Just give me time, and you will see how I will carry the war into their camp.

Mrs. Stockmann. Yes, you carry the war into their camp, and you get your dismissal—that is what you will do.

Dr. Stockmann. In any case I shall have done my duty towards the public—towards the community. I, who am called its enemy!

Mrs. Stockmann. But towards your family, Thomas? Towards your own home! Do you think that is doing your duty towards those you have to provide for?

Petra. Ah, don't think always first of us, mother.

Mrs. Stockmann. Oh, it is easy for you to talk; you are able to shift for yourself, if need be. But remember the boys, Thomas; and think a little, too, of yourself, and of me—

Dr. Stockmann. I think you are out of your senses, Katherine! If I were to be such a miserable coward as to go on my knees to Peter and his damned crew, do you suppose I should ever know an hour's peace of mind all my life afterwards?

Mrs. Stockmann. I don't know anything about that; but God preserve us from the peace of mind we shall have, all the same, if you go on defying him! You will find yourself again without the means of subsistence, with no income to count upon. I should think we had had enough of that in the old days. Remember that, Thomas; think what that means.

Dr. Stockmann (collecting himself with a struggle and clenching his fists). And this is what this slavery can bring upon a free, honourable man! Isn't it horrible, Katherine?

Mrs. Stockmann. Yes, it is sinful to treat you so, it is perfectly true. But, good heavens, one has to put up with so much injustice in this world.—There are the boys, Thomas! Look at them! What is to become of them? Oh, no, no, you can never have the heart—. (EJLIF *and* MORTEN *have come in while she was speaking, with their school books in their hands.*)

Dr. Stockmann. The boys—! (*Recovers himself suddenly.*) No, even if the whole world goes to pieces, I will never bow my neck to this yoke! (*Goes towards his room.*)

Mrs. Stockmann (following him). Thomas—what are you going to do!

Dr. Stockmann (at his door). I mean to have the right to look my sons in the face when they are grown men. (*Goes into his room.*)

Mrs. Stockmann (bursting into tears). God help us all!

Petra. Father is splendid! He will not give in.

(*The boys look on in amazement;* PETRA *signs to them not to speak.*)

ACT III

(SCENE.—*The editorial office of the " People's Messenger." The entrance door is on the left-hand side of the back wall; on the right-hand side is another door with glass panels through which the printing-room can be seen. Another door in the right-hand wall. In the middle of the room is a large table covered with papers, newspapers and books. In the foreground on the left a window, before which stands a desk and a high stool. There are a couple of easy chairs by the table, and other chairs standing along the wall. The room is dingy and uncomfortable; the furniture is old, the chairs stained and torn. In the printing-room the compositors are seen at work, and a printer is working a hand-press.* HOVSTAD *is sitting at the desk, writing.* BILLING *comes in from the right with* DR. STOCKMANN'S *manuscript in his hand.*)

Billing. Well, I must say!

Hovstad (still writing). Have you read it through?

Billing (laying the MS. on the desk). Yes, indeed I have.

Hovstad. Don't you think the Doctor hits them pretty hard?

Billing. Hard?   Bless my soul, he's crushing!   Every word falls like—how shall I put it?—like the blow of a sledgehammer.

Hovstad. Yes, but they are not the people to throw up the sponge at the first blow.

Billing. That is true; and for that reason we must strike blow upon blow until the whole of this aristocracy tumbles to pieces.   As I sat in there reading this, I almost seemed to see a revolution in being.

Hovstad (turning round). Hush!—Speak so that Aslaksen cannot hear you.

Billing (lowering his voice). Aslaksen is a chicken-hearted chap, a coward; there is nothing of the man in him.   But this time you will insist on your own way, won't you?   You will put the Doctor's article in?

Hovstad. Yes, and if the Mayor doesn't like it—

Billing. That will be the devil of a nuisance.

Hovstad. Well, fortunately we can turn the situation to good account, whatever happens.   If the Mayor will not fall in with the Doctor's project, he will have all the small tradesmen down on him—the whole of the House-holders' Association and the rest of them.   And if he does fall in with it, he will fall out with the whole crowd of large shareholders in the Baths, who up to now have been his most valuable supporters—

Billing. Yes, because they will certainly have to fork out a pretty penny—

Hovstad. Yes, you may be sure they will.   And in this

way the ring will be broken up, you see, and then in every issue of the paper we will enlighten the public on the Mayor's incapability on one point and another, and make it clear that all the positions of trust in the town, the whole control of municipal affairs, ought to be put in the hands of the Liberals.

Billing. That is perfectly true! I see it coming—I see it coming; we are on the threshold of a revolution!

(*A knock is heard at the door.*)

Hovstad. Hush! (*Calls out.*) Come in! (DR. STOCKMANN *comes in by the street door.* HOVSTAD *goes to meet him.*) Ah, it is you, Doctor! Well?

Dr. Stockmann. You may set to work and print it, Mr. Hovstad!

Hovstad. Has it come to that, then?

Billing. Hurrah!

Dr. Stockmann. Yes, print away. Undoubtedly it has come to that. Now they must take what they get. There is going to be a fight in the town, Mr. Billing!

Billing. War to the knife, I hope! We will get our knives to their throats, Doctor!

Dr. Stockmann. This article is only a beginning. I have already got four or five more sketched out in my head. Where is Aslaksen?

Billing (*calls into the printing-room*). Aslaksen, just come here for a minute!

Hovstad. Four or five more articles, did you say? On the same subject?

Dr. Stockmann. No—far from it, my dear fellow. No, they are about quite another matter. But they all spring from the question of the water-supply and the drainage. One thing leads to another, you know. It is like beginning to pull down an old house, exactly.

Billing. Upon my soul, it's true; you find you are not done till you have pulled all the old rubbish down.

Aslaksen (*coming in*). Pulled down? You are not thinking of pulling down the Baths surely, Doctor?

Hovstad. Far from it, don't be afraid.

Dr. Stockmann. No, we meant something quite different. Well, what do you think of my article, Mr. Hovstad?

Hovstad. I think it is simply a masterpiece—

Dr. Stockmann. Do you really think so? Well, I am very pleased, very pleased.

Hovstad. It is so clear and intelligible. One need have no special knowledge to understand the bearing of it. You will have every enlightened man on your side.

Aslaksen. And every prudent man too, I hope?

Billing. The prudent and the imprudent—almost the whole town.

Aslaksen. In that case we may venture to print it.

Dr. Stockmann. I should think so!

Hovstad. We will put it in to-morrow morning.

Dr. Stockmann. Of course—you must not lose a single day. What I wanted to ask you, Mr. Aslaksen, was if you would supervise the printing of it yourself.

Aslaksen. With pleasure.

Dr. Stockmann. Take care of it as if it were a treasure! No misprints—every word is important. I will look in again a little later; perhaps you will be able to let me see a proof. I can't tell you how eager I am to see it in print, and see it burst upon the public—

Billing. Burst upon them—yes, like a flash of lightning!

Dr. Stockmann. —and to have it submitted to the judgment of my intelligent fellow-townsmen. You cannot imagine what I have gone through to-day. I have been threatened first with one thing and then with another; they have tried to rob me of my most elementary rights as a man—

Billing. What! Your rights as a man!

Dr. Stockmann. —they have tried to degrade me, to make a coward of me, to force me to put personal interests before my most sacred convictions—

Billing. That is too much—I'm damned if it isn't.

Hovstad. Oh, you mustn't be surprised at anything from that quarter.

Dr. Stockmann. Well, they will get the worst of it

with me; they may assure themselves of that. I shall consider the " People's Messenger " my sheet-anchor now, and every single day I will bombard them with one article after another, like bomb-shells—

Aslaksen. Yes, but—

Billing. Hurrah!—it is war, it is war!

Dr. Stockmann. I shall smite them to the ground—I shall crush them—I shall break down all their defences, before the eyes of the honest public! That is what I shall do!

Aslaksen. Yes, but in moderation, Doctor—proceed with moderation—

Billing. Not a bit of it, not a bit of it! Don't spare the dynamite!

Dr. Stockmann. Because it is not merely a question of water-supply and drains now, you know. No—it is the whole of our social life that we have got to purify and disinfect—

Billing. Spoken like a deliverer!

Dr. Stockmann. All the incapables must be turned out, you understand—and that in every walk of life! Endless vistas have opened themselves to my mind's eye to-day. I cannot see it all quite clearly yet, but I shall in time. Young and vigorous standard-bearers—those are what we need and must seek, my friends; we must have new men in command at all our outposts.

Billing. Hear, hear!

Dr. Stockmann. We only need to stand by one another, and it will all be perfectly easy. The revolution will be launched like a ship that runs smoothly off the stocks. Don't you think so?

Hovstad. For my part I think we have now a prospect of getting the municipal authority into the hands where it should lie.

Aslaksen. And if only we proceed with moderation, I cannot imagine that there will be any risk.

Dr. Stockmann. Who the devil cares whether there is any risk or not! What I am doing, I am doing in the name of truth and for the sake of my conscience.

Hovstad. You are a man who deserves to be supported, Doctor.

Aslaksen. Yes, there is no denying that the Doctor is a true friend to the town—a real friend to the community, that he is.

Billing. Take my word for it, Aslaksen, Dr. Stockmann is a friend of the people.

Aslaksen. I fancy the Householders' Association will make use of that expression before long.

Dr. Stockmann (affected, grasps their hands). Thank you, thank you, my dear staunch friends. It is very refreshing to me to hear you say that; my brother called me something quite different. By Jove, he shall have it back, with interest! But now I must be off to see a poor devil—. I will come back, as I said. Keep a very careful eye on the manuscript, Aslaksen, and don't for worlds leave out any of my notes of exclamation! Rather put one or two more in! Capital, capital! Well, good-bye for the present—good-bye, good-bye!

(They show him to the door, and bow him out.)

Hovstad. He may prove an invaluably useful man to us.

Aslaksen. Yes, so long as he confines himself to this matter of the Baths. But if he goes farther afield, I don't think it would be advisable to follow him.

Hovstad. Hm!—that all depends—

Billing. You are so infernally timid, Aslaksen!

Aslaksen. Timid? Yes, when it is a question of the local authorities, I am timid, Mr. Billing; it is a lesson I have learnt in the school of experience, let me tell you. But try me in higher politics, in matters that concern the government itself, and then see if I am timid.

Billing. No, you aren't, I admit. But this is simply contradicting yourself.

Aslaksen. I am a man with a conscience, and that is the whole matter. If you attack the government, you don't do the community any harm, anyway; those fellows pay no attention to attacks, you see—they go on just as they are, in spite of them. But *local* authorities are different; they *can* be turned out, and then perhaps you may get an ignorant lot into office who may do irreparable harm to the householders and everybody else.

Hovstad. But what of the education of citizens by self government—don't you attach any importance to that?

Aslaksen. When a man has interests of his own to protect, he cannot think of everything, Mr. Hovstad.

Hovstad. Then I hope I shall never have interests of my own to protect!

Billing. Hear, hear!

Aslaksen (with a smile). Hm! *(Points to the desk.)* Mr. Sheriff Stensgaard was your predecessor at that editorial desk.

Billing (spitting). Bah! That turncoat.

Hovstad. I am not a weathercock—and never will be.

Aslaksen. A politician should never be too certain of anything, Mr. Hovstad. And as for you, Mr. Billing, I should think it is time for you to be taking in a reef or two in your sails, seeing that you are applying for the post of secretary to the Bench.

Billing. I—?

Hovstad. Are you, Billing?

Billing. Well, yes—but you must clearly understand I am only doing it to annoy the bigwigs.

Aslaksen. Anyhow, it is no business of mine. But if I am to be accused of timidity and of inconsistency in my principles, this is what I want to point out: my political past is an open book. I have never changed, except perhaps to become a little more moderate, you see. My heart is still with the people; but I don't deny that my reason has a certain bias towards the authorities—the local ones, I mean. *(Goes into the printing-room.)*

Billing. Oughtn't we to try and get rid of him, Hovstad?

Hovstad. Do you know anyone else who will advance the money for our paper and printing bill?

Billing. It is an infernal nuisance that we don't possess some capital to trade on.

Hovstad (sitting down at his desk). Yes, if we only had that, then—

Billing. Suppose you were to apply to Dr. Stockmann?

Hovstad (turning over some papers). What is the use? He has got nothing.

Billing. No, but he has got a warm man in the background, old Morten Kiil—"the Badger," as they call him.

Hovstad (writing). Are you so sure *he* has got anything?

Billing. Good Lord, of course he has! And some of it must come to the Stockmanns. Most probably he will do something for the children, at all events.

Hovstad (turning half round). Are you counting on that?

Billing. Counting on it? Of course I am not counting on anything.

Hovstad. That is right. And I should not count on the secretaryship to the Bench either, if I were you; for I can assure you—you won't get it.

Billing. Do you think I am not quite aware of that? My object is precisely *not* to get it. A slight of that kind stimulates a man's fighting power—it is like getting a supply of fresh bile—and I am sure one needs that badly enough in a hole-and-corner place like this, where it is so seldom anything happens to stir one up.

Hovstad (writing). Quite so, quite so.

Billing. Ah, I shall be heard of yet!—Now I shall go and write the appeal to the Householders' Association. *(Goes into the room on the right.)*

Hovstad (sitting at his desk, biting his penholder, says slowly). Hm!—that's it, is it. *(A knock is heard.)* Come in! (PETRA *comes in by the outer door.* HOVSTAD *gets up.)* What, you!—here?

Petra. Yes, you must forgive me—

Hovstad (pulling a chair forward). Won't you sit down?

Petra. No, thank you; I must go again in a moment.

Hovstad. Have you come with a message from your father, by any chance?

Petra. No, I have come on my own account. (*Takes a book out of her coat pocket.*) Here is the English story.

Hovstad. Why have you brought it back?

Petra. Because I am not going to translate it.

Hovstad. But you promised me faithfully—

Petra. Yes, but then I had not read it. I don't suppose you have read it either?

Hovstad. No, you know quite well I don't understand English; but—

Petra. Quite so. That is why I wanted to tell you that you must find something else. (*Lays the book on the table.*) You can't use this for the " People's Messenger."

Hovstad. Why not?

Petra. Because it conflicts with all your opinions.

Hovstad. Oh, for that matter—

Petra. You don't understand me. The burden of this story is that there is a supernatural power that looks after the so-called good people in this world and makes everything happen for the best in their case—while all the so-called bad people are punished.

Hovstad. Well, but that is all right. That is just what our readers want.

Petra. And are you going to be the one to give it to them? For myself, I do not believe a word of it. You know quite well that things do not happen so in reality.

Hovstad. You are perfectly right; but an editor cannot always act as he would prefer. He is often obliged to bow to the wishes of the public in unimportant matters. Politics are the most important thing in life—for a newspaper, anyway; and if I want to carry my public with me on the path that leads to liberty and progress, I must not frighten them away. If they find a moral tale of this sort in the serial at the bottom of the page, they will be all the more ready to read what is printed above it; they feel more secure, as it were.

Petra. For shame! You would never go and set a snare like that for your readers; you are not a spider!

Hovstad (smiling). Thank you for having such a good opinion of me.   No; as a matter of fact that is Billing's idea and not mine.

Petra. Billing's?

Hovstad. Yes; anyway he propounded that theory here one day.   And it is Billing who is so anxious to have that story in the paper; I don't know anything about the book.

Petra. But how can Billing, with his emancipated views—

Hovstad. Oh, Billing is a many-sided man.   He is applying for the post of secretary to the Bench, too, I hear.

Petra. I don't believe it, Mr. Hovstad.   How could he possibly bring himself to do such a thing?

Hovstad. Ah, you must ask him that.

Petra. I should never have thought it of him.

Hovstad (looking more closely at her). No?   Does it really surprise you so much?

Petra. Yes.   Or perhaps not altogether.   Really, I don't quite know—

Hovstad. We journalists are not much worth, Miss Stockmann.

Petra. Do you really mean that?

Hovstad. I think so sometimes.

Petra. Yes, in the ordinary affairs of everyday life, perhaps; I can understand that.   But now, when you have taken a weighty matter in hand—

Hovstad. This matter of your father's, you mean?

Petra. Exactly.   It seems to me that now you must feel you are a man worth more than most.

Hovstad. Yes, to-day I do feel something of that sort.

Petra. Of course you do, don't you?   It is a splendid vocation you have chosen—to smooth the way for the march of unappreciated truths, and new and courageous lines of thought.   If it were nothing more than because you stand fearlessly in the open and take up the cause of an injured man—

Hovstad. Especially when that injured man is—ahem!—I don't rightly know how to—

Petra. When that man is so upright and so honest, you mean?

Hovstad (more gently). Especially when he is your father, I meant.

Petra (suddenly checked). That?

Hovstad. Yes, Petra—Miss Petra.

Petra. Is it *that,* that is first and foremost with you? Not the matter itself? Not the truth?—not my father's big generous heart?

Hovstad. Certainly—of course—that too.

Petra. No, thank you; you have betrayed yourself, Mr. Hovstad, and now I shall never trust you again in anything.

Hovstad. Can you really take it so amiss in me that it is mostly for your sake—?

Petra. What I am angry with you for, is for not having been honest with my father. You talked to him as if the truth and the good of the community were what lay nearest to your heart. You have made fools of both my father and me. You are not the man you made yourself out to be. And that I shall never forgive you— never!

Hovstad. You ought not to speak so bitterly, Miss Petra—least of all now.

Petra. Why not now, especially?

Hovstad. Because your father cannot do without my help.

Petra (looking him up and down). Are you that sort of man too? For shame!

Hovstad. No, no, I am not. This came upon me so unexpectedly—you must believe that.

Petra. I know what to believe. Good-bye.

Aslaksen (coming from the printing-room, hurriedly and with an air of mystery). Damnation, Hovstad!— (*Sees* PETRA.) Oh, this is awkward—

Petra. There is the book; you must give it to some one else. (*Goes towards the door.*)

Hovstad (following her). But, Miss Stockmann—

Petra. Good-bye. (*Goes out.*)

Aslaksen. I say—Mr. Hovstad—

Hovstad. Well, well!—what is it?

Aslaksen. The Mayor is outside in the printing-room.

Hovstad. The Mayor, did you say?

Aslaksen. Yes, he wants to speak to you. He came in by the back door—didn't want to be seen, you understand.

Hovstad. What can he want? Wait a bit—I will go myself. (*Goes to the door of the printing-room, opens it, bows and invites* PETER STOCKMANN *in.*) Just see, Aslaksen, that no one—

Aslaksen. Quite so. (*Goes into the printing-room.*)

Peter Stockmann. You did not expect to see me here, Mr. Hovstad?

Hovstad. No, I confess I did not.

Peter Stockmann (*looking round*). You are very snug in here—very nice indeed.

Hovstad. Oh—

Peter Stockmann. And here I come, without any notice, to take up your time!

Hovstad. By all means, Mr. Mayor. I am at your service. But let me relieve you of your— (*takes* STOCKMANN'S *hat and stick and puts them on a chair*). Won't you sit down?

Peter Stockmann (*sitting down by the table*). Thank you. (HOVSTAD *sits down.*) I have had an extremely annoying experience to-day, Mr. Hovstad.

Hovstad. Really? Ah well, I expect with all the various business you have to attend to—

Peter Stockmann. The Medical Officer of the Baths is responsible for what happened to-day.

Hovstad. Indeed? The Doctor?

Peter Stockmann. He has addressed a kind of report to the Baths Committee on the subject of certain supposed defects in the Baths.

Hovstad. Has he indeed?

Peter Stockmann. Yes—has he not told you? I thought he said—

Hovstad. Ah, yes—it is true he did mention something about—

Aslaksen (coming from the printing-room). I ought to have that copy—

Hovstad (angrily). Ahem!—there it is on the desk.

Aslaksen (taking it). Right.

Peter Stockmann. But look there—that is the thing I was speaking of!

Aslaksen. Yes, that is the Doctor's article, Mr. Mayor.

Hovstad. Oh, is *that* what you were speaking about?

Peter Stockmann. Yes, that is it. What do you think of it?

Hovstad. Oh, I am only a layman—and I have only taken a very cursory glance at it.

Peter Stockmann. But you are going to print it?

Hovstad. I cannot very well refuse a distinguished man—

Aslaksen. I have nothing to do with editing the paper, Mr. Mayor—

Peter Stockmann. I understand.

Aslaksen. I merely print what is put into my hands.

Peter Stockmann. Quite so.

Aslaksen. And so I must— (*moves off towards the printing-room*).

Peter Stockmann. No, but wait a moment, Mr. Aslaksen. You will allow me, Mr. Hovstad?

Hovstad. If you please, Mr. Mayor.

Peter Stockmann. You are a discreet and thoughtful man, Mr. Aslaksen.

Aslaksen. I am delighted to hear you think so, sir.

Peter Stockmann. And a man of very considerable influence.

Aslaksen. Chiefly among the small tradesmen, sir.

Peter Stockmann. The small tax-payers are the majority—here as everywhere else.

Aslaksen. That is true.

Peter Stockmann. And I have no doubt you know the general trend of opinion among them, don't you?

Aslaksen. Yes I think I may say I do, Mr. Mayor.

Peter Stockmann. Yes. Well, since there is such a

praiseworthy spirit of self-sacrifice among the less wealthy citizens of our town—

Aslaksen. What?

Hovstad. Self-sacrifice?

Peter Stockmann. It is pleasing evidence of a public-spirited feeling, extremely pleasing evidence. I might almost say I hardly expected it. But you have a closer knowledge of public opinion than I.

Aslaksen. But, Mr. Mayor—

Peter Stockmann. And indeed it is no small sacrifice that the town is going to make.

Hovstad. The town?

Aslaksen. But I don't understand. Is it the Baths—?

Peter Stockmann. At a provisional estimate, the alterations that the Medical Officer asserts to be desirable will cost somewhere about twenty thousand pounds.

Aslaksen. That is a lot of money, but—

Peter Stockmann. Of course it will be necessary to raise a municipal loan.

Hovstad (*getting up*). Surely you never mean that the town must pay—?

Aslaksen. Do you mean that it must come out of the municipal funds?—out of the ill-filled pockets of the small tradesmen?

Peter Stockmann. Well, my dear Mr. Aslaksen, where else is the money to come from?

Aslaksen. The gentlemen who own the Baths ought to provide that.

Peter Stockmann. The proprietors of the Baths are not in a position to incur any further expense.

Aslaksen. Is that absolutely certain, Mr. Mayor?

Peter Stockmann. I have satisfied myself that it is so. If the town wants these very extensive alterations, it will have to pay for them.

Aslaksen. But, damn it all—I beg your pardon—this is quite another matter, Mr. Hovstad!

Hovstad. It is, indeed.

Peter Stockmann. The most fatal part of it is that we shall be obliged to shut the Baths for a couple of years.

Hovstad. Shut them? Shut them altogether?

Aslaksen. For two years?

Peter Stockmann. Yes, the work will take as long as that—at least.

Aslaksen. I'm damned if we will stand that, Mr. Mayor! What are we householders to live upon in the meantime?

Peter Stockmann. Unfortunately that is an extremely difficult question to answer, Mr. Aslaksen. But what would you have us do? Do you suppose we shall have a single visitor in the town, if we go about proclaiming that our water is polluted, that we are living over a plague spot, that the entire town—

Aslaksen. And the whole thing is merely imagination?

Peter Stockmann. With the best will in the world, I have not been able to come to any other conclusion.

Aslaksen. Well then I must say it is absolutely un-justifiable of Dr. Stockmann—I beg your pardon, Mr. Mayor—

Peter Stockmann. What you say is lamentably true, Mr. Aslaksen. My brother has unfortunately always been a headstrong man.

Aslaksen. After this, do you mean to give him your support, Mr. Hovstad?

Hovstad. Can you suppose for a moment that I—?

Peter Stockmann. I have drawn up a short *résumé* of the situation as it appears from a reasonable man's point of view. In it I have indicated ho v certain possible defects might suitably be remedied without out-running the resources of the Baths Committee.

Hovstad. Have you got it with you, Mr. Mayor.

Peter Stockmann (fumbling in his pocket). Yes, I brought it with me in case you should—

Aslaksen. Good Lord, there he is!

Peter Stockmann. Who? My brother?

Hovstad. Where? Where?

Aslaksen. He has just gone through the printing-room.

Peter Stockmann. How unlucky! I don't want to

meet him here, and I had still several things to speak to you about.

Hovstad (*pointing to the door on the right*). Go in there for the present.

Peter Stockmann. But—?

Hovstad. You will only find Billing in there.

Aslaksen. Quick, quick, Mr. Mayor—he is just coming.

Peter Stockmann. Yes, very well; but see that you get rid of him quickly. (*Goes out through the door on the right, which* ASLAKSEN *opens for him and shuts after him.*)

Hovstad. Pretend to be doing something, Aslaksen. (*Sits down and writes.* ASLAKSEN *begins foraging among a heap of newspapers that are lying on a chair.*)

Dr. Stockmann (*coming in from the printing-room*). Here I am again. (*Puts down his hat and stick.*)

Hovstad (*writing*). Already, Doctor? Hurry up with what we were speaking about, Aslaksen. We are very pressed for time to-day.

Dr. Stockmann (*to* ASLAKSEN). No proof for me to see yet, I hear.

Aslaksen (*without turning round*). You couldn't expect it yet, Doctor.

Dr. Stockmann. No, no; but I am impatient, as you can understand. I shall not know a moment's peace of mind till I see it in print.

Hovstad. Hm!—It will take a good while yet, won't it, Aslaksen?

Aslaksen. Yes, I am almost afraid it will.

Dr. Stockmann. All right, my dear friends; I will come back. I do not mind coming back twice if necessary. A matter of such great importance—the welfare of the town at stake— it is no time to shirk trouble. (*Is just going, but stops and comes back.*) Look here— there is one thing more I want to speak to you about.

Hovstad. Excuse me, but could it not wait till some other time?

Dr. Stockmann. I can tell you in half a dozen words.

It is only this. When my article is read to-morrow and it is realised that I have been quietly working the whole winter for the welfare of the town—

Hovstad. Yes but, Doctor—

Dr. Stockmann. I know what you are going to say. You don't see how on earth it was any more than my duty—my obvious duty as a citizen. Of course it wasn't; I know that as well as you. But my fellow citizens, you know—! Good Lord, think of all the good souls who think so highly of me—!

Aslaksen. Yes, our townsfolk have had a very high opinion of you so far, Doctor.

Dr. Stockmann. Yes, and that is just why I am afraid they—. Well, this is the point; when this reaches them, especially the poorer classes, and sounds in their ears like a summons to take the town's affairs into their own hands for the future—

Hovstad (getting up). Ahem! Doctor, I won't conceal from you the fact—

Dr. Stockmann. Ah!—I knew there was something in the wind! But I won't hear a word of it. If anything of that sort is being set on foot—

Hovstad. Of what sort?

Dr. Stockmann. Well, whatever it is—whether it is a demonstration in my honour, or a banquet, or a subscription list for some presentation to me—whatever it is, you must promise me solemnly and faithfully to put a stop to it. You too, Mr. Aslaksen; do you understand?

Hovstad. You must forgive me, Doctor, but sooner or later we must tell you the plain truth—

(He is interrupted by the entrance of MRS. STOCKMANN, *who comes in from the street door.)*

Mrs. Stockmann (seeing her husband). Just as I thought!

Hovstad (going towards her). You too, Mrs. Stockmann?

Dr. Stockmann. What on earth do *you* want here, Katherine?

Mrs. Stockmann. I should think you know very well what I want.

Hovstad. Won't you sit down? Or perhaps—

Mrs. Stockmann. No, thank you; don't trouble. And you must not be offended at my coming to fetch my husband; I am the mother of three children, you know.

Dr. Stockmann. Nonsense!—we know all about that.

Mrs. Stockmann. Well, one would not give you credit for much thought for your wife and children to-day; if you had had that, you would not have gone and dragged us all into misfortune.

Dr. Stockmann. Are you out of your senses, Katherine? Because a man has a wife and children, is he not to be allowed to proclaim the truth—is he not to be allowed to be an actively useful citizen—is he not to be allowed to do a service to his native town!

Mrs. Stockmann. Yes, Thomas—in reason.

Aslaksen. Just what I say. Moderation in everything.

Mrs. Stockmann. And that is why you wrong us, Mr. Hovstad, in enticing my husband away from his home and making a dupe of him in all this.

Hovstad. I certainly am making a dupe of no one—

Dr. Stockmann. Making a dupe of me! Do you suppose *I* should allow myself to be duped!

Mrs. Stockmann. It is just what you do. I know quite well you have more brains than anyone in the town, but you are extremely easily duped, Thomas. (*To Hovstad.*) Please to realise that he loses his post at the Baths if you print what he has written—

Aslaksen. What?

Hovstad. Look here, Doctor—

Dr. Stockmann (*laughing*). Ha—ha!—just let them try! No, no—they will take good care not to. I have got the compact majority behind me, let me tell you!

Mrs. Stockmann. Yes, that is just the worst of it— your having any such horrid thing behind you.

Dr. Stockmann. Rubbish, Katherine!—Go home and look after your house and leave me to look after the community. How can you be so afraid, when I am so confident and happy? (*Walks up and down, rubbing his hands.*) Truth and the People will win the fight, you may be certain! I see the whole of the broadminded middle class marching like a victorious army—! (*Stops beside a chair.*) What the deuce is that lying there?

Aslaksen Good Lord!

Hovstad. Ahem!

Dr. Stockmann. Here we have the topmost pinnacle of authority! (*Takes the Mayor's official hat carefully between his finger-tips and holds it up in the air.*)

Mrs. Stockmann. The Mayor's hat!

Dr. Stockmann. And here is the staff of office, too. How in the name of all that's wonderful—?

Hovstad. Well, you see—

Dr. Stockmann. Oh, I understand. He has been here trying to talk you over. Ha—ha!—he made rather a mistake there! And as soon as he caught sight of me in the printing-room—. (*Bursts out laughing.*) Did he run away, Mr. Aslaksen?

Aslaksen (*hurriedly*). Yes, he ran away, Doctor.

Dr. Stockmann. Ran away without his stick or his—. Fiddlesticks! Peter doesn't run away and leave his belongings behind him. But what the deuce have you done with him? Ah!—in there, of course. Now you shall see, Katherine!

Mrs. Stockmann. Thomas—please don't—!

Aslaksen. Don't be rash, Doctor.

(DR. STOCKMANN *has put on the Mayor's hat and taken his stick in his hand. He goes up to the door, opens it, and stands with his hand to his hat at the salute.* PETER STOCKMANN *comes in, red with anger.* BILLING *follows him.*)

Peter Stockmann. What does this tomfoolery mean?

Dr. Stockmann. Be respectful, my good Peter. I am the chief authority in the town now. (*Walks up and down.*)

Mrs. Stockmann (*almost in tears*). Really, Thomas!

Peter Stockmann (*following him about*). Give me my hat and stick.

Dr. Stockmann (*in the same tone as before*). If you are chief constable, let me tell you that I am the Mayor— I am the master of the whole town, please understand!

Peter Stockmann. Take off my hat, I tell you. Remember it is part of an official uniform.

Dr. Stockmann. Pooh! Do you think the newly awakened lion-hearted people are going to be frightened by an official hat? There is going to be a revolution in the town to-morrow, let me tell you. You thought you could turn me out; but now I shall turn you out— turn you out of all your various offices. Do you think I cannot? Listen to me. I have triumphant social forces behind me. Hovstad and Billing will thunder in the " People's Messenger," and Aslaksen will take the field at the head of the whole Householders' Association—

Aslaksen. That I won't, Doctor.

Dr. Stockmann. Of course you will—

Peter Stockmann. Ah!—may I ask then if Mr. Hovstad intends to join this agitation.

Hovstad. No, Mr. Mayor.

Aslaksen. No, Mr. Hovstad is not such a fool as to go and ruin his paper and himself for the sake of an imaginary grievance.

Dr. Stockmann (*looking round him*). What does this mean?

Hovstad. You have represented your case in a false light, Doctor, and therefore I am unable to give you my support.

Billing. And after what the Mayor was so kind as to tell me just now, I—

Dr. Stockmann. A false light! Leave that part of it to me. Only print my article; I am quite capable of defending it.

Hovstad. I am not going to print it. I cannot and will not and dare not print it.

Dr. Stockmann. You dare not? What nonsense!— you are the editor; and an editor controls his paper, I suppose!

Aslaksen. No, it is the subscribers, Doctor.

Peter Stockmann. Fortunately, yes.

Aslaksen. It is public opinion—the enlightened public—householders and people of that kind; they control the newspapers.

Dr. Stockmann (composedly). And I have all these influences against me?

Aslaksen. Yes, you have. It would mean the absolute ruin of the community if your article were to appear.

Dr. Stockmann. Indeed.

Peter Stockmann. My hat and stick, if you please. (DR. STOCKMANN *takes off the hat and lays it on the table with the stick.* PETER STOCKMANN *takes them up.*) Your authority as mayor has come to an untimely end.

Dr. Stockmann. We have not got to the end yet. (*To* HOVSTAD.) Then it is quite impossible for you to print my article in the " People's Messenger " ?

Hovstad. Quite impossible—out of regard for your family as well.

Mrs. Stockmann. You need not concern yourself about his family, thank you, Mr. Hovstad.

Peter Stockmann (taking a paper from his pocket). It will be sufficient, for the guidance of the public, if this appears. It is an official statement. May I trouble you?

Hovstad (taking the paper). Certainly; I will see that it is printed.

Dr. Stockmann. But not mine. Do you imagine that you can silence me and stifle the truth! You will not find it so easy as you suppose. Mr. Aslaksen, kindly take my manuscript at once and print it as a pamphlet—at my expense. I will have four hundred copies—no, five—six hundred.

Aslaksen. If you offered me its weight in gold, I could not lend my press for any such purpose, Doctor. It would be flying in the face of public opinion. You will not get it printed anywhere in the town.

Dr. Stockmann. Then give it me back.

Hovstad (giving him the MS.). Here it is.

Dr. Stockmann (taking his hat and stick). It shall be

made public all the same. I will read it out at a mass meeting of the townspeople. All my fellow-citizens shall hear the voice of truth!

Peter Stockmann. You will not find any public body in the town that will give you the use of their hall for such a purpose.

Aslaksen. Not a single one, I am certain.

Billing. No, I'm damned if you will find one.

Mrs. Stockmann. But this is too shameful! Why should every one turn against you like that?

Dr. Stockmann (angrily). I will tell you why. It is because all the men in this town are old women— like you; they all think of nothing but their families, and never of the community.

Mrs. Stockmann (putting her arm into his). Then I will show them that an—an old woman can be a man for once. I am going to stand by you, Thomas!

Dr. Stockmann. Bravely said, Katherine! It shall be made public—as I am a living soul! If I can't hire a hall, I shall hire a drum, and parade the town with it and read it at every street-corner.

Peter Stockmann. You are surely not such an arrant fool as that!

Dr. Stockmann. Yes, I am.

Aslaksen. You won't find a single man in the whole town to go with you.

Billing. No, I'm damned if you will.

Mrs. Stockmann. Don't give in, Thomas. I will tell the boys to go with you.

Dr. Stockmann. That is a splendid idea!

Mrs. Stockmann. Morten will be delighted; and Ejlif will do whatever he does.

Dr. Stockmann. Yes, and Petra!—and you too, Katherine!

Mrs. Stockmann. No, I won't do that; but I will stand at the window and watch you, that's what I will do.

Dr. Stockmann (puts his arms round her and kisses her). Thank you, my dear! Now you and I are going to try a fall, my fine gentlemen! I am going to see whether a pack of cowards can succeed in gagging a patriot who wants to purify society! (*He and his wife go out by the street door.*)

Peter Stockmann (*shaking his head seriously*). Now he has sent *her* out of her senses, too.

ACT IV

(SCENE.—*A big old-fashioned room in* CAPTAIN HORSTER'S *house. At the back folding-doors, which are standing open, lead to an ante-room. Three windows in the left-hand wall. In the middle of the opposite wall a platform has been erected. On this is a small table with two candles, a water-bottle and glass, and a bell. The room is lit by lamps placed between the windows. In the foreground on the left there is a table with candles and a chair. To the right is a door and some chairs standing near it. The room is nearly filled with a crowd of towns- people of all sorts, a few women and schoolboys being amongst them. People are still streaming in from the back, and the room is soon filled.*)

1st Citizen (*meeting another*). Hullo, Lamstad! You here too?

2nd Citizen. I go to every public meeting, I do.

3rd Citizen. Brought your whistle too, I expect!

2nd Citizen. I should think so. Haven't you?

3rd Citizen. Rather! And old Evensen said he was going to bring a cow-horn, he did.

2nd Citizen. Good old Evensen! (*Laughter among the crowd.*)

4th Citizen (*coming up to them*). I say, tell me what is going on here to-night.

2nd Citizen. Dr. Stockmann is going to deliver an address attacking the Mayor.

4th Citizen. But the Mayor is his brother.

1st Citizen. That doesn't matter; Dr. Stockmann's not the chap to be afraid.

3rd Citizen. But he is in the wrong; it said so in the " People's Messenger."

2nd Citizen. Yes, I expect he must be in the wrong this time, because neither the Householders' Association nor the Citizens' Club would lend him their hall for his meeting.

1st Citizen. He couldn't even get the loan of the hall at the Baths.

2nd Citizen. No, I should think not.

A Man in another part of the crowd. I say—who are we to back up in this?

Another Man, beside him. Watch Aslaksen, and do as he does.

Billing (*pushing his way through the crowd, with a writing-case under his arm*). Excuse me, gentlemen— do you mind letting me through? I am reporting for the " People's Messenger." Thank you very much! (*He sits down at the table on the left.*)

A Workman. Who was that?

Second Workman. Don't you know him? It's Billing, who writes for Aslaksen's paper.

(CAPTAIN HORSTER *brings in* MRS. STOCKMANN *and* PETRA *through the door on the right.* EJLIF *and* MORTEN *follow them in.*)

Horster. I thought you might all sit here; you can slip out easily from here, if things get too lively.

Mrs. Stockmann. Do you think there will be a disturbance?

Horster. One can never tell—with such a crowd. But sit down, and don't be uneasy.

Mrs. Stockmann (*sitting down*). It was extremely kind of you to offer my husband the room.

Horster. Well, if nobody else would—

Petra (*who has sat down beside her mother*). And it was a plucky thing to do, Captain Horster.

Horster. Oh, it is not such a great matter as all that.

(HOVSTAD *and* ASLAKSEN *make their way through the crowd.*)

Aslaksen (going up to HORSTER). Has the Doctor not come yet?

Horster. He is waiting in the next room. (*Movement in the crowd by the door at the back.*)

Hovstad. Look—here comes the Mayor!

Billing. Yes, I'm damned if he hasn't come after all!

(PETER STOCKMANN *makes his way gradually through the crowd, bows courteously, and takes up a position by the wall on the left. Shortly afterwards* DR. STOCKMANN *comes in by the right-hand door. He is dressed in a black frock-coat, with a white tie. There is a little feeble applause, which is hushed down. Silence is obtained.*)

Dr. Stockmann (in an undertone). How do you feel, Katherine?

Mrs. Stockmann. All right, thank you. (*Lowering her voice.*) Be sure not to lose your temper, Thomas.

Dr. Stockmann. Oh, I know how to control myself. (*Looks at his watch, steps on to the platform, and bows.*) It is a quarter past—so I will begin. (*Takes his MS. out of his pocket*).

Aslaksen. I think we ought to elect a chairman first.

Dr. Stockmann. No, it is quite unnecessary.

Some of the Crowd. Yes—yes!

Peter Stockmann. I certainly think, too, that we ought to have a chairman.

Dr. Stockmann. But I have called this meeting to deliver a lecture, Peter.

Peter Stockmann. Dr. Stockmann's lecture may possibly lead to a considerable conflict of opinion.

Voices in the Crowd. A chairman! A chairman!

Hovstad. The general wish of the meeting seems to be that a chairman should be elected.

Dr. Stockmann (restraining himself). Very well—let the meeting have its way.

Aslaksen. Will the Mayor be good enough to undertake the task?

Three Men (clapping their hands). Bravo! Bravo!

Peter Stockmann. For various reasons, which you will easily understand, I must beg to be excused. But fortunately we have amongst us a man who I think will be acceptable to you all.　I refer to the President of the Householders' Association, Mr. Aslaksen.

Several voices. Yes—Aslaksen!　Bravo Aslaksen!

(DR. STOCKMANN *takes up his MS. and walks up and down the platform.*)

Aslaksen. Since my fellow-citizens choose to entrust me with this duty, I cannot refuse.

(*Loud applause.* ASLAKSEN *mounts the platform.*)

Billing (*writing*). " Mr. Aslaksen was elected with enthusiasm."

Aslaksen. And now, as I am in this position, I should like to say a few brief words.　I am a quiet and peaceable man, who believes in discreet moderation, and—and—in moderate discretion.　All my friends can bear witness to that.

Several Voices. That's right!　That's right, Aslaksen!

Aslaksen. I have learnt in the school of life and experience that moderation is the most valuable virtue a citizen can possess—

Peter Stockmann. Hear, hear!

Aslaksen. —And moreover that discretion and moderation are what enable a man to be of most service to the community.　I would therefore suggest to our esteemed fellow-citizen, who has called this meeting, that he should strive to keep strictly within the bounds of moderation.

A Man by the door. Three cheers for the Moderation Society!

A Voice. Shame!

Several Voices. Sh!—Sh!

Aslaksen. No interruptions, gentlemen, please!　Does anyone wish to make any remarks?

Peter Stockmann. Mr. Chairman.

Aslaksen. The Mayor will address the meeting.

Peter Stockmann. In consideration of the close relationship in which, as you all know, I stand to the present Medical Officer of the Baths, I should have preferred not to speak this evening. But my official position with regard to the Baths and my solicitude for the vital interests of the town compel me to bring forward a motion. I venture to presume that there is not a single one of our citizens present who considers it desirable that unreliable and exaggerated accounts of the sanitary condition of the Baths and the town should be spread abroad.

Several Voices. No, no! Certainly not! We protest against it!

Peter Stockmann. Therefore I should like to propose that the meeting should not permit the Medical Officer either to read or to comment on his proposed lecture.

Dr. Stockmann (impatiently). Not permit—! What the devil—!

Mrs. Stockmann (coughing). Ahem!—ahem!

Dr. Stockmann (collecting himself). Very well. Go ahead!

Peter Stockmann. In my communication to the "People's Messenger," I have put the essential facts before the public in such a way that every fair-minded citizen can easily form his own opinion. From it you will see that the main result of the Medical Officer's proposals—apart from their constituting a vote of censure on the leading men of the town—would be to saddle the ratepayers with an unnecessary expenditure of at least some thousands of pounds.

(Sounds of disapproval among the audience, and some cat-calls.)

Aslaksen (ringing his bell). Silence, please, gentlemen! I beg to support the Mayor's motion. I quite agree with him that there is something behind this agitation started by the Doctor. He talks about the Baths; but it is a revolution he is aiming at—he wants to get the administration of the town put into new hands. No one doubts the honesty of the Doctor's intentions—no one will suggest that there can be any two opinions as to that. I myself am a believer in self-government for the people,

provided it does not fall too heavily on the ratepayers.
But that would be the case here; and that is why I
will see Dr. Stockmann damned—I beg your pardon—
before I go with him in the matter. You can pay too
dearly for a thing sometimes; that is my opinion.

(*Loud applause on all sides.*)

Hovstad. I, too, feel called upon to explain my
position. Dr. Stockmann's agitation appeared to be
gaining a certain amount of sympathy at first, so I
supported it as impartially as I could. But presently
we had reason to suspect that we had allowed ourselves
to be misled by misrepresentation of the state of affairs—

Dr. Stockmann. Misrepresentation—!

Hovstad. Well, let us say a not entirely trustworthy
representation. The Mayor's statement has proved
that. I hope no one here has any doubt as to my liberal
principles; the attitude of the " People's Messenger "
towards important political questions is well known to
every one. But the advice of experienced and thoughtful
men has convinced me that in purely local matters a
newspaper ought to proceed with a certain caution.

Aslaksen. I entirely agree with the speaker.

Hovstad. And, in the matter before us, it is now an
undoubted fact that Dr. Stockmann has public opinion
against him. Now, what is an editor's first and most
obvious duty, gentlemen ? Is it not to work in harmony
with his readers ? Has he not received a sort of tacit
mandate to work persistently and assiduously for the
welfare of those whose opinions he represents ? Or is it
possible I am mistaken in that ?

Voices from the crowd. No, no ! You are quite right !

Hovstad. It has cost me a severe struggle to break
with a man in whose house I have been lately a frequent
guest—a man who till to-day has been able to pride
himself on the undivided goodwill of his fellow-citizens—
a man whose only, or at all events whose essential, fail-
ing is that he is swayed by his heart rather than his
head.

A few scattered voices. That is true ! Bravo, Stockmann !

Hovstad. But my duty to the community obliged me to break with him. And there is another consideration that impels me to oppose him, and, as far as possible, to arrest him on the perilous course he has adopted; that is, consideration for his family—

Dr. Stockmann. Please stick to the water-supply and drainage!

Hovstad. —consideration, I repeat, for his wife and his children for whom he has made no provision.

Morten. Is that us, mother?

Mrs. Stockmann. Hush!

Aslaksen. I will now put the Mayor's proposition to the vote.

Dr. Stockmann. There is no necessity! To-night I have no intention of dealing with all that filth down at the Baths. No; I have something quite different to say to you.

Peter Stockmann (aside). What is coming now?

A Drunken Man (by the entrance door). I am a rate-payer! And therefore I have a right to speak too! And my entire—firm—inconceivable opinion is—

A number of voices. Be quiet, at the back there!

Others. He is drunk! Turn him out! (*They turn him out.*)

Dr. Stockmann. Am I allowed to speak?

Aslaksen (ringing his bell). Dr. Stockmann will address the meeting.

Dr. Stockmann. I should like to have seen anyone, a few days ago, dare to attempt to silence me as has been done to-night! I would have defended my sacred rights as a man, like a lion! But now it is all one to me; I have something of even weightier importance to say to you. (*The crowd presses nearer to him,* MORTEN KIIL *conspicuous among them.*)

Dr. Stockmann (continuing). I have thought and pondered a great deal, these last few days—pondered over such a variety of things that in the end my head seemed too full to hold them—

Peter Stockmann (with a cough). Ahem!

Dr. Stockmann. —but I got them clear in my mind at last, and then I saw the whole situation lucidly. And that is why I am standing here to-night. I have a great revelation to make to you, my fellow-citizens! I will impart to you a discovery of a far wider scope than the trifling matter that our water-supply is poisoned and our medicinal Baths are standing on pestiferous soil.

A number of voices (shouting). Don't talk about the Baths! We won't hear you! None of that!

Dr. Stockmann. I have already told you that what I want to speak about is the great discovery I have made lately—the discovery that all the sources of our *moral* life are poisoned and that the whole fabric of our civic community is founded on the pestiferous soil of false-hood.

Voices of disconcerted Citizens. What is that he says?

Peter Stockmann. Such an insinuation—!

Aslaksen (with his hand on his bell). I call upon the speaker to moderate his language.

Dr. Stockmann. I have always loved my native town as a man only can love the home of his youthful days. I was not old when I went away from here; and exile, longing and memories cast as it were an additional halo over both the town and its inhabitants. (*Some clapping and applause.*) And there I stayed, for many years, in a horrible hole far away up north. When I came into contact with some of the people that lived scattered about among the rocks, I often thought it would of been more service to the poor half-starved creatures if a veterinary doctor had been sent up there, instead of a man like me. (*Murmurs among the crowd.*)

Billing (laying down his pen). I'm damned if I have ever heard—!

Hovstad. It is an insult to a respectable population!

Dr. Stockmann. Wait a bit! I do not think anyone will charge me with having forgotten my native town up there. I was like one of the eider-ducks brooding on its nest, and what I hatched was—the plans for these Baths. (*Applause and protests.*) And then when fate at last decreed for me the great happiness of coming home again—I assure you, gentlemen, I thought I had nothing more in the world to wish for. Or rather, there was one thing I wished for—eagerly, untiringly, ardently—and that was to be able to be of service to my native town and the good of the community.

Peter Stockmann (looking at the ceiling). You chose a strange way of doing it—ahem!

Dr. Stockmann. And so, with my eyes blinded to the real facts, I revelled in happiness. But yesterday morning—no, to be precise, it was yesterday afternoon—the eyes of my mind were opened wide, and the first thing I realised was the colossal stupidity of the authorities—. (*Uproar, shouts and laughter.* MRS. STOCKMANN *coughs persistently.*)

Peter Stockmann. Mr. Chairman!

Aslaksen (ringing his bell). By virtue of my authority—!

Dr. Stockmann. It is a petty thing to catch me up on a word, Mr. Aslaksen. What I mean is only that I got scent of the unbelievable piggishness our leading men had been responsible for down at the Baths. I can't stand leading men at any price!—I have had enough of such people in my time. They are like billy-goats in a young plantation; they do mischief everywhere. They stand in a free man's way, whichever way he turns, and what I should like best would be to see them exterminated like any other vermin—. (*Uproar.*)

Peter Stockmann. Mr. Chairman, can we allow such expressions to pass?

Aslaksen (with his hand on his bell). Doctor—!

Dr. Stockmann. I cannot understand how it is that I have only now acquired a clear conception of what these gentry are, when I had almost daily before my eyes in this town such an excellent specimen of them— my brother Peter—slow-witted and hide-bound in prejudice—. (*Laughter, uproar and hisses.* MRS. STOCKMANN *sits coughing assiduously.* ASLAKSEN *rings his bell violently.*)

The Drunken Man (who has got in again). Is it me he is talking about? My name's Petersen, all right—but devil take me if I—

Angry Voices. Turn out that drunken man! Turn him out. (*He is turned out again.*)

Peter Stockmann. Who was that person?

1st Citizen. I don't know who he is, Mr. Mayor.

2nd Citizen. He doesn't belong here.

3rd Citizen. I expect he is a navvy from over at— (*the rest is inaudible*).

Aslaksen. He had obviously had too much beer.— Proceed, Doctor; but please strive to be moderate in your language.

Dr. Stockmann. Very well, gentlemen, I will say no more about our leading men.   And if anyone imagines, from what I have just said, that my object is to attack these people this evening, he is wrong—absolutely wide of the mark. For I cherish the comforting conviction that these parasites—all these venerable relics of a dying school of thought—are most admirably paving the way for their own extinction; they need no doctor's help to hasten their end. Nor is it folk of that kind who constitute the most pressing danger to the community. It is not they who are most instrumental in poisoning the sources of our moral life and infecting the ground on which we stand. It is not they who are the most dangerous enemies of truth and freedom amongst us.

Shouts from all sides. Who then? Who is it? Name! Name!

Dr. Stockmann. You may depend upon it I shall name them! That is precisely the great discovery I made yesterday. (*Raises his voice.*) The most dangerous enemy of truth and freedom amongst us is the compact majority—yes, the damned compact Liberal majority—that is it! Now you know! (*Tremendous uproar. Most of the crowd are shouting, stamping and hissing. Some of the older men among them exchange stolen glances and seem to be enjoying themselves.* MRS. STOCKMANN *gets up, looking anxious.* EJLIF *and* MORTEN

*advance threateningly upon some schoolboys who are
playing pranks.* ASLAKSEN *rings his bell and begs for
silence.* HOVSTAD *and* BILLING *both talk at once, but are
inaudible. At last quiet is restored.*)

Aslaksen. As chairman, I call upon the speaker to
withdraw the ill-considered expressions he has just
used.

Dr. Stockmann. Never, Mr. Aslaksen! It is the majority
in our community that denies me my freedom and seeks
to prevent my speaking the truth.

Hovstad. The majority always has right on its side.

Billing. And truth too, by God!

Dr. Stockmann. The majority *never* has right on its
side. Never, I say! That is one of these social lies
against which an independent, intelligent man must
wage war. Who is it that constitute the majority of
the population in a country? Is it the clever folk or the
stupid? I don't imagine you will dispute the fact that
at present the stupid people are in an absolutely overwhelming majority all the world over. But, good Lord!
—you can never pretend that it is right that the stupid
folk should govern the clever ones! (*Uproar and cries.*)
Oh, yes—you can shout me down, I know! but you
cannot answer me. The majority has *might* on its side—
unfortunately; but *right* it has *not*. I am in the right—
I and a few other scattered individuals. The minority
is always in the right. (*Renewed uproar.*)

Hovstad. Aha!—so Dr. Stockmann has become an
aristocrat since the day before yesterday!

Dr. Stockmann. I have already said that I don't
intend to waste a word on the puny, narrow-chested,
short-winded crew whom we are leaving astern. Pulsating life no longer concerns itself with them. I am
thinking of the few, the scattered few amongst us, who
have absorbed new and vigorous truths. Such men
stand, as it were, at the outposts, so far ahead that the
compact majority has not yet been able to come up
with them; and there they are fighting for truths that
are too newly-born into the world of consciousness to

have any considerable number of people on their side as yet.

Hovstad. So the Doctor is a revolutionary now!

Dr. Stockmann. Good heavens—of course I am, Mr. Hovstad! I propose to raise a revolution against the lie that the majority has the monopoly of the truth. What sort of truths are they that the majority usually supports? They are truths that are of such advanced age that they are beginning to break up. And if a truth is as old as that, it is also in a fair way to become a lie, gentlemen. (*Laughter and mocking cries.*) Yes, believe me or not, as you like; but truths are by no means as long-lived as Methuselah—as some folk imagine. A normally constituted truth lives, let us say, as a rule seventeen or eighteen, or at most twenty years; seldom longer. But truths as aged as that are always worn frightfully thin, and nevertheless it is only then that the majority recognises them and recommends them to the community as wholesome moral nourishment. There is no great nutritive value in that sort of fare, I can assure you; and, as a doctor, I ought to know. These " majority truths " are like last year's cured meat—like rancid, tainted ham; and they are the origin of the moral scurvy that is rampant in our communities.

Aslaksen. It appears to me that the speaker is wandering a long way from his subject.

Peter Stockmann. I quite agree with the Chairman.

Dr. Stockmann. Have you gone clean out of your senses, Peter? I am sticking as closely to my subject as I can; for my subject is precisely this, that it is the masses, the majority—this infernal compact majority—that poisons the sources of our moral life and infects the ground we stand on.

Hovstad. And all this because the great, broad-minded majority of the people is prudent enough to show deference only to well-ascertained and well-approved truths?

Dr. Stockmann. Ah, my good Mr. Hovstad, don't talk

nonsense about well-ascertained truths! The truths of which the masses now approve are the very truths that the fighters at the outposts held to in the days of our grandfathers. We fighters at the outposts nowadays no longer approve of them; and I do not believe there is any other well-ascertained truth except this, that no community can live a healthy life if it is nourished only on such old marrowless truths.

Hovstad. But instead of standing there using vague generalities, it would be interesting if you would tell us what these old marrowless truths are, that we are nourished on.

(*Applause from many quarters.*)

Dr. Stockmann. Oh, I could give you a whole string of such abominations; but to begin with I will confine myself to one well-approved truth, which at bottom is a foul lie, but upon which nevertheless Mr. Hovstad and the " People's Messenger " and all the " Messenger's " supporters are nourished.

Hovstad. And that is—?

Dr. Stockmann. That is, the doctrine you have inherited from your forefathers and proclaim thoughtlessly far and wide—the doctrine that the public, the crowd, the masses, are the essential part of the population—that they constitute the People—that the common folk, the ignorant and incomplete element in the community, have the same right to pronounce judgment and to approve, to direct and to govern, as the isolated, intellectually superior personalities in it.

Billing. Well, damn me if ever I—

Hovstad (*at the same time, shouting out*). Fellow-citizens, take good note of that!

A number of voices (*angrily*). Oho!—we are not the People! Only the superior folk are to govern, are they!

A Workman. Turn the fellow out, for talking rubbish!

Another. Out with him!

Another (*calling out*). Blow your horn, Evensen!

(*A horn is blown loudly, amidst hisses and an angry uproar.*)

Dr. Stockmann (*when the noise has somewhat abated*). Be reasonable! Can't you stand hearing the voice of truth for once? I don't in the least expect you to agree with me all at once ; but I must say I did expect Mr. Hovstad to admit I was right, when he had recovered his composure a little. He claims to be a freethinker—

Voices (*in murmurs of astonishment*). Freethinker, did he say? Is Hovstad a freethinker?

Hovstad (*shouting*). Prove it, Dr. Stockmann! When have I said so in print?

Dr. Stockmann (*reflecting*). No, confound it, you are right!—you have never had the courage to. Well, I won't put you in a hole, Mr. Hovstad. Let us say it is I that am the freethinker, then. I am going to prove to you, scientifically, that the " People's Messenger " leads you by the nose in a shameful manner when it tells you that you—that the common people, the crowd, the masses, are the real essence of the People. That is only a newspaper lie, I tell you! The common people are nothing more than the raw material of which a People is made. (*Groans, laughter and uproar.*) Well, isn't that the case? Isn't there an enormous difference between a well-bred and an ill-bred strain of animals? Take, for instance, a common barn-door hen. What sort of eating do you get from a shrivelled up old scrag of a fowl like that? Not much, do you! And what sort of eggs does it lay? A fairly good crow or a raven can lay pretty nearly as good an egg. But take a well-bred Spanish or Japanese hen, or a good pheasant or a turkey—then you will see the difference. Or take the case of dogs, with whom we humans are on such intimate terms. Think first of an ordinary common cur—I mean one of the horrible, coarse-haired, low-bred curs that do nothing but run about the streets and befoul the walls of the houses. Compare one of these curs with a poodle whose sires for many generations have been bred in a gentleman's house, where they have had the best of food and had the opportunity of hearing soft voices and music. Do you not think that the poodle's brain is developed to quite a different degree from that of the cur? Of course it is. It is puppies of well-bred poodles like that, that showmen train to do incredibly clever tricks—things that a common cur could never learn to do even if it stood on its head. (*Uproar and mocking cries.*)

A Citizen (*calls out*). Are you going to make out we are dogs, now?

Another Citizen. We are not animals, Doctor!

Dr. Stockmann. Yes but, bless my soul, we *are*, my friend! It is true we are the finest animals anyone could wish for; but, even amongst us, exceptionally fine animals are rare. There is a tremendous difference between poodle-men and cur-men. And the amusing part of it is, that Mr. Hovstad quite agrees with me as long as it is a question of four-footed animals—

Hovstad. Yes, it is true enough as far as they are concerned.

Dr. Stockmann. Very well. But as soon as I extend the principle and apply it to two-legged animals, Mr. Hovstad stops short. He no longer dares to think independently, or to pursue his ideas to their logical conclusion; so he turns the whole theory upside down and proclaims in the "People's Messenger" that it is the barn-door hens and street curs that are the finest specimens in the menagerie. But that is always the way, as long as a man retains the traces of common origin and has not worked his way up to intellectual distinction.

Hovstad. I lay no claim to any sort of distinction. I am the son of humble countryfolk, and I am proud that the stock I come from is rooted deep among the common people he insults.

Voices. Bravo, Hovstad! Bravo! Bravo!

Dr. Stockmann. The kind of common people I mean are not only to be found low down in the social scale; they crawl and swarm all around us—even in the highest social positions. You have only to look at your own fine, distinguished Mayor! My brother Peter is every bit as plebeian as anyone that walks in two shoes—(*laughter and hisses*)

Peter Stockmann. I protest against personal allusions of this kind.

Dr. Stockmann (imperturbably).—and that, not because he is, like myself, descended from some old rascal of a pirate from Pomerania or thereabouts—because that is who we are descended from—

Peter Stockmann. An absurd legend. I deny it!

Dr. Stockmann. —but because he thinks what his superiors think and holds the same opinions as they. People who do that are, intellectually speaking, common people; and that is why my magnificent brother Peter is in reality so very far from any distinction—and consequently also so far from being liberal-minded.

Peter Stockmann. Mr. Chairman—!

Hovstad. So it is only the distinguished men that are liberal-minded in this country? We are learning something quite new! (*Laughter.*)

Dr. Stockmann. Yes, that is part of my new discovery too. And another part of it is that broad-mindedness is almost precisely the same thing as morality. That is why I maintain that it is absolutely inexcusable in the " People's Messenger " to proclaim, day in and day out, the false doctrine that it is the masses, the crowd, the compact majority, that have the monopoly of broad-mindedness and morality—and that vice and corruption and every kind of intellectual depravity are the result of culture, just as all the filth that is draining into our Baths is the result of the tanneries up at Mölledal! (*Uproar and interruptions.* DR. STOCKMANN *is undisturbed, and goes on, carried away by his ardour, with a smile.*) And yet this same " People's Messenger " can go on preaching that the masses ought to be elevated to higher conditions of life! But, bless my soul, if the " Messenger's " teaching is to be depended upon, this very raising up the masses would mean nothing more or less than setting them straightway upon the paths of depravity! Happily the theory that culture demoralises is only an old falsehood that our forefathers believed in and we have inherited. No, it is ignorance, poverty, ugly conditions of life, that do the devil's work! In a house which does not get aired and swept every day—my wife Katherine maintains that the floor ought to be scrubbed as well, but that is a debatable question—in such a house, let me tell you, people will lose within two or three years the power of thinking or acting in a moral manner. Lack of oxygen weakens the conscience. And there must be a plentiful lack of oxygen in very many houses in this town, I should think, judging from the fact that the whole compact majority can be unconscientious enough to wish to build the town's prosperity on a quagmire of falsehood and deceit.

Aslaksen. We cannot allow such a grave accusation to be flung at a citizen community.

A Citizen. I move that the Chairman direct the speaker to sit down.

Voices (angrily). Hear, hear! Quite right! Make him sit down!

Dr. Stockmann (losing his self-control). Then I will go and shout the truth at every street corner! I will write it in other towns' newspapers! The whole country shall know what is going on here!

Hovstad. It almost seems as if Dr. Stockmann's intention were to ruin the town.

Dr. Stockmann. Yes, my native town is so dear to me that I would rather ruin it than see it flourishing upon a lie.

Aslaksen. This is really serious. (*Uproar and catcalls.* MRS. STOCKMANN *coughs, but to no purpose; her husband does not listen to her any longer.*)

Hovstad (shouting above the din). A man must be a public enemy to wish to ruin a whole community!

Dr. Stockmann (with growing fervour). What does the destruction of a community matter, if it lives on lies! It ought to be razed to the ground, I tell you! All who live by lies ought to be exterminated like vermin! You will end by infecting the whole country; you will bring about such a state of things that the whole country will deserve to be ruined. And if things come to that pass, I shall say from the bottom of my heart: Let the whole country perish, let all these people be exterminated!

Voices from the crowd. That is talking like an out-and-out enemy of the people!

Billing. There sounded the voice of the people, by all that's holy!

The whole crowd (*shouting*). Yes, yes! He is an enemy of the people! He hates his country! He hates his own people!

Aslaksen. Both as a citizen and as an individual, I am profoundly disturbed by what we have had to listen to. Dr. Stockmann has shown himself in a light I should never have dreamed of. I am unhappily obliged to subscribe to the opinion which I have just heard my estimable fellow-citizens utter; and I propose that we should give expression to that opinion in a resolution. I propose a resolution as follows: " This meeting declares that it considers Dr. Thomas Stockmann, Medical Officer of the Baths, to be an enemy of the people." (*A storm of cheers and applause. A number of men surround the* DOCTOR *and hiss him.* MRS. STOCKMANN *and* PETRA *have got up from their seats.* MORTEN *and* EJLIF *are fighting the other schoolboys for hissing; some of their elders separate them.*)

Dr. Stockmann (*to the men who are hissing him*). Oh, you fools! I tell you that—

Aslaksen (*ringing his bell*). We cannot hear you now, Doctor. A formal vote is about to be taken; but, out of regard for personal feelings, it shall be by ballot and not verbal. Have you any clean paper, Mr. Billing?

Billing. I have both blue and white here.

Aslaksen (*going to him*). That will do nicely; we shall get on more quickly that way. Cut it up into small strips—yes, that's it. (*To the meeting.*) Blue means no, white means yes. I will come round myself and collect votes. (PETER STOCKMANN *leaves the hall.* ASLAKSEN *and one or two others go round the room with the slips of paper in their hats.*)

1st Citizen (*to* HOVSTAD). I say, what has come to the Doctor? What are we to think of it?

Hovstad. Oh, you know how headstrong he is.

2nd Citizen (*to* BILLING). Billing, you go to their house—have you ever noticed if the fellow drinks?

Billing. Well I'm hanged if I know what to say. There are always spirits on the table when you go.

3rd Citizen. I rather think he goes quite off his head sometimes.

1st Citizen. I wonder if there is any madness in his family?

Billing. I shouldn't wonder if there were.

4th Citizen. No, it is nothing more than sheer malice; he wants to get even with somebody for something or other.

Billing. Well certainly he suggested a rise in his salary on one occasion lately, and did not get it.

The Citizens (*together*). Ah!—then it is easy to understand how it is!

The Drunken Man (*who has got amongst the audience again*). I want a blue one, I do! And I want a white one!

Voices. It's that drunken chap again! Turn him out!

Morten Kiil (*going up to* DR. STOCKMANN). Well, Stockmann, do you see what these monkey tricks of yours lead to?

Dr. Stockmann. I have done my duty.

Morten Kiil. What was that you said about the tanneries at Mölledal?

Dr. Stockmann. You heard well enough. I said they were the source of all the filth.

Morten Kiil. My tannery too?

Dr. Stockmann. Unfortunately your tannery is by far the worst.

Morten Kiil. Are you going to put that in the papers?

Dr. Stockmann. I shall conceal nothing.

Morten Kiil. That may cost you dear, Stockmann. (*Goes out.*)

A Stout Man (*going up to* CAPTAIN HORSTER, *with-*

**ₕ 552

out taking any notice of the ladies).   Well, Captain, so you lend your house to enemies of the people?

Horster. I imagine I can do what I like with my own possessions, Mr. Vik.

The Stout Man. Then you can have no objection to my doing the same with mine.

Horster. What do you mean, sir?

The Stout Man. You shall hear from me in the morning. (*Turns his back on him and moves off.*)

Petra. Was that not your owner, Captain Horster?

Horster. Yes, that was Mr. Vik the ship-owner.

Aslaksen (*with the voting-papers in his hands, gets up on to the platform and rings his bell*). Gentlemen, allow me to announce the result. By the votes of every one here except one person—

A Young Man. That is the drunk chap!

Aslaksen. By the votes of every one here except a tipsy man, this meeting of citizens declares Dr. Thomas Stockmann to be an enemy of the people. (*Shouts and applause.*) Three cheers for our ancient and honourable citizen community! (*Renewed applause.*) Three cheers for our able and energetic Mayor, who has so loyally suppressed the promptings of family feeling! (*Cheers.*) The meeting is dissolved. (*Gets down.*)

Billing. Three cheers for the Chairman!

The whole crowd. Three cheers for Aslaksen! Hurrah!

Dr. Stockmann. My hat and coat, Petra! Captain, have you room on your ship for passengers to the New World?

Horster. For you and yours we will make room, Doctor.

Dr. Stockmann (*as* PETRA *helps him into his coat*). Good. Come, Katherine! Come, boys!

Mrs. Stockmann (*in an undertone*). Thomas, dear, let us go out by the back way.

Dr. Stockmann. No back ways for me, Katherine. (*Raising his voice.*) You will hear more of this enemy of the people, before he shakes the dust off his shoes upon you! I am not so forgiving as a certain Person;

I do not say: " I forgive you, for ye know not what ye
do."

Aslaksen (shouting). That is a blasphemous comparison,
Dr. Stockmann!

Billing. It is, by God! It's dreadful for an earnest
man to listen to.

A Coarse Voice. Threatens us now, does he!

Other Voices (excitedly). Let's go and break his windows! Duck him in the fjord!

Another Voice. Blow your horn, Evensen! Pip, pip!

*(Horn-blowing, hisses, and wild cries. DR. STOCKMANN
goes out through the hall with his family, HORSTER
elbowing a way for them.)*

The Whole Crowd (howling after them as they go).
Enemy of the People! Enemy of the People!

Billing (as he puts his papers together). Well, I'm
damned if I go and drink toddy with the Stockmanns to-
night!

*(The crowd press towards the exit. The uproar con-
tinues outside; shouts of " Enemy of the People! "
are heard from without.)*

ACT V

*(SCENE.—DR. STOCKMANN'S study. Bookcases, and
cabinets containing specimens, line the walls. At the
back is a door leading to the hall; in the foreground on the
left, a door leading to the sitting-room. In the right-hand
wall are two windows, of which all the panes are broken.
The DOCTOR'S desk, littered with books and papers, stands
in the middle of the room, which is in disorder. It is
morning. DR. STOCKMANN in dressing-gown, slippers
and a smoking-cap, is bending down and raking with an
umbrella under one of the cabinets. After a little while he
rakes out a stone.)*

*Dr. Stockmann (calling through the open sitting-room
door).* Katherine, I have found another one.

Mrs. Stockmann (*from the sitting-room*). Oh, you will find a lot more yet, I expect.

Dr. Stockmann (*adding the stone to a heap of others on the table*). I shall treasure these stones as relics. Ejlif and Morten shall look at them every day, and when they are grown up they shall inherit them as heirlooms. (*Rakes about under a bookcase.*) Hasn't—what the deuce is her name?—the girl, you know—hasn't she been to fetch the glazier yet?

Mrs. Stockmann (*coming in*). Yes, but he said he didn't know if he would be able to come to-day.

Dr. Stockmann. You will see he won't dare to come.

Mrs. Stockmann. Well, that is just what Randine thought—that he didn't dare to, on account of the neighbours. (*Calls into the sitting-room.*) What is it you want, Randine? Give it to me. (*Goes in, and comes out again directly.*) Here is a letter for you, Thomas.

Dr. Stockmann. Let me see it. (*Opens and reads it.*) Ah!—of course.

Mrs. Stockmann. Who is it from?

Dr. Stockmann. From the landlord. Notice to quit.

Mrs. Stockmann. Is it possible? Such a nice man—

Dr. Stockmann (*looking at the letter*). Does not dare do otherwise, he says. Doesn't like doing it, but dare not do otherwise—on account of his fellow-citizens—out of regard for public opinion. Is in a dependent position—dare not offend certain influential men—

Mrs. Stockmann. There, you see, Thomas!

Dr. Stockmann. Yes, yes, I see well enough; the whole lot of them in the town are cowards; not a man among them dares do anything for fear of the others. (*Throws the letter on to the table.*) But it doesn't matter to us, Katherine. We are going to sail away to the New World, and—

Mrs. Stockmann. But, Thomas, are you sure we are well advised to take this step?

Dr. Stockmann. Are you suggesting that I should stay here, where they have pilloried me as an enemy of the people—branded me—broken my windows! And just look here, Katherine—they have torn a great rent in my black trousers too!

Mrs. Stockmann. Oh, dear!—and they are the best pair you have got!

Dr. Stockmann. You should never wear your best trousers when you go out to fight for freedom and truth. It is not that I care so much about the trousers, you know; you can always sew them up again for me. But that the common herd should dare to make this attack on me, as if they were my equals—that is what I cannot, for the life of me, swallow!

Mrs. Stockmann. There is no doubt they have behaved very ill to you, Thomas; but is that sufficient reason for our leaving our native country for good and all?

Dr. Stockmann. If we went to another town, do you suppose we should not find the common people just as insolent as they are here? Depend upon it, there is not much to choose between them. Oh, well, let the curs snap—that is not the worst part of it. The worst is that, from one end of this country to the other, every man is the slave of his Party. Although, as far as that goes, I daresay it is not much better in the free West either; the compact majority, and liberal public opinion, and all that infernal old bag of tricks are probably rampant there, too. But there things are done on a larger scale, you see. They may kill you, but they won't put you to death by slow torture. They don't squeeze a free man's soul in a vice, as they do here. And, if need be, one can live in solitude. (*Walks up and down.*) If only I knew where there was a virgin forest or a small South Sea island for sale, cheap—

Mrs. Stockmann. But think of the boys, Thomas!

Dr. Stockmann (*standing still*). What a strange woman you are, Katherine! Would you prefer to have the boys grow up in a society like this? You saw for yourself last night that half the population are out of their minds; and if the other half have not lost their senses, it is because they are mere brutes, with no sense to lose.

Mrs. Stockmann. But, Thomas dear, the imprudent things you said had something to do with it, you know.

Dr. Stockmann. Well, isn't what I said perfectly true? Don't they turn every idea topsy-turvy? Don't they make a regular hotch-potch of right and wrong? Don't they say that the things I know are true, are lies? The craziest part of it all is the fact of these " liberals," men of full age, going about in crowds imagining that they are the broad-minded party! Did you ever hear anything like it, Katherine?

Mrs. Stockmann. Yes, yes, it's mad enough of them, certainly; but—(PETRA *comes in from the sitting-room*). Back from school already?

Petra. Yes. I have been given notice of dismissal.

Mrs. Stockmann. Dismissal?

Dr. Stockmann. You too?

Petra. Mrs. Busk gave me my notice; so I thought it was best to go at once.

Dr. Stockmann. You were perfectly right, too!

Mrs. Stockmann. Who would have thought Mrs. Busk was a woman like that!

Petra. Mrs. Busk isn't a bit like that, mother; I saw quite plainly how it hurt her to do it. But she didn't dare do otherwise, she said; and so I got my notice.

Dr. Stockmann (*laughing and rubbing his hands*). She didn't dare do otherwise, either! It's delicious!

Mrs. Stockmann. Well, after the dreadful scenes last night—

Petra. It was not only that. Just listen to this, father!

Dr. Stockmann. Well?

Petra. Mrs. Busk showed me no less than three letters she received this morning—

Dr. Stockmann. Anonymous, I suppose?

Petra. Yes.

Dr. Stockmann. Yes, because they didn't dare to risk signing their names, Katherine!

Petra. And two of them were to the effect that a man, who has been our guest here, was declaring last night at the Club that my views on various subjects are extremely emancipated—

Dr. Stockmann. You did not deny that, I hope?

Petra. No, you know I wouldn't. Mrs. Busk's own views are tolerably emancipated, when we are alone together; but now that this report about me is being spread, she dare not keep me on any longer.

Mrs. Stockmann. And some one who had been a guest of ours! That shows you the return you get for your hospitality, Thomas!

Dr. Stockmann. We won't live in such a disgusting hole any longer. Pack up as quickly as you can, Katherine; the sooner we can get away, the better.

Mrs. Stockmann. Be quiet—I think I hear some one in the hall. See who it is, Petra.

Petra (opening the door). Oh, it's you, Captain Horster! Do come in.

Horster (coming in). Good morning. I thought I would just come in and see how you were.

Dr. Stockmann (shaking his hand). Thanks—that is really kind of you.

Mrs. Stockmann. And thank you, too, for helping us through the crowd, Captain Horster.

Petra. How did you manage to get home again?

Horster. Oh, somehow or other. I am fairly strong, and there is more sound than fury about these folk.

Dr. Stockmann. Yes, isn't their swinish cowardice astonishing? Look here, I will show you something! There are all the stones they have thrown through my windows. Just look at them! I'm hanged if there are more than two decently large bits of hardstone in the whole heap; the rest are nothing but gravel—wretched little things. And yet they stood out there bawling and swearing that they would do me some violence; but as for *doing* anything—you don't see much of that in this town.

Horster. Just as well for you this time, doctor!

Dr. Stockmann. True enough. But it makes one angry all the same; because if some day it should be a question of a national fight in real earnest, you will see that public opinion will be in favour of taking to one's heels, and the compact majority will turn tail like a flock of sheep, Captain Horster. That is what is so mournful to think of; it gives me so much concern, that —. No, devil take it, it is ridiculous to care about it! They have called me an enemy of the people, so an enemy of the people let me be!

Mrs. Stockmann. You will never be that, Thomas.

Dr. Stockmann. Don't swear to that, Katherine. To be called an ugly name may have the same effect as a pin-scratch in the lung. And that hateful name—I can't get quit of it. It is sticking here in the pit of my stomach, eating into me like a corrosive acid. And no magnesia will remove it.

Petra. Bah!—you should only laugh at them, father.

Horster. They will change their minds some day, Doctor.

Mrs. Stockmann. Yes, Thomas, as sure as you are standing here.

Dr. Stockmann. Perhaps, when it is too late. Much good may it do them! They may wallow in their filth then and rue the day when they drove a patriot into exile. When do you sail, Captain Horster?

Horster. Hm!—that was just what I had come to speak about—

Dr. Stockmann. Why, has anything gone wrong with the ship?

Horster. No; but what has happened is that I am not to sail in it.

Petra. Do you mean that you have been dismissed from your command?

Horster (smiling). Yes, that's just it.

Petra. You too.

Mrs. Stockmann. There, you see, Thomas!

Dr. Stockmann. And that for the truth's sake! Oh, if I had thought such a thing possible—

Horster. You mustn't take it to heart; I shall be sure to find a job with some ship-owner or other, elsewhere.

Dr. Stockmann. And that is this man Vik—a wealthy

man, independent of every one and everything—!
Shame on him!

Horster. He is quite an excellent fellow otherwise;
he told me himself he would willingly have kept me on,
if only he had dared—

Dr. Stockmann. But he didn't dare? No, of course
not.

Horster. It is not such an easy matter, he said, for a
party man—

Dr. Stockmann. The worthy man spoke the truth. A
party is like a sausage machine; it mashes up all sorts
of heads together into the same mincemeat—fatheads
and blockheads, all in one mash!

Mrs. Stockmann. Come, come, Thomas dear!

Petra (*to* HORSTER). If only you had not come home
with us, things might not have come to this pass.

Horster. I do not regret it.

Petra (*holding out her hand to him*). Thank you for
that!

Horster (*to* DR. STOCKMANN). And so what I came to
say was that if you are determined to go away, I have
thought of another plan—

Dr. Stockmann. That's splendid!—if only we can get
away at once.

Mrs. Stockmann. Hush!—wasn't that some one knocking?

Petra. That is uncle, surely.

Dr. Stockmann. Aha! (*Calls out.*) Come in!

Mrs. Stockmann. Dear Thomas, promise me definitely—.

(PETER STOCKMANN *comes in from the hall.*)

Peter Stockmann. Oh, you are engaged. In that case,
I will—

Dr. Stockmann. No, no, come in.

Peter Stockmann. But I wanted to speak to you alone.

Mrs. Stockmann. We will go into the sitting-room
in the meanwhile.

Horster. And I will look in again later.

Dr. Stockmann. No, go in there with them, Captain
Horster; I want to hear more about—

Horster. Very well, I will wait, then. (*He follows* MRS. STOCKMANN *and* PETRA *into the sitting-room.*)

Dr. Stockmann. I daresay you find it rather draughty here to-day. Put your hat on.

Peter Stockmann. Thank you, if I may. (*Does so.*) I think I caught cold last night; I stood and shivered—

Dr. Stockmann. Really? I found it warm enough.

Peter Stockmann. I regret that it was not in my power to prevent those excesses last night.

Dr. Stockmann. Have you anything particular to say to me besides that?

Peter Stockmann (*taking a big letter from his pocket*). I have this document for you, from the Baths Committee.

Dr. Stockmann. My dismissal?

Peter Stockmann. Yes, dating from to-day. (*Lays the letter on the table.*) It gives us pain to do it; but, to speak frankly, we dared not do otherwise on account of public opinion.

Dr. Stockmann (*smiling*). Dared not? I seem to have heard that word before, to-day.

Peter Stockmann. I must beg you to understand your position clearly. For the future you must not count on any practice whatever in the town.

Dr. Stockmann. Devil take the practice! But why are you so sure of that?

Peter Stockmann. The Householders' Association is circulating a list from house to house. All right-minded citizens are being called upon to give up employing you; and I can assure you that not a single head of a family will risk refusing his signature. They simply dare not.

Dr. Stockmann. No, no; I don't doubt it. But what then?

Peter Stockmann. If I might advise you, it would be best to leave the place for a little while—

Dr. Stockmann. Yes, the propriety of leaving the place *has* occurred to me.

Peter Stockmann. Good. And then, when you have had six months to think things over, if, after mature consideration, you can persuade yourself to write a few words of regret, acknowledging your error—

Dr. Stockmann. I might have my appointment restored to me, do you mean?

Peter Stockmann. Perhaps. It is not at all impossible.

Dr. Stockmann. But what about public opinion, then? Surely you would not dare to do it on account of public feeling?

Peter Stockmann. Public opinion is an extremely mutable thing. And, to be quite candid with you, it is a matter of great importance to us to have some admission of that sort from you in writing.

Dr. Stockmann. Oh, that's what you are after, is it? I will just trouble you to remember what I said to you lately about foxy tricks of that sort!

Peter Stockmann. Your position was quite different then. At that time you had reason to suppose you had the whole town at your back—

Dr. Stockmann. Yes, and now I feel I have the whole town *on* my back—(*flaring up*). I would not do it if I had the devil and his dam on my back—! Never—never, I tell you!

Peter Stockmann. A man with a family has no right to behave as you do. You have no right to do it, Thomas.

Dr. Stockmann. I have no right! There is only one single thing in the world a free man has no right to do. Do you know what that is?

Peter Stockmann. No.

Dr. Stockmann. Of course you don't, but I will tell you. A free man has no right to soil himself with filth; he has no right to behave in a way that would justify his spitting in his own face.

Peter Stockmann. This sort of thing sounds extremely plausible, of course; and if there were no other explanation for your obstinacy—. But as it happens that there is.

Dr. Stockmann. What do you mean?

Peter Stockmann. You understand very well what I

mean. But, as your brother and as a man of discretion, I advise you not to build too much upon expectations and prospects that may so very easily fail you.

Dr. Stockmann. What in the world is all this about?

Peter Stockmann. Do you really ask me to believe that you are ignorant of the terms of Mr. Kiil's will?

Dr. Stockmann. I know that the small amount he possesses is to go to an institution for indigent old workpeople. How does that concern me?

Peter Stockmann. In the first place, it is by no means a small amount that is in question. Mr. Kiil is a fairly wealthy man.

Dr. Stockmann. I had no notion of that!

Peter Stockmann. Hm!—hadn't you really? Then I suppose you had no notion, either, that a considerable portion of his wealth will come to your children, you and your wife having a life-rent of the capital. Has he never told you so?

Dr. Stockmann. Never, on my honour! Quite the reverse; he has consistently done nothing but fume at being so unconscionably heavily taxed. But are you perfectly certain of this, Peter?

Peter Stockmann. I have it from an absolutely reliable source.

Dr. Stockmann. Then, thank God, Katherine is provided for—and the children too! I must tell her this at once—(*calls out*) Katherine, Katherine!

Peter Stockmann (*restraining him*). Hush, don't say a word yet!

Mrs. Stockmann (*opening the door*). What is the matter?

Dr. Stockmann. Oh, nothing, nothing; you can go back. (*She shuts the door.* DR. STOCKMANN *walks up and down in his excitement.*) Provided for!—Just think of it, we are all provided for! And for life! What a blessed feeling it is to know one is provided for!

Peter Stockmann. Yes, but that is just exactly what you are not. Mr. Kiil can alter his will any day he likes.

Dr. Stockmann. But he won't do that, my dear Peter.

The "Badger" is much too delighted at my attack on you and your wise friends.

Peter Stockmann (*starts and looks intently at him*). Ah, that throws a light on various things.

Dr. Stockmann. What things?

Peter Stockmann. I see that the whole thing was a combined manœuvre on your part and his. These violent, reckless attacks that you have made against the leading men of the town, under the pretence that it was in the name of truth—

Dr. Stockmann. What about them?

Peter Stockmann. I see that they were nothing else than the stipulated price for that vindictive old man's will.

Dr. Stockmann (*almost speechless*). Peter—you are the most disgusting plebeian I have ever met in all my life.

Peter Stockmann. All is over between us. Your dismissal is irrevocable—we have a weapon against you now. (*Goes out.*)

Dr. Stockmann. For shame! For shame! (*Calls out.*) Katherine, you must have the floor scrubbed after him! Let—what's her name—devil take it, the girl who has always got soot on her nose—

Mrs. Stockmann (*in the sitting-room*). Hush, Thomas, be quiet!

Petra (*coming to the door*). Father, grandfather is here, asking if he may speak to you alone.

Dr. Stockmann. Certainly he may. (*Going to the door.*) Come in, Mr. Kiil. (MORTEN KIIL *comes in.* DR. STOCKMANN *shuts the door after him.*) What can I do for you? Won't you sit down?

Morten Kiil. I won't sit. (*Looks around.*) You look very comfortable here to-day, Thomas.

Dr. Stockmann. Yes, don't we!

Morten Kiil. Very comfortable—plenty of fresh air. I should think you have got enough to-day of that oxygen you were talking about yesterday. Your conscience must be in splendid order to-day, I should think.

Dr. Stockmann. It is.

Morten Kiil. So I should think. (*Taps his chest.*)
Do you know what I have got here?

Dr. Stockmann. A good conscience, too, I hope.

Morten Kiil. Bah!—No, it is something better than
that. (*He takes a thick pocket-book from his breast-
pocket, opens it, and displays a packet of papers.*)

Dr. Stockmann (*looking at him in astonishment*). Shares
in the Baths?

Morten Kiil. They were not difficult to get to-day.

Dr. Stockmann. And you have been buying—?

Morten K il. As many as I could pay for.

Dr. Stockmann. But, my dear Mr. Kiil—consider the
state of the Baths' affairs!

Morten Kiil. If you behave like a reasonable man, you
can soon set the Baths on their feet again.

Dr. Stockmann. Well, you can see for yourself that I
have done all I can, but—. They are all mad in this
town!

Morten Kiil. You said yesterday that the worst of this
pollution came from my tannery. If that is true, then
my grandfather and my father before me, and I myself,
for many years past, have been poisoning the town like
three destroying angels. Do you think I am going to sit
quiet under that reproach?

Dr. Stockmann. Unfortunately I am afraid you will
have to.

Morten Kiil. No, thank you. I am jealous of my name
and reputation. They call me " the Badger," I am told.
A badger is a kind of pig, I believe; but I am not going
to give them the right to call me that. I mean to live
and die a clean man.

Dr. Stockmann. And how are you going to set about
it?

Morten Kiil. You shall cleanse me, Thomas.

Dr. Stockmann. I?

Morten Kiil. Do you know what money I have bought
these shares with? No, of course you can't know—
but I will tell you. It is the money that Katherine and

Petra and the boys will have when I am gone. Because
I have been able to save a little bit after all, you know.

Dr. Stockmann (flaring up). And you have gone and
taken Katherine's money for *this!*

Morten Kiil. Yes, the whole of the money is invested
in the Baths now. And now I just want to see whether
you are quite stark, staring mad, Thomas! If you
still make out that these animals and other nasty things
of that sort come from my tannery, it will be exactly as
if you were to flay broad strips of skin from Katherine's
body, and Petra's, and the boys'; and no decent man
would do that—unless he were mad.

Dr. Stockmann (walking up and down). Yes, but I *am*
mad; I *am* mad!

Morten Kiil. You cannot be so absurdly mad as all
that, when it is a question of your wife and children.

Dr. Stockmann (standing still in front of him). Why
couldn't you consult me about it, before you went and
bought all that trash?

Morten Kiil. What is done cannot be undone.

Dr. Stockmann (walks about uneasily). If only I
were not so certain about it—! But I am absolutely
convinced that I am right.

Morten Kiil (weighing the pocket-book in his hand).
If you stick to your mad idea, this won't be worth
much, you know. *(Puts the pocket-book in his pocket.)*

Dr. Stockmann. But, hang it all! it might be possible
for science to discover some prophylactic, I should
think—or some antidote of some kind—

Morten Kiil. To kill these animals, do you mean?

Dr. Stockmann. Yes, or to make them innocuous.

Morten Kiil. Couldn't you try some rat's-bane?

Dr. Stockmann. Don't talk nonsense! They all say
it is only imagination, you know. Well, let it go at that!
Let them have their own way about it! Haven't the
ignorant, narrow-minded curs reviled me as an enemy
of the people?—and haven't they been ready to tear
the clothes off my back, too?

Morten Kiil. And broken all your windows to pieces!

Dr. Stockmann. And then there is my duty to my family. I must talk it over with Katherine; she is great on those things.

Morten Kiil. That is right; be guided by a reasonable woman's advice.

Dr. Stockmann (advancing towards him). To think you could do such a preposterous thing! Risking Katherine's money in this way, and putting me in such a horribly painful dilemma! When I look at you, I think I see the devil himself—.

Morten Kiil. Then I had better go. But I must have an answer from you before two o'clock—yes or no. If it is no, the shares go to a charity, and that this very day.

Dr. Stockmann. And what does Katherine get?

Morten Kiil. Not a halfpenny. (*The door leading to the hall opens, and* HOVSTAD *and* ASLAKSEN *make their appearance.*) Look at those two!

Dr. Stockmann (staring at them). What the devil!— have *you* actually the face to come into my house?

Hovstad. Certainly.

Aslaksen. We have something to say to you, you see.

Morten Kiil (in a whisper). Yes or no—before two o'clock.

Aslaksen (glancing at HOVSTAD*).* Aha! (MORTEN KIIL *goes out.*)

Dr. Stockmann. Well, what do you want with me? Be brief.

Hovstad. I can quite understand that you are annoyed with us for our attitude at the meeting yesterday—

Dr. Stockmann. Attitude, do you call it? Yes, it was a charming attitude! I call it weak, womanish—damnably shameful!

Hovstad. Call it what you like, we could not do otherwise.

Dr. Stockmann. You *dared* not do otherwise—isn't that it?

Hovstad. Well, if you like to put it that way.

Aslaksen. But why did you not let us have word of it beforehand?—just a hint to Mr. Hovstad or to me?

Dr. Stockmann. A hint? Of what?

Aslaksen. Of what was behind it all.

Dr. Stockmann. I don't understand you in the least.

Aslaksen (with a confidential nod). Oh yes, you do, Dr. Stockmann.

Hovstad. It is no good making a mystery of it any longer.

Dr. Stockmann (looking first at one of them and then at the other). What the devil do you both mean?

Aslaksen. May I ask if your father-in-law is not going round the town buying up all the shares in the Baths?

Dr. Stockmann. Yes, he has been buying Baths shares to-day; but—

Aslaksen. It would have been more prudent to get some one else to do it—some one less nearly related to you.

Hovstad. And you should not have let your name appear in the affair. There was no need for anyone to know that the attack on the Baths came from you. You ought to have consulted me, Dr. Stockmann.

Dr. Stockmann (looks in front of him; then a light seems to dawn on him and he says in amazement:) Are such things conceivable? Are such things possible?

Aslaksen (with a smile). Evidently they are. But it is better to use a little *finesse*, you know.

Hovstad. And it is much better to have several persons in a thing of that sort; because the responsibility of each individual is lessened, when there are others with him.

Dr. Stockmann (composedly). Come to the point, gentlemen. What do you want?

Aslaksen. Perhaps Mr. Hovstad had better—

Hovstad. No, you tell him, Aslaksen.

Aslaksen. Well, the fact is that, now we know the bearings of the whole affair, we think we might venture to put the " People's Messenger " at your disposal.

Dr. Stockmann. Do you dare do that now? What about public opinion? Are you not afraid of a storm breaking upon our heads?

Hovstad. We will try to weather it.

Aslaksen. And you must be ready to go off quickly on a new tack, Doctor. As soon as your invective has done its work—

Dr. Stockmann. Do you mean, as soon as my father-in-law and I have got hold of the shares at a low figure?

Hovstad. Your reasons for wishing to get the control of the Baths are mainly scientific, I take it.

Dr. Stockmann. Of course; it was for scientific reasons that I persuaded the old " Badger " to stand in with me in the matter. So we will tinker at the conduit-pipes a little, and dig up a little bit of the shore, and it shan't cost the town a sixpence. That will be all right— eh?

Hovstad. I think so—if you have the " People's Messenger " behind you.

Aslaksen. The Press is a power in a free community, Doctor.

Dr. Stockmann. Quite so. And so is public opinion. And you, Mr. Aslaksen—I suppose you will be answerable for the Householders' Association?

Aslaksen. Yes, and for the Temperance Society. You may rely on that.

Dr. Stockmann. But, gentlemen—I really am ashamed to ask the question—but, what return do you—?

Hovstad. We should prefer to help you without any return whatever, believe me. But the " People's Messenger " is in rather a shaky condition; it doesn't go really well; and I should be very unwilling to suspend the paper now, when there is so much work to do here in the political way.

Dr. Stockmann. Quite so; that would be a great trial to such a friend of the people as you are. (*Flares up.*) But I am an enemy of the people, remember! (*Walks about the room.*) Where have I put my stick? Where the devil is my stick?

Hovstad. What's that?

Aslaksen. Surely you never mean—?

Dr. Stockmann (*standing still*). And suppose I ·don't

give you a single penny of all I get out of it? Money
is not very easy to get out of us rich folk, please to
remember!

Hovstad. And you please to remember that this affair
of the shares can be represented in two ways!

Dr. Stockmann. Yes, and you are just the man to do it.
If I don't come to the rescue of the " People's Messenger,"
you will certainly take an evil view of the affair; you
will hunt me down, I can well imagine—pursue me—
try to throttle me as a dog does a hare.

Hovstad. It is a natural law; every animal must fight
for its own livelihood.

Aslaksen. And get its food where it can, you know.

Dr. Stockmann (walking about the room). Then you go
and look for yours in the gutter; because I am going to
show you which is the strongest animal of us three!
(*Finds an umbrella and brandishes it above his head.*)
Ah, now—!

Hovstad. You are surely not going to use violence!

Aslaksen. Take care what you are doing with that
umbrella.

Dr. Stockmann. Out of the window with you, Mr.
Hovstad!

Hovstad (edging to the door). Are you quite mad!

Dr. Stockmann. Out of the window, Mr. Aslaksen!
Jump, I tell you! You will have to do it, sooner or
later.

Aslaksen (running round the writing-table). Moderation, Doctor—I am a delicate man—I can stand so
little—(*calls out*) help, help!

(MRS. STOCKMANN, PETRA *and* HORSTER *come in from
the sitting-room.*)

Mrs. Stockmann. Good gracious, Thomas! What is
happening?

Dr. Stockmann (brandishing the umbrella). Jump out,
I tell you! Out into the gutter!

Hovstad. An assault on an unoffending man! I call you
to witness, Captain Horster. (*Hurries out through the
hall.*)

Aslaksen (*irresolutely*). If only I knew the way about here—. (*Steals out through the sitting-room.*)

Mrs. Stockmann (*holding her husband back*). Control yourself, Thomas!

Dr. Stockmann (*throwing down the umbrella*). Upon my soul, they have escaped after all.

Mrs. Stockmann. What did they want you to do?

Dr. Stockmann. I will tell you later on; I have something else to think about now. (*Goes to the table and writes something on a calling-card.*) Look there, Katherine; what is written there?

Mrs. Stockmann. Three big *Noes;* what does that mean.

Dr. Stockmann. I will tell you that too, later on. (*Holds out the card to* PETRA.) There, Petra; tell sooty-face to run over to the " Badger's " with that, as quick as she can. Hurry up! (PETRA *takes the card and goes out to the hall.*)

Dr. Stockmann. Well, I think I have had a visit from every one of the devil's messengers to-day! But now I am going to sharpen my pen till they can feel its point; I shall dip it in venom and gall; I shall hurl my inkpot at their heads!

Mrs. Stockmann. Yes, but we are going away, you know, Thomas.

(PETRA *comes back.*)

Dr. Stockmann. Well?

Petra. She has gone with it.

Dr. Stockmann. Good.—Going away, did you say? No, I'll be hanged if we are going away! We are going to stay where we are, Katherine!

Petra. Stay here?

Mrs. Stockmann. Here, in the town?

Dr. Stockmann. Yes, here. This is the field of battle— this is where the fight will be. This is where I shall triumph! As soon as I have had my trousers sewn up I shall go out and look for another house. We must have a roof over our heads for the winter.

Horster. That you shall have in my house.

Dr. Stockmann. Can I?

Horster. Yes, quite well. I have plenty of room, and I am almost never at home.

Mrs. Stockmann. How good of you, Captain Horster!

Petra. Thank you!

Dr. Stockmann (*grasping his hand*). Thank you, thank you! That is one trouble over! Now I can set to work in earnest at once. There is an endless amount of things to look through here, Katherine! Luckily I shall have all my time at my disposal; because I have been dismissed from the Baths, you know.

Mrs. Stockmann (*with a sigh*). Oh yes, I expected that.

Dr. Stockmann. And they want to take my practice away from me, too. Let them! I have got the poor people to fall back upon, anyway—those that don't pay anything; and, after all, they need me most, too. But, by Jove, they will have to listen to me; I shall preach to them in season and out of season, as it says somewhere.

Mrs. Stockmann. But, dear Thomas, I should have thought events had showed you what use it is to preach.

Dr. Stockmann. You are really ridiculous, Katherine. Do you want me to let myself be beaten off the field by public opinion and the compact majority and all that devilry? No, thank you! And what I want to do is so simple and clear and straightforward. I only want to drum into the heads of these curs the fact that the liberals are the most insidious enemies of freedom—that party programmes strangle every young and vigorous truth—that considerations of expediency turn morality and justice upside down—and that they will end by making life here unbearable. Don't you think, Captain Horster, that I ought to be able to make people understand that?

Horster. Very likely; I don't know much about such things myself.

Dr. Stockmann. Well, look here—I will explain! It is the party leaders that must be exterminated. A party leader is like a wolf, you see—like a voracious wolf.

He requires a certain number of smaller victims to prey upon every year, if he is to live. Just look at Hovstad and Aslaksen! How many smaller victims have they not put an end to—or at any rate maimed and mangled until they are fit for nothing except to be house-holders or subscribers to the " People's Messenger "! (*Sits down on the edge of the table.*) Come here, Katherine—look how beautifully the sun shines to-day! And this lovely spring air I am drinking in!

Mrs. Stockmann. Yes, if only we could live on sun-shine and spring air, Thomas.

Dr. Stockmann. Oh, you will have to pinch and save a bit—then we shall get along. That gives me very little concern. What is much worse is, that I know of no one who is liberal-minded and high-minded enough to venture to take up my work after me.

Petra. Don't think about that, father; you have plenty of time before you.—Hullo, here are the boys already!

(EJLIF *and* MORTEN *come in from the sitting-room.*)

Mrs. Stockmann. Have you got a holiday?

Morten. No; but we were fighting with the other boys between lessons—

Ejlif. That isn't true; it was the other boys were fighting with us.

Morten. Well, and then Mr. Rörlund said we had better stay at home for a day or two.

Dr. Stockmann (*snapping his fingers and getting up from the table*). I have it! I have it, by Jove! You shall never set foot in the school again!

The Boys. No more school!

Mrs. Stockmann. But, Thomas—

Dr. Stockmann. Never, I say. I will educate you myself; that is to say, you shan't learn a blessed thing—

Morten. Hooray!

Dr. Stockmann. —but I will make liberal-minded and high-minded men of you. You must help me with that, Petra.

Petra. Yes, father, you may be sure I will.

Dr. Stockmann. And my school shall be in the room where they insulted me and called me an enemy of the people. But we are too few as we are; I must have at least twelve boys to begin with.

Mrs. Stockmann. You will certainly never get them in this town.

Dr. Stockmann. We shall. (*To the boys.*) Don't you know any street urchins—regular ragamuffins—?

Morten. Yes, father, I know lots!

Dr. Stockmann. That's capital! Bring me some specimens of them. I am going to experiment with curs, just for once; there may be some exceptional heads amongst them.

Morten. And what are we going to do, when you have made liberal-minded and high-minded men of us?

Dr. Stockmann. Then you shall drive all the wolves out of the country, my boys!

(EJLIF *looks rather doubtful about it;* MORTEN *jumps about crying* " Hurrah! ")

Mrs. Stockmann. Let us hope it won't be the wolves that will drive you out of the country, Thomas.

Dr. Stockmann. Are you out of your mind, Katherine? Drive me out! Now—when I am the strongest man in the town!

Mrs. Stockmann. The strongest—now?

Dr. Stockmann. Yes, and I will go so far as to say that now I am the strongest man in the whole world.

Morten. I say!

Dr. Stockmann (*lowering his voice*). Hush! You mustn't say anything about it yet; but I have made a great discovery.

Mrs. Stockmann. Another one?

Dr. Stockmann. Yes. (*Gathers them round him, and says confidentially:*) It is this, let me tell you—that the strongest man in the world is he who stands most alone.

Mrs. Stockmann (*smiling and shaking her head*). Oh, Thomas, Thomas!

Petra (*encouragingly, as she grasps her father's hands*). Father!

VERYMAN'S LIBRARY: A Selected List

ls List covers a selection of volumes available in Everyman's Library. Those
umes marked with a ★ indicate that a paperback edition of this title is also available.
mbers only of hardback editions are given.

BIOGRAPHY

ESSAYS AND CRITICISM

FICTION

1

Brontë, Emily (1818–48). ★WUTHERING HEIGHTS, 1847; and POEMS.

Bunyan, John (1628–88). GRACE ABOUNDING, 1666; and THE LIFE AND DEATH
MR BADMAN, 1680. 815.   ★PILGRIM'S PROGRESS, Parts I and II, 1678–84. R
edition.

Butler, Samuel (1835–1902). EREWHON, 1872 (revised 1901); and EREWHON REVISIT
1901. 881.   THE WAY OF ALL FLESH, 1903. 895

Cervantes, Saavedra Miguel de (1547–1616). DON QUIXOTE DE LA MANCHA. Transla
by *P. A. Motteux*.   2 vols. 38

Collins, Wilkie (1824–89). THE MOONSTONE, 1868. 979.   ★THE WOMAN IN WHITE, 1

Conrad, Joseph (1857–1924). ★LORD JIM, 1900. Typically set in the East Indies.
★THE NIGGER OF THE 'NARCISSUS'; TYPHOON; and THE SHADOW LINE. 980. N
TROMO, 1904. Conrad's greatest novel. 38.   THE ROVER, 1923. Early Napoleo
Era. 395.   ★THE SECRET AGENT, 1907. With a Preface by the author.
★VICTORY. An Island Tale. 228

Defoe, Daniel (1661?–1731). ★THE FORTUNES AND MISFORTUNES OF MOLL FLANDE
1722. 837.   JOURNAL OF THE PLAGUE YEAR, 1722. 289.   ★THE LIFE, ADVENTU
AND PIRACIES OF THE Famous CAPTAIN SINGLETON, 1720. 74.   ★ROBINSON CRU
and THE FARTHER ADVENTURES OF ROBINSON CRUSOE, 1719. Parts I and II compl
59

Dickens, Charles (1812–70). WORKS. (*See separate List*)

Dostoyevsky, Fyodor (1821–81). THE BROTHERS KARAMAZOV, 1879–80. Translated
Constance Garnett. 2 vols. 802–3.   ★CRIME AND PUNISHMENT, 1866. Translated
Constance Garnett. 501.   THE IDIOT, 1873. Translated by *Eva M. Martin*. 6
★LETTERS FROM THE UNDERWORLD, 1864; and OTHER TALES. Translated by *C.
Hogarth*. 654.   ★POOR FOLK, 1845; and THE GAMBLER, 1867. Translated by *C.
Hogarth*. 711.   THE POSSESSED, 1871. Translated by *Constance Garnett*. 2 vols. 86

Dumas, Alexandre (1802–70). ★THE BLACK TULIP, 1850. The brothers De Witt in B
land, 1672–5. 174.   THE COUNT OF MONTE CRISTO, 1844. Napoleon's later ph
2 vols. 393–4.   THE THREE MUSKETEERS, 1844. The France of Cardinal Richelieu.

Eliot, George. ★ADAM BEDE, 1859. 27.   DANIEL DERONDA, 1876. 2 vols. 539–
FELIX HOLT, 1866. 353.   MIDDLEMARCH, 1872. 2 vols. 854–5.   ★THE MILL ON
FLOSS, 1860. 325.   ROMOLA, 1863. The Florence of Savonarola. 231.   ★SI
MARNER, THE WEAVER OF RAVELOE, 1861. 121

Fielding, Henry (1707–54). AMELIA, 1751. Amelia is drawn from Fielding's first w
2 vols. 852–3.   ★JONATHAN WILD, 1743; and JOURNAL OF A VOYAGE TO LISB
1755. 877.   ★JOSEPH ANDREWS, 1742. A skit on Richardson's *Pamela*. 467.   ★T
JONES, 1749. The first great English novel of humour. 2 vols. 355–6

Flaubert, Gustave (1821–80). ★MADAME BOVARY, 1857. Translated by *Eleanor Ma
Aveling*. 808.   SALAMMBÔ, 1862. Translated by *J. C. Chartres*. 869.   ★SENTIMENT
EDUCATION, 1869. Translated by *Anthony Goldsmith*, 969

Forster, Edward Morgan (*b.* 1879). A PASSAGE TO INDIA, 1924.

Gaskell, Mrs Elizabeth (1810–65). ★CRANFORD, 1853.

Gogol, Nikolay (1809–52). DEAD SOULS, 1842.

Goldsmith, Oliver (1728–74). ★THE VICAR OF WAKEFIELD, 1766.

Gorky, Maxim (1868–1936). ★THROUGH RUSSIA.

Hugo, Victor Marie (1802–85). LES MISÉRABLES, 1862. 2 vols. 363–4.   ★NOTRE DA
DE PARIS, 1831. 422.   TOILERS OF THE SEA, 1866. 509

James, Henry (1843–1916). ★THE AMBASSADORS, 1903. 987.   ★THE TURN OF T
SCREW, 1898; and THE ASPERN PAPERS, 1888. 912

Jerome, Jerome K. (1859–1927). ★THREE MEN IN A BOAT, 1889, and THREE MEN
THE BUMMEL, 1900.

Kingsley, Charles (1819–75). HEREWARD THE WAKE, 1866. 296.   WESTWARD H
1855. 20

Lytton, Edward Bulwer, Baron (1803–73). ★THE LAST DAYS OF POMPEII, 1834.

Maugham, W. Somerset (1874–1965). CAKES AND ALE, 1930.

Maupassant, Guy de (1850–93). ★SHORT STORIES. Translated by *Marjorie Laurie*.

Melville, Herman (1819–91). ★MOBY DICK; OR THE WHITE WHALE, 1851. 179. TYP
1846; and BILLY BUDD (*published* 1924). South Seas adventures. 180

Meredith, George (1828–1909). THE ORDEAL OF RICHARD FEVEREL, 1859.

★**Modern Short Stories.** Selected by *John Hadfield*. Twenty stories.

Moore, George (1852–1933). ESTHER WATERS, 1894.

Priestley, J. B. (*b.* 1894). ANGEL PAVEMENT, 1931. A finely conceived London novel
938.   BRIGHT DAY, 1946. The author's favourite novel. 671

Rabelais, François (1494?–1553). THE HEROIC DEEDS OF GARGANTUA AND PAN
GRUEL, 1532–5. *Urquhart and Motteux's* unabridged translation, 1653–94.
                                                                   2 vols. 82

Russian Short Stories. Translated by *Rochelle S. Townsend*.

Scott, Sir Walter (1771–1832). WORKS. (*See separate List*)

Shelley, Mary Wollstonecraft (1797–1851). ★FRANKENSTEIN, 1818.

Smollett, Tobias (1721–71). ★THE EXPEDITION OF HUMPHRY CLINKER, 1771. 9
PEREGRINE PICKLE, 1751. 2 vols. 838–9.   ★RODERICK RANDOM, 1742. 790

Stendhal (pseudonym of Henri Beyle, 1783–1842). SCARLET AND BLACK, 1831. Tra
lated by *C. K. Scott Moncrieff*,   2 vols. 94

*Poems of our Time, 1900–60. An Anthology edited by *Richard Church*, C.B.E., *M. Bozman* and *Edith Sitwell*, D.LITT., D.B.E. Nearly 400 poems by about 130 poets.
Rossetti, Dante Gabriel (1828–82). POEMS.
Shakespeare, William (1564–1616). A Complete Edition. Cambridge Text. Glossa 3 vols.: Comedies, 153; Histories, Poems and Sonnets, 154; Tragedies, 155
Spenser, Edmund (1552–99). THE FAËRIE QUEENE, 1590–6. Glossary. 2 vols. 443 THE SHEPHERD'S CALENDAR, 1579; and OTHER POEMS. 879
Synge, J. M. (1871–1909). PLAYS, POEMS AND PROSE.
Tchekhov, Anton (1860–1904). *PLAYS AND STORIES. Translated by *S. S. Kotelian*

*Twenty-four One-Act Plays. From Gordon Bottomley to W. B. Yeats.
Webster, John (1580?–1625?), and **Ford, John** (1586–1639). *SELECTED PLAYS.
Wilde, Oscar (1854–1900). *PLAYS, PROSE WRITINGS AND POEMS.
Wordsworth, William (1770–1850). POEMS. Edited by *Philip Wayne*, M.A.
3 vols. 203, 311,

RELIGION AND PHILOSOPHY

Aristotle (384–322 B.C.). POLITICS and THE ATHENIAN CONSTITUTION. 605. ETH 547. METAPHYSICS. 1000. PRIOR AND POSTERIOR ANALYTICS. 450. All Edited a translated by *John Warrington*.
Augustine, Saint (353–430). CONFESSIONS. *Dr Pusey's* translation, 1838. 200. THE C OF GOD. Complete text. 2 vols. 982–3
Berkeley, George (1685–1753). A NEW THEORY OF VISION AND OTHER WRITINGS, 17

Browne, Sir Thomas (1605–82). RELIGIO MEDICI, 1642.
Bunyan, John. (*See under* Fiction.)
Burton, Robert (1577–1640). THE ANATOMY OF MELANCHOLY, 1621. Edited by *Holbr Jackson*. 3 vols. 88
Chinese Philosophy in Classical Times. Covering the period 1500 B.C.–A.D. 100.
Descartes, René (1596–1650). A DISCOURSE ON METHOD, 1637; MEDITATIONS ON T FIRST PHILOSOPHY, 1641; and PRINCIPLES OF PHILOSOPHY, 1644. Translated *Prof. J. Veitch*.
Francis, Saint (1182–1226). THE LITTLE FLOWERS OF ST. FRANCIS; THE MIRROR PERFECTION (by Leo of Assisi); and THE LIFE OF ST FRANCIS (by St Bonaventu

Hobbes, Thomas (1588–1679). LEVIATHAN, 1651.
Hooker, Richard (1554–1600). OF THE LAWS OF ECCLESIASTICAL POLITY, 1597.
2 vols. 20

Koran, The. *Rodwell's* translation, 1861.
Law, William (1686–1761). A SERIOUS CALL TO A DEVOUT AND HOLY LIFE, 1728.
Leibniz, Gottfried Wilhelm (1646–1716). PHILOSOPHICAL WRITINGS. Selected and tra lated by *Mary Morris*.
Marcus Aurelius (121–80). MEDITATIONS. *A. S. L. Farquharson* translation.
Plato (427–347 B.C.). THE LAWS. Translated by *A. E. Taylor* (1869–1945). 275. T REPUBLIC. Translated by *A. D. Lindsay*, C.B.E., LL.D. 64. THE TRIAL AND DEA OF SOCRATES. Translated by *John Warrington*. 457. THE SYMPOSIUM AND OT DIALOGUES. Translation by *Michael Joyce, Michael Oakley* and *John Warrington*
Spinoza, Benedictus de (1632–77). ETHICS, 1677; and ON THE CORRECTION OF T UNDERSTANDING, 1687. Translated by *Andrew Boyle*.

SCIENCE

Darwin, Charles (1809–82). THE ORIGIN OF SPECIES, 1859. Embodies Darwin's f additions.
Eddington, Sir Arthur (1882–1944). THE NATURE OF THE PHYSICAL WORLD, 1928.
Locke, John (1632–1704). TWO TREATISES OF CIVIL GOVERNMENT, 1690.
Marx, Karl (1818–83). CAPITAL, 1867. Translated by *Eden* and *Cedar Paul*.
2 vols. 84

Mill, John Stuart (1806–73). UTILITARIANISM, 1863; LIBERTY, 1859; and REP SENTATIVE GOVERNMENT, 1861.
Owen, Robert (1771–1858). A NEW VIEW OF SOCIETY, 1813; and OTHER WRITINGS.
Smith, Adam (1723–90). THE WEALTH OF NATIONS, 1766. 2 vols. 412
Wollstonecraft, Mary (1759–97). THE RIGHTS OF WOMAN, 1792; and **Mill, John Stu** (1806–73), THE SUBJECTION OF WOMEN, 1869.

TRAVEL AND TOPOGRAPHY

Borrow, George (1803–81). THE BIBLE IN SPAIN, 1843. 151. WILD WALES. 1862.
Boswell, James (1740–95). JOURNAL OF A TOUR TO THE HEBRIDES WITH SAMU JOHNSON, 1785.
Cobbett, William (1762–1835). RURAL RIDES, 1830. 2 vols. 63
Darwin, Charles (1809–82). *THE VOYAGE OF THE 'BEAGLE', 1839.
Kinglake, Alexander (1809–91). EOTHEN, 1844.
Polo, Marco (1254–1324). TRAVELS.
Portuguese Voyages, 1498–1663. Edited by *Charles David Ley*.
Stow, John (1525?–1605). *THE SURVEY OF LONDON. Elizabethan London.

4